Social Exclusion and Status Formation

Social Exclusion and Status Formation:

Emerging a New Social Status among Dalits in North Bihar

Jitendra Ram

ISBN: 978-81-212-6472-3

First Published, 2023

Published by

Gyan Publishing House
5, Ansari Road
Daryaganj, New Delhi-110002
Phone: 011-47034999, 9811692060
www.gyanbooks.com
E-mail: books@gyanbooks.com

Printed at: Gyan Press, Delhi.

DEDICATED TO

MY PARENTS
VASUDEO RAM & RADHIKA DEVI
WHO HAVE BEEN CONSTANT SOURCE
OF INSPIRATION AND ENERGY
THROUGHOUT MY LIFE.

Contents

Foreword

The term 'social exclusion', its origin, and its multi-dimensional approaches are provided or formulated by many scholars, researchers and policy makers in European countries in the mid-1970s, then in India and elsewhere. Social exclusion, a multi-dimensional concept in social sciences, has adversely affected all human societies in the world more or less, and the society of India is no exception. In Indian society, it revolves around socio-cultural, economic, educational and political domains in which an individual or individuals/ groups/ communities largely get discriminated, segregated, subordinated and even exploitered in various aspects of their life. Furthermore, social exclusion which means exclusion or throwing away or boycotting permanently members from a caste or community. Such policy has remained in operation since the early period of the Indo-Aryan and later Hindu society in India. This operates even today, especially among the lower caste, both in rural and urban India. In this regard, Dalit communities, by and large, have been the most excluded castes or communities of the society in India. The Dalits have been the most discriminated, exploited, subordinated and physically segregated communities. Due to it, they have remained deprived in terms of their socio-economic, educational, political and cultural domains in comparison to the people of other castes and communities. It is altogether dependent on caste system which is a peculiar institution of Indian society that plays a dominant part of exclusion among the lower caste people. Caste system, for example, has a rigid hierarchy which sole stress on birth for status determination. It is well specified form of social inequality and the interest of each caste in the caste system are mutually opposed. Likewise, class or social class in India society is operationally an open caste and has not transcended the social and cultural reflexivity of caste even today. In other words, Dr. Ambedkar rightly points out that 'caste in a singular number is an unreality. Caste exits only in plural number.'

In this given situation, there is no doubt that even today social exclusion vis-à-vis social discrimination broadly happens against Dalits or Scheduled Castes in India in general and Bihar in particular. At present, Dalits are known as one of the most vulnerable section of people. Bihar is one of those states which has termed as a caste-ridden society, is the third most populous state with respect to Dalits or Scheduled Castes population. Besides, this simply means that with the improved in class or socio-economic status of the Dalits, there is considerable degree of improvement in their caste status, although the status or rank of their caste remains the same in the caste-hierarchy as it exists in the town. This also means that the impact of their social exclusion, due to low status or rank of their caste in the caste hierarchy, has loosened its grip over status formation among a sizable number of the Dalits in the town.

There is not much sociological literature on social exclusion and status formation among the people in general and Dalits in particular in Indian society. However, a few writings on the issues about both India and elsewhere do provide some insights into comprehending social exclusion and formation of status among the various segments of population, especially among the marginalized ones. The present book on *Social Exclusion and Status Formation: Emerging a New Social Status among Dalits in North Bihar* by Dr. Jitendra Ram relies primarily on the empirical data collected from both rural and urban areas of Bihar to understand social exclusion as well as status formation among Dalits or Scheduled Castes. This study, located in East Champaran District of North Bihar, reveals the various natures and forms or extents of exclusion, discrimination, untouchability, subordination, deprivation and even exploitation both in rural and urban locations in Bihar. This book examines various factors responsible for exclusion of Dalits as well as their status formation in both caste and class or socio-economic status hierarchy and how both contribute in forming a new kind of status among Dalits in Bihar. This book, based on recent literature, is not only a significant contribution to theme of the study but also a valuable addition to the knowledge base and it may be well received by both the social scientists as well as general readers.

NANDU RAM
Former Dean of SSS
And Former Professor of Dr. Ambedkar Chair
Jawaharlal Nehru University, New Delhi

Acknowledgements

This piece of work owes to the valuable guidance and constant source of encouragement of host personalities without whom I could have ever been able to bring this to an end. This book is largely based on my doctoral research submitted in Jawaharlal Nehru University, New Delhi and some of the works were published earlier in Journals such as Social Action and Economic and Political Weekly.

First and foremost, I convey my heartfelt sense of gratitude and thanks to my former supervisor Prof. Nandu Ram (Dr. Ambedkar Chair Professor, CSSS, Dean, SSS), who provided guidance, feedback and support which made it possible to write my Ph.D. Thesis. I also express my sincere gratitude and thanks to my present supervisor Prof. Vivek Kumar who extended guidance and support which made it possible to write my Thesis. Without their interest and guidance, it was not possible on my part to give it a final shape. I am highly indebted to both of them.

I would like to thank the faculty members of the Centre for the Study of Social Systems (CSSS) for their generous help in each and every field of academic endeavour during my academic career. I have dependent upon countless acts of support, generosity and guidance from Prof. M.N. Panini, Prof. Dipankar Gupta, Prof. Anand Kumar, Prof. S.S. Jodhka, Prof. Ehsanul Haq, Prof. Avijit Pathak, Prof. Susan Vishvanathan, Prof. Tiplut Nongbri, Prof. Renuka Singh, Prof. Nilika Mehrotra, Prof Amit Kumar Sharma, Prof. V. Sujatha, with whom I did my M.A and M. Phil. works from 2004 to 2008. The guidance and support received from Dr. G. Srinivas, Dr. Bimal Akoijam, Prof. Harish Narayan Das and all creditable teachers of JNU who contributed to this thesis work. I am deeply grateful for their constant support and help. I would also like to thank the office staffs of CSSS and SSS, especially Mr. Balbir, Mr. Suredra Mrs Anita, Mr. Digamber, Mr. Rajvir, Mr. Bharat and Mr. Sumer, Mr. Manish and Mr. Bhupendra for all time support and cooperation. I convey my thanks to the staff of JNU Library, DSA Library, Nehru Memorial Museum & Library, Teen Murti House, New Delhi and Bihar Information Centre, New Delhi. I wish to thank the staffs of all these libraries for their unconditional help and co-operation.

I extend my especial gratitude and thanks to my dear friend, Mr. Rajesh Roushan who encouraged me and offered his support during my study. My sincere gratitude and thanks also go to Mr. Sudamdeo Ray, Md. Sagir Alam, Mr. Madan Singh, Mr. Pancham Yadav for their co-operation. I also convey my thanks to Dr. Jayashree Ambewadikar, Dr. Ajay Chaudhary, Mr. Siddharth Ram, Mr. Anand Ram, Dr. Mukhtyar Singh, Dr. Babu Bagmare, Dr. Anil Anna, Dr Ramkishore Maholiya, Mrs. Nisha Kumari, Dr. Vinod Arya, Mr. Suresh Ahirwar, Dr. Anil Kumar, Dr. Pramod Kumar and all my JNU friends, seniors and juniors who helped me in different ways.

I am most indebted to my family, especially my parents, Vasudeo Ram and Radhika Devi who suffered a lot in their lives without caring their comfort and pushed me for higher education. All the credit goes to my parents who took burden to nurture me what I am today. They gave me a light of understanding, a sense of feeling and a ray of hope throughout my career. I am also indebted to my elder brother, Sikandar Ram and younger brothers, Upendra Ram, Gautam Ram, my nieces, Anisha, Kavya, nephews, Utkarsh, Ujjawal, Shreyansh, sister-in-law, Babita Devi, sister, Uma Devi and brother-in-law, Naresh Ram for their valuable emotional support in each and every step of my life. My sincere gratitude and thanks also go to father-in-law, Birendra Pratap, mother-in-law, late Indu Devi, brother-in-law, Manish Kumar, sister-in-law, Preeti Kumari and all my nearest and dearest who offered their valuable support in different ways. I am deeply indebted to all of them. I also express my gratitude and thanks, especially to my youngest uncle, late Nageshwar Ram for his constant encouragement and emotional support during my schooling. He always played his role as a catalyst in my academic life. My sincere thanks also go to another uncles, Sahdeo Ram, Baleshwar Ram and Bhuneshwar Ram for their backup in different ways. I am very grateful to my wife, Dr. Poonam Kumari, daughter, Prajakta and son, Prajwal who have been showering love, support, affection throughout my academic journey. Without their unconditional support, this book never would have come to be.

Finally, I would like to thank Mr. B. P. Garg and the editorial team at Gyan Publishing House for their efficient and friendly handling of the book.

Having been privileged in receiving such love and support, I own responsibility for all the errors or omissions that might have crept in the work.

JITENDRA RAM

List of Tables

Map

Appendix-A

Abbreviations

AMO - Assistant Mining Officer
ARO - Assistant Rationing Officer
AY - Anganwardi Yojna
BDO - Block Development Officer
BPL - Below Poverty Line
BSBRT - Bihar State Board of Religious Trusts
DAO - District Account Officer
DC - Deputy Collector
DDO - District Development Officer
DIO - District Industries Officer
DM - District Magistrate
DPO - District Panchayat Officer
DPRO - District Public Relation Officer
DRO - District Rationing Officer
DSO - District Statistical Officer
DWO - District Welfare Office
DWO - District Welfare Officer
DWO - District Welfare Officer
GOI - Government of India
GP - Gram Panchayat
IAY - Indira Awas Yojna
IILS - International Institute of Labour Studies
ILO - International Labour Organisation

IRDP - Integrated Rural Development Programme
JRY - Jawahar Rojgar Yojna
LAO - Land Acquisition Officer
LB - Lower Backward
LS - Lok Sabha
MGNREGA- Mahatma Gandhi National Rural Employment Guarantee Act
MLA - Member of Legislative Assembly
MRD - Ministry of Rural Development
NGO - Non-Governmental Organisation
NREP - National Rural Employment Programme
PC - Planning Commission
PD - Protective Discrimination
RCD - Removal of Civil Disabilities
RD - Rural Development
SC - Scheduled Caste
SOPP - Special Office Package Programme
ST - Scheduled Tribe
TO - Treasury Officer
UB - Upper Backward
UC - Upper Caste
VLW - Village Level Worker
VS - Vidhan Sabha

Chapter - 1

Introduction

Social exclusion is a global phenomenon, which affects adversely individuals, groups and communities. Being accepted as a multi-dimensional concept in social sciences, social exclusion basically explains the institutionalised attempt to keep a few segments of population away from their participation in the various aspects of life in a given society. It is a way of segregating an individual or a group of individuals or a community from the socio-political, economic and cultural domains of social life. Such segregation may be in the form of social distancing, expressed both in physical and social separation, and from the institutional functioning.

More specifically, the term 'social exclusion' is relatively of recent origin in the mid1970s in Western Europe, and it implies to the deprivation of the poor and the marginalised section of people in the world. Rene Lenoir (1974) is the first initiator of the concept of social exclusion in the study of excluded people such as mentally and physically handicapped, suicidal people or people with the suicidal tendency, aged people who remain invalid with regard to performing actively the productive role, abused children and the abusers, delinquents, single parents, multi-problem households, marginals, asocial persons and other socially 'misfits' in France before the 1970s.[1] Similarly, Arjan De Haan[2] defines it as "the denial of equal opportunities imposed by certain groups of society upon others, which leads to inability of individuals to participate in the basic social, civil, political, economic and cultural functioning of society in which they live". Further, Silver[3] describes it by saying that people may be excluded in the following spheres of life earning their livelihood; securing permanent employment and earnings needed for the minimal or prevailing consumption levels; owning property like land, housing, etc. achieving education, skills and cultural capital; participating democratically in the functioning of the welfare state; attaining citizenship and legal equality; and acquiring sociability, human respect, and understanding. The above mentioned definitions of social exclusion clearly show that individuals or groups or even communities are wholly or partially excluded from the various spheres of life in a given society.

Similarly, the term status simply means a socially defined position of a person in a group or a social system or society such as female, student, teacher, child, mother, father, etc. A status occupant is expected by others to behave in a specific way in the given situation. For instance, the relation of a father and a child is reciprocal and gives to each other a position in the family or group. In other words, position is always relative whereas status implies a group or a society. It is in this sense certain privileges, rights and duties are associated with every status. Many sociologists have used the terms position and status synonymously, but some have also made distinction between them. More specifically, the term position denotes one's situation placed in the role-structure, while status refers to the evaluative aspect of the position. Johnson [4] has distinguished the three related terms role, status and position. For him, position or social position is the one filled in by an individual member of a social group or community. It consists of two main elements, i.e., (1) expectations and obligations held by other members of the group or community and the concerning behaviour of the incumbent, and (2) right or the legitimate expectations of the incumbent and the concerning behaviour of other members. Johnson calls the first element as the role of a position, while the second element as the status of a person. It actually denotes the prestige of a position of an individual.

Further, Davis [5] explains that status is a position in the general institutional system, recognised and supported by the entire society. Similarly, for Horton and Hunt[6] status is the rank or position of the individual in a group; and for Weber, status refers to the esteem or social honour given to individuals or groups. There is, however, a little difference between status and social status. For instance, the term status simply indicates the position a person occupies in a group, whereas social status is the amount of honour and prestige he or she receives from members of the group or community and from the larger society having a stratified system. Social status denotes not only the position but also the relative social 'standing' of a person on a publicly recognised scale or social hierarchy. In sum, social status of a person is determined by a wide range of factors and conditions such as original nature and physical characteristics, accidental conditions, physique, mentality and temperament, etc. So also, sex or gender, age, race, caste, class, economic position, etc. are important factors that affect the social standing of a person in a society or community he or she lives.

In the Hindu caste system in India, a person's status is based on his or her birth in a particular caste (*Jati),* which has a definite rank in the caste-hierarchy. This is termed 'ascribed status' with which he or she is born and dies. A person in India also possesses another type of status which he or she achieves in the various domains of his/her life. This is termed 'achieved status', and it is this type of status which is formed through his/ her various types of efforts over a period of time. In this way, the formation of status of an individual is determined on the basis of a number of attributes acquired by him or her, and the interaction or social interaction between him/her and others, besides his or her status ascribed by the caste.[7]

The Problem

In the light of the above explanations, we may briefly analyze that social exclusion is a process by which individuals or groups are wholly or partially excluded from their participation in the society in which they live (European Foundation1995). The concept of social exclusion in India deals with the form of segregating a group of people from the social, economic, educational, political, cultural and religious domains of their social life. In the discussion on the theme, often there is overlap between the exclusion of a person due to his or her individual attributes and the exclusion of the groups due to group attributes. It is necessary to recognize that in the case of group exclusion, all individuals belonging to a particular social or cultural group are excluded because of their group identity and not because of their individual attributes, which may qualify then to be inclusive ones. In other words, the exclusion of an individual is essentially different from that of group. Individuals (from excluded and non-excluded groups) often get excluded from their access to social and economic opportunities for various reasons specific for them (and not because of their particular group's social and cultural identity). For example, individuals may be excluded from job or employment due to lack of requisite education and skills. They may face exclusion in their access to education due to lack of minimum qualifications and merit or their inability to pay for costly education. They may also be excluded from their access to consumer markets due to their lack of income and purchasing power. On the other hand, in the case of exclusion of a group or social group, the variables associated with social and cultural identities such as social origin like caste, colour, race, ethnicity, religion and gender become important, which would exclude all persons belonging to the concerned groups.[8] It is, therefore, necessary to enquire into which of the attributes and variables play more significant role in exclusion of the group as well as of individual from access to various opportunities and the status system as well.

Nature and forms of social exclusion of Dalits in the Indian society or social system, particularly in the Hindu social system, are discrimination, deprivation, exploitation, untouchability, etc., which are deeply rooted in the Hindu caste system. The form of discrimination in the Indian society, which has received much attention, is the caste-based discrimination. By way of differential forms of social relation and interaction among people of various castes, the caste-based discrimination is not confined only to the social sphere but is also extended to the cultural, economic and political spheres. In cultural sphere, there is intolerance of the upper castes to worship commondeities, perform religious rituals or to participate in festivals by the Dalits. It is ever since pervasive against the Dalits or Scheduled Castes who are located at the bottom of the caste-hierarchy, and is seen more in rural than in urban areas. Discrimination is also experienced by Dalits in their access to owing land, trade and business, food security schemes, public water resources, housing facilities, health services, postal and telephone services, road and communication, education and intellectual power, political empowerment, etc. (Shah 2006). Hence, in the Indian context, the caste-based exclusion is more pungent and etched in the collective conscious, which is culturally conditioned.

In the economic sphere, according to Ram,[9] Dalits face discrimination, at two levels, in both the public and private sectors organisations. One, at the time of recruitment itself when the recruiters or selectors remain non-Dalits who are invariably guided by their traditional prejudices against the Dalits. At the second level, the discrimination rather social discrimination against Dalits comes from their fellow employees and superiors in the work organisations. Deprivation and exploitation are other sources of social exclusion of Dalits in the country. It is a fact that the Dalits have been denied of their equal access to social, economic, educational and political domains of life in Indian society as stated above, and still the processes of their explicit deprivation and exploitation are visible more in the rural areas.

The notion of untouchability is another source of social exclusion of Dalits in India. The root cause of untouchability is embedded in the Varnashram Darma, which is based on the superior and inferior gradation or ranking of one varna over the other in descending order (performing religiously the duty of one's varna, out of four of Brahmin, Kshatriya, Vaishya and Shudra varnas). According to the general understanding, the institution of caste is supposedly derived from the varna, which is relied on the fact that the hierarchy of caste system is analogous to that of the varna system and so also is the gradation or rank of each caste in the system. In addition, the caste system is based on observance of purity and pollution.[10] Such notions exclude the Dalits on the basis of their caste identity rather than including them in the social system. As we know, the contact of any kind through touching, dining, drinking and fetching water from the common well and so on between the institutionally-distanced castes, i.e., Dalit and non-Dalit castes, along with the former's spatial segregation supposedly confirm the notion of untouchability. It is a fact that the people belonging to twice-born castes do not accept cooked food or water from the Dalits. They also do not have commensal or inter-dining relationship with them. Although people of the higher castes invite Dalits for ceremonial dinners, but the latter are served meals separately and that too in the end in rural areas. This shows that the exclusion of Dalits is on the basis of their group attributes and not on their individual attributes.

That is why, the extent or degree of social exclusion is the highest against the Dalit communities in the country and more so in the rural areas. It is, therefore, proposed to find out the nature, forms and extent of social exclusion based on untouchability both in rural and urban areas.

We may now briefly look at the formation of social status in the Indian context. But before that, we shall explain the types or forms of status in a society. Thus, according to Linton[11], there are two types of status, i.e., ascribed and achieved statuses. The ascribed status is based on birth, age, sex or gender, kinship, race, caste, etc., as stated earlier. These are "assigned" to a person by the society, irrespective of his or her unique talents or characteristics. For example, status of a boy or a girl in a family is his or her ascribed status in terms of both sex and age. Likewise, the status of an American Negro or Black American or an Indian Dalit is the ascribed status. On the other hand, the achieved status of an individual is a result of his or her personal accomplishments in the open market competition. It is a social position which he or she attains through his or her own efforts, individual choice and competition. In this way, the achieved status is always changeable, while the ascribed status is static or stagnant. The achieved status of a person is, however, determined by a wide range of factors and conditions which are rooted in his or her original nature and socio-cultural moorings. In the whole scenario, the ascribed status always dominates over or influences the nature and form of the achieved status of the person in a society. That is why, Dalits have historically or traditionally been excluded communities and the process of their exclusion still exists in India due to their ascribed status, in spite of their possessing talents or attributes of achievement resulting rite achieved status.

Weber[12] deals with status in terms of a quality of social honour. In contrast to classes, the status groups, according to him, are normally communities of an amorphous kind. He further argues that the economically determined class situation leads to status situation which is atypical component of the life situation of men and women. This, in turn, is determined by a specific positive or negative social estimation of honour. This honour may be connected with quality shared by a plurality and, of course, can be linked in the most varied ways with the status distinction.[13] In the theory of reference group behaviour (and attitudes) and relative deprivation, Merton[14] also has suggested that certain individuals and groups tend to adopt the behaviour (and attitudes) of other groups or individuals in order to achieve a similar position or status. But if they fail to achieve such a position, they suffer from relative deprivation because they find others, belonging to their group, achieving success in similar situations. This type of reference group applies to achieve their respective status or social status.

Dumont[15] reverses the term status for religious status, i.e., rank of caste in caste hierarchy in terms of the superiority of the pure over the impure. On the other hand, Saberwal[16] has stated that, "For one thing, the unit of social appraisal in urban India is increasingly not the corporate group but the individual; and the determinants of this appraisal include education, economic resources, political influence, general knowledgeability, etc., besides religious status. This composite evaluation of one's social standing by others and one's awareness of this evaluation by them will here be designated status with a capital". Unlike Weberian formulation of status of social class, the formation of status or of social status of an individual in India, in Saberwal's sense, is based on the secular characteristics or criteria, i.e., education, economic resources, employment, power or authority or political influence which are achievable by him or her in the society, although his or her corporate group (caste) status does influence it positively or negatively. Hence, an individual may go up or down but groups or communities remain, by and large, static or stagnant due to their ascribed status and their members inherit it in the Indian social system, in spite of a microscopic minority intends to disown it. Therefore, in the this study, the enquiry is to be made as to why Dalits are socially excluded and whether their ascribed status, in some way or the other, contributes to improving or downgrading their social status in the Indian society as a whole. It would also find out the changes in their ascribed status (caste status) on the basis of their interaction with non-Dalits or Scheduled Castes.

After Independence, the government of India and the state governments have adopted and implemented various policies and programmes for socio-economic progress of the Dalits. But it is not clear as how many people from the Dalit communities have got benefited from them. It is also true that a few Dalits have improved their socio-economic condition but bulks of them are still at the bottom line. So also, how many of them have succeeded in getting out of their social, economic and political exclusion and been included wholly or ever partially in these domains. By taking these issues into consideration, the present study would probe into the emerging patterns of formation of socio-economic and political status of the Dalits. It would also investigate how far have they achieved the aforesaid statuses as the present democratic system does not allow or create hurdles in the process of the enhancement of their social development and achieved status. Accordingly, the study would outline the other issues related to government policies and programmes for poverty alleviation, land ownership, employment, etc. in favour of Dalits in the country.

Objectives

In view of the above, the present study aims at exploring the various nature, forms, degree or extents and factors responsible for social exclusion and status formation among Dalits. The following are the specific objectives of this study.

1. To enquire into the nature and form(s) of discrimination, exploitation and subordination of the Dalits in the Hindu caste system and its relationship to the nature and basis of their 'ascribed status'.
2. To find out the forms and degree of their access to various dimensions or aspects of the 'achieved status' in the contemporary period.
3. To elucidate the nature and forms of relationship between their ascribed and achieved statuses.
4. And, to examine the nature and degree or extent of the formation of social status among them and the various kinds of hurdles or bottle-necks coming in it.

Research Questions

Following research questions would be raised and the attempts made to find out their answer in course of pursuing the present study:

1. What is the traditional status of the Dalits in a given socio-cultural milieu in a region?

2. Do the Dalits face more social exclusion in rural than in urban areas?
3. Whether the practice of untouchability and other forms of discrimination and thereby exclusion or social exclusion still exist, in varying nature, against the Dalits living in the Post-independence period, in various regions in the country or in a given state?
4. Do they still face more caste-based oppression, exploitation and isolation in rural than in urban areas?
5. What is their present socio-economic status? Whether it is improving or deteriorating further or is stationary?
6. Although the Dalits have equal political rights of voting and contesting elections at various levels, to what extent have they been able to acquire political consciousness, and power and authority at the local, regional, state and country levels?
7. What has been their traditional caste occupation? Whether they still practice it or is there change in that?
8. Have the Dalits in rural areas benefited from the land reform measures and various other states sponsored and implemented economic measures?
9. Whether their initial low and differential educational level between their males and females have improved and disparity removed in the recent decades?
10. Has the achieved status of the Dalits really enhanced their social prestige in the Hindu caste system in terms of being unconditionally acknowledged and accepted by the non-Dalits in the country?
11. Finally, what is the nature and form of status formation, through the convergence of both ascribed and achieved statuses, of the Dalits in both the rural and urban areas?

Review of Literature

There is not much sociological literature on social exclusion of and status formation among the people in general and Dalits in particular in Indian society. However, a few writings on the issues about both India and elsewhere do provide some insights into comprehending social exclusion and formation of status among the various segments of population, especially among the marginalised ones. We shall provide below a brief review of these writings, including a few about the people in India, and enquire into how these are helpful in understanding social exclusion of and status formation especially among the Dalits in a relatively backward socio-economic region in India.

More specifically, as stated earlier, De Haan[17] explains social exclusion in terms of denial of equal opportunities imposed by certain groups of people upon others in a society. This leads to their inability to participate in the basic social, civil, political, economic and cultural functioning of a society in which they live. On the other hand, Silver[18] illustrates social exclusion by saying that people may be excluded from earning their livelihood, at the prevailing consumption levels, through securing permanent employment; acquiring property like land, housing, etc. and getting credits, achieving education, skills and cultural capital, and so on. But in the view of Byrne[19] social exclusion is about the nature of social system and about the dynamic development of social structure which has implications for the various agencies providing reinforcement and sustenance to it.

However, social exclusion, for Sen[20], is a relational root of deprivation. Sen explains by distinguishing the constitutive relevance of exclusion (exclusion or deprivation is of intrinsic importance in its own rights) from its instrumental importance (exclusion itself is not impoverishing but it can lead to the impoverishment of human life). He also differentiates between unfavourable exclusion and unfavourable inclusion and active and passive exclusion. In other words, exclusion is something that is done by some people to the other people. Similarly, Naila Kabeer[21] states that social exclusion happens at global, national and local levels. According to her, the concept is deeply rooted in institutions like state, markets, community/ civil society, etc. These institutions are structured in the relationship between macro-economic change and the patterns of economic growth as well as the changing life circumstances of individuals, households and groups. She further points out that the "various institutional mechanisms through which resources are allotted and values assigned operate in such a way as to systematically deny particular groups of people the resources and recognition which would allow them to participate fully in the life of that society".

After the brief exposition of the concept of social exclusion when we look at a few writings about an excluded community like Dalits in India, we find that they have been perennially excluded and deprived from almost every aspects of life. For instance, Prakash Louis[22] reveals that social exclusion of Dalits is entirely embedded in the various institutions of the Indian social system, particularly the Hindu social system. He further points out that the Dalits get excluded from the social, political, economic and cultural domains of their life. According to him, social exclusion or segregation is an institutionalised form of social distancing which keeps out a particular section of population from the usual functioning of a social order. Similarly, Thorat[23] examines the nature of social exclusion in the Hindu social system. According to him, the exclusion of an individual takes place from access to economic and social opportunities due to his or her individual attributes. On the other hand, in the case of group exclusion, all individuals belonging to a particular social or cultural group are excluded due to their group identity. This simply means that the individuals or persons belonging to certain groups are excluded, irrespective of their individual positive attributes, simply because their groups are excluded.

Further, confirming social exclusion to religious domain, James Massey[24] stated that religion is as much a source of bondage and exclusion of liberation-inclusion, especially in the case of the casteless Christians or Dalits Christians. In his view, the history of their problem and the basic question of their identity also include the role of religion as an agent of their bondage or liberation. He mainly discusses the role of Hindu religion in the historical development of the Dalit problems in the caste system. Emphasizing on casteless Christians, he argues that the Christian Dalits or Dalit Christians are casteless because they belong to a community which, in their pre-Dalit state, was of the casteless and classless people. It is in this sense the Christians are supposed to be the most egalitarian and so also is the Christianity or Christian religion.

But contrary to this, changes have also occurred among the Scheduled Castes or Dalits due to their self- initiatives. For instance, in a study of the Jatavs of Agra city, Lynch [25] illustrates social change among them through their political participation in the state of Uttar Pradesh. He mainly examines their identity in the Hindu caste system in the state. According to him, changes have taken place among people of the Jatav caste due to adoption of the Parliamentary Democracy after Independence. He has found that the people of this caste had begun a process of self-evaluation and self-reformation in order to gain respectability and higher status in the Hindu caste system. He further explains that they have got mobility not through sanskritisation but through the active and separate political participation. In this way, the Jatavs have achieved political power and authority through the politics and job opportunities in the state of Uttar Pradesh.

Plight of the Dalits has become a regular feature in rural India. Their plight is distinctively visible in the social, economic, political, religious and cultural aspects of their life. Such plight has been examined by Vidyarthi and Mishra[26] in the four cultural and linguistic zones of Magahi, Maithali, Bhojpuri and tribal zone of the in divided state of Bihar. In their study, both Vidyarthi and Mishra describe the different Scheduled Castes or categories (such as Bhogtas, *Panswansis, Ghasis Turi-Mahlis* and *Chamars* in the tribal zone, and *Musahars, Chamars, Rajwars and Dusadhas* in the Magahi area) and compare their social, economic, political and cultural disparity among them. According to them, the Scheduled Castes or Dalits of the tribal zone are self-employed as artisan communities, compared to those of the Magahi zone where they are casual labourers in the agricultural fields of the upper caste people. In any case, the Scheduled Castes in all these cultural zones are socially excluded in almost all domains of life.

It is a fact that the Dalits or Scheduled Castes in India have been socially, economically and educationally backward communities for centuries and still it is an ongoing process. They are the most vulnerable section of society compared to other castes and communities. Due to the various schemes adopted and implemented under the various developmental programmes like *Integrated Rural Development Programmes,* (IRDP), *National Rural Employment Programmes* (NREP), *Jawahar Rojgar Yojna* (JRY*), Indira Awas Yojna (*IAY), etc., changes have taken place among people of the various caste categories of the Scheduled Castes in several states in the country. In the state of Bihar, these programmes have primarily brought changes in their position of occupation and income, educational and training for self-employment, health and nutrition, social awareness and participation, etc.[27]

On the other hand, Harold Isaacs[28] interviewed 50 educated members of scheduled castes from different professional background. It is a travel account of scheduled castes living in urban centres. He writes "I went to India early in 1963 to find out what has been happening to educated ex-untouchable in these first years of Indian Independence. My inquiry was a modest one and so is this report in which I simply pass on what I learned from talking with some fifty individuals going through the experience of students, teachers, civil servants, politicians, who have come up through the openings in Indian society created by new educated opportunities. My brief report obviously does not exhaust the subject but it does introduce it. There is also the connection between the experience of 'untouchables' in India today and that of the Negroes in the United States". In his book, Isaacs gives a brief account on the origin of the untouchability and the details of dialogue which took place between Gandhi and Ambedkar during the crisis of 1932. He also gives the accounts by mentioning that the educated scheduled castes individuals who being segregated and looked down in the society prefer to maintain anonymous without disclosing their untouchable identity. Most of them would not like to maintain relationships with their rural and urban kinsmen although they deeply feel interested to revolt against the caste Hindu society. The accounts given by Isaacs are of immense relevance because they trace the grievances of the disillusioned untouchables or Scheduled Castes and their failure of the system to evolve a casteless society.

Bernard S. Cohn[29] deals with an interesting and vivid account of the changing status of *Chamars of Madhopur* in a Rajput village in Jounpur district of Uttar Pradesh. The Chamars occupy a subordinate place in all the economic and political affairs of the village. He explains various fundamental issues regarding Chamar community, related with their kinship organisation, religious customs and social status. He states by mentioning that "chamar are regarded as defiled especially because of their repugnant traditional occupations of skinning, tanning and midwifery and eating carrion beef". He further elaborates on economic aspects by saying that the Chamar are economically tied to the village, especially to the *Thakurs,* as tenants, traditional workers and labourers. Economically, a Chamar family cultivates about one acre of land and the income from this sustains them only for four months of the year and in remaining part of the year they work as agricultural coolies. In recent years, urban employment has increased. They have started to work in cotton and jute mills in the mines and in the cities as construction workers and rickshaw pullers. In the political domain, Cohn notes that the status of the Chamars is subservient to Thakurs. The infrastructural development has facilitated spatial mobility and changes in the work position of Chamars of Madhopur village. The Arya Samaj movements of religious reform grew strong, elections brought political competition on a wider scale and the nationalist struggle became a reality for the villagers. Due to these outside influences, population in the village and surrounding areas steadily rose. Even caste status and religious customs have undergone notable change. This study primarily highlights the process of transformation from their traditional servile status to a new status and direction of development.

On the other hand, Sunanda Patwarthan[30] has studied the changing position of scheduled castes in Poona city. In this study, she deals with mobility and the nature of change that has taken place among the Harijans of a particular region of Maharashtra. With a sample of 360 families drawn from *Mahar*, *Mang*, *Chamabhar*, *Dhor* and *Holar* communities in Poona city she has analyzed the change as well as continuity among the Scheduled Castes at behavioural and socio-cultural levels. She perceives changes occurring at two different levels, i.e., materialist level and at the level of value system. She seeks to answer the fundamental questions how far the Indian social system as a system of values has changed during the last few decades. She further raises the question, is it possible for individuals and groups belonging to the low polluting castes, with low income categories, to move up in terms of socio-economic status and change in their polluting occupations in spite of ritual restriction and structured constraints. Again, is it possible for the *Mang* or the *Mahar* or the Harijan or the Neo-Buddhist in Maharashtra to have access to the new technologies into Indian society. She has analyzed the upward mobility of the untouchable in terms of changes in their occupation, education, political participation as well as Sanskritisation and conversion to other religions and caste associations.

Andre Beteille[31] has studied caste, class and power along with changing relations as micro level in the village of Sripuram in Tanjore district of Tamil Nandu. In the traditional structure, class and power are subsumed in the caste but in a changing society they are to some extent caste free. He argues that the predominant castes in the village were the Brahmins, Non-Brahmins and Adi-Dravidas (untouchables). By explaining physical structure of the village, he gives an account of the disposition of different communities inhabiting the village. There is a clear-cut physical segregation from one village to another village. The caste structure of the village in terms of these three caste groups was analyzed along with an analysis of the heterogeneous characters of each caste group. Beteille further examines the economic organisation in terms of production, distribution and exchange, concentrating chiefly on the class system as system of social relations. He also deals with the process of change of ownership of land taken place from Brahmins to Non-Brahmins. In this process, the economic position of Adi-Dravidas has not undergone any change. Despite that he mentions that power has also shifted from Brahmins to Non-Brahmins through the creation of new institutions such as the panchayats. Political parties have made inroads into the old power blocks. The Adi-Dravidas with their numerical strength could make their voice felt in the elections.

Further, Mishra[32] explains the socio-economic status, educational level and religious affiliations of the Dalits of Gaya district in south and Darbhanga district in north Bihar. According to him, Dalits are economically and educationally most backward castes or communities in these two districts where they are more in numbers. Apart from this, he also elucidates the problem of their exploitation and oppression, besides atrocities committed on them by other castes in the state. More so, atrocities on the Dalits are now a general phenomenon, but more importantly atrocities on Dalit women are more common in rural areas. But what he has not unfolded is the reasons for their backwardness and the nature or forms and degree of their social exclusion. He has, however, pointed out the process of change in economic, educational and religious status of Dalits going on in the state as a whole.

F.G. Bailey[33] studied Bisipara village in a remote hills of the western Orissa where he found the warrior caste at the top while the Boad untouchables occupying the lowest position and working as farm labourers in the village social hierarchy. During the last hundred years, the process of the change initiated through administration and trade had changed the structure of the caste groups in the village. Due to the monopoly of trade, the Boad outcastes raised themselves, to some extent, in the economic ladder but they have been prevented from finding a social level appropriate to their new economic status because of the barrier of pollution. Because of that they tended more often to invoke the protection of the administration and to use their rights as citizens of the state to overcome the disabilities improved by the rest of the village. Interestingly, The Boad outcastes did not receive justice through the village council, but through courts of law. Even they attempted to go beyond the political frontier of the village and seek to establish themselves as citizens of the state. The Boad outcastes, according to Bailey "are tending to separate themselves from the rest of the village and try to order their relationship with their caste groups in the village not in term of village structure but within the framework of administration".

Satish Saberwal[34], whose study contains comparative and empirical details about the Scheduled Castes, focuses on the social mobility among two Scheduled Castes -*Ad Dharmis* and *Balmikis* and a backward caste, *Ramgarhias* in a small township of Modelpur in Punjab. In this effort, he makes an interesting observation of the conflicting, results affecting these specific communities. He argues that the forces of urbanisation and industrialisation have enabled the Ramgarhias to develop entrepreneurial capacity in their traditional occupations of carpentry and blacksmithy. This has also helped the Ad Dharmis to leave their traditional occupation of weaving and shoe-making and to adopt new occupations. But these processes have remained in effected in the case of Balmikis who still continue in their traditional occupation of scavenging.

Contrary to this, Sinha and Sinha[35] have mentioned about some new untoward incidents which highlight the diminishing surviving conditions of Dalits in rural Bihar, let alone their development of socio-economic and political conditions. For instance, they have stated about the Bathani Tola Massacre (1995) in Bhojpur district of central Bihar which highlights the ongoing suppression of the struggles of the underprivileged by the private armies of upper castes in alliance with the middle castes and the state apparatus. Their argument makes clear about the dangerous trend among the upper and middle level castes in connivance with the state machinery that has emerged as a powerful force to suppress the Scheduled Castes or Dalits in the rural areas.

Earlier, Sachchidananda[36] had focused on the elite formation among the Scheduled Castes in Bihar. He had chosen the elite from amongst the Dalit government employees, politicians and social workers, who had also been socio-politically more conscious Scheduled Castes in urban area in the state. Due to their socio-economic and political well-being, both quantitative and qualitative socio-psychological changes have been taking place among the 'Harijan elite'. It has also enhanced the educational level of both men and women, social position of the educated and socially and politically conscious Dalit women besides the caste solidarity and political consciousness among the Dalits as a whole. According to him, the above mentioned attributes have elevated their social status also through the various government measures and their internalisation of the *Sanskritic* and modern values. According to him, the socio-economic condition of the Scheduled Castes has improved in Bihar, yet, the practice of child marriage, widow remarriage, etc., is still in vague among them in the state.

William L. Rowe [37] presents the purer but rarely documented case of actual changes taken place in the rank by part of an endogamous Shudra caste of Noniayas (Non-Scheduled Castes) of the northern India. In his study, he explains how elite within caste of Noniayas used its economic power to claim and eventually gain a partially successful entry into the higher Kshatriya varna rank within a period of half a century. He describes three factors by which the Noniayas claim high rank in the society. First, a western-influenced secular model with some de-emphasis on ritual and on the importance of caste has gained adherents as among wealthy, educated, high-caste persons elsewhere in India. Second, some persons lack the economic ability or perhaps the desire to undertake the expense of validating the claims to high rank. Third, there exists a desire to retain eligibility for the advantageous opportunities sponsored by the government for

Depressed or Scheduled Castes. Even the notion of Sanskritisation played the key role in changing their behaviour and customs.

However, focusing on the condition of Dalits in India in general and in Bihar in particular, Ramashray Roy[38] has mentioned that there is not much improvement in the socio-economic condition of Scheduled Castes more than half a century after the independence. He tries to explain and find out the loopholes in the relationship between development and democracy which, according to him, is dissatisfactory. For instance, only a few privileged people from among the Dalits have made substantial gains and the remaining others have been marginalised, he says. He further states that their continued depressed socio-economic condition has been unaffected by the various welfare and development schemes in Bihar. On the other hand, Lal[39] illustrates the economic, political and social exploitation of the Dalits done by the upper strata of society in Bihar. According to him, Dalits are the worst sufferer than any other community and their suffering is deeply embedded in the institution of Hindu caste system. He advances his idea by stating that land is the main source of income of people in the rural areas, and in the context of land, the upper castes possess most of the land while Dalits are mainly agricultural labourers and are in the vulnerable condition.

In the state of Bihar, criminalisation of politics is a fact of life. Elections are only as an instrument for legitimizing the criminality of politics, wherein the muscle power had remained the part of electoral process before 1990 in which the upper castes allowed conditionally the Dalits and even the backward caste people to cast their votes in elections. After 1990, a drastic change took place in the process of elections in the state. Indu Bharti[40] has reported about the Dalits' assertion in the elections to the Lok Shabha and Vidhan Shabha held in 1990 in which the hundreds of thousands of Dalits were able to cast their votes, resisting threats to their lives and defeating the murderous booth-capturing campaign of the upper castes landlords. This has given the Dalits a new *Izzat* (dignity) in the state.

Finally, if we see the jajmani system in Bihar or in different parts of India, we find that it is the system of social ties among the people of different caste groups which is changing. Under this system, each caste group within a village or outside is expected to give certain specialised services to the families of other castes. In this way, each caste is traditionally associated with the practice of a particular occupation. For instance, in his study of four villages of the Buxar district of Bihar, Sahay[41] reflects on the relationship between caste and occupation as well as the status of each caste in the jajmani system today. He also finds that caste-based occupations no longer exist in the villages. In other words, jajmani system in rural Bihar has undergone notable change, especially regarding the linkages between caste and occupations.

Similarly, the Raigars of north India, especially of Rajasthan and Delhi, have shown an emerging pattern of their becoming a dominant Scheduled Caste. For this purpose, Shyamlal[42] has stated about the different phases of development among the Raigars. He has also analysed the caste consciousness and caste-based solidarity among the different untouchable castes or communities in general and Raigars in particular in Rajasthan and Delhi.

Sharma[43] has tried to present the problem of Scheduled Castes in a different perspective in which he makes a distinction between caste and class on the basis of empirical data from rural Bihar. He analyses such data in the historical perspective. He argues that historically four upper castes in rural Bihar have remained dominant in rural as well as urban areas. They are Brahmans, Bhumihars, Rajputs and Kayasthas who are socially and economically more powerful than other castes in regard with having great stock of land in their possession in the state. The second most dominant castes are the backward castes which are both numerically and economically better off. According to him, the forward castes are essentially the big peasants and landlords, and the backward castes like Yadav and Koeri are mainly the middle level peasants. The Scheduled Castes are essentially agricultural labourers in agrarian hierarchy in the state.

Research Methodology

The present study is exploratory and descriptive. The purpose of such research design is to describe the nature, forms and extent of social exclusion of Scheduled Castes or Dalits and the formation of social status among them within and outside the Hindu social system. It also reveals social, economic, political and cultural aspects of their life and, in turn, examines how these facilitate them in forming their social status, both within and outside the caste system. In this study, a number of social indicators such as education, employment and income, power or authority, location or rank in the hierarchy of caste system, nature and extent of untouchability, gender disparity, etc. have been identified to explore the nature and forms of social exclusion of Dalits and formation of their social status in a region or state in India.

Universe of the Study

For the purpose of the present study, a region in the state of Bihar has been selected due to its socio-economic and educational backwardness in general and of the Dalits in particular. Bihar is traditionally divided into North Gangetic (North Bihar) and South Gangetic (South Bihar) plain. The North Bihar Plain covers an area of 56,320 square kilometers and South Bihar Plain occupies an area of 33,320 square kilometers. The Chotanganpur plateau (now in Jharkhand) covers about 46 percent of the total area but only 25 percent of the total population of the state. North Bihar is chronically affected by floods but does not have proper irrigation facilities, contrary to the South Bihar which is free from flood devastation and has good irrigation facilities.[44] Due to well irrigation facilities and location of industries, South Bihar is more developed than the North Bihar. The society in Bihar as a whole is considered to be a semi-feudal in its structure and functions. Bihar is one of those states where the upper castes, numerically not being large, have traditionally enjoyed the ritual and socio-economic as well as political superiority and social prestige. Their numerical weakness is more than compensated by their ritual status, social prestige, and economic and political power in the state. On the other hand, the Dalits in Bihar are considered, as mentioned above, to be the most backward Scheduled Castes, compared to those in other states in India. Due to their low socio-economic, political, and educational and hierarchical positions in the existing social system, they have been, for centuries, the victim of the feudal or semi-feudal social order in India in general and in Bihar in particular.

According to 2001 Census, the total population of the country is 1028 million persons (532.1 million males and 496.4 million females) in which 16.6 million (8.6 million males and 8.0 million females) were Scheduled Castes, constituting 16.20 percent of the total population of the Scheduled Castes in the country. The Scheduled Castes or Dalits are 14.77 percent (Jharkhand included) of the total population of the state. In India, 45.20 percent of the Scheduled Castes were literate, compared to only 28.5 percent literates in Bihar. Bihar is divided into thirty eight districts out of which the East Champaran district, situated in North Bihar has been selected for the present study. Presently, the East Champaran district, with its headquarters at Motihari, consists of six sub-divisions and twenty-seven blocks. According to 2001 Census, total population of the East Champaran district was 36,88,687 persons (19,41,681 males and 17,47,006 females) in which 4,95,799 persons were Scheduled Castes (2,61,132 males and 2,34,667 females). There were 36.40 percent (male 51.38 percent and female 19.97 percent) main workers in engaged in primary, secondary and tertiary sectors of employment in Bihar. In case of the East Champaran district, there were 38.24 percent of the Dalits or Scheduled Castes (male 56.15 percent and female17.93%) who were engaged in the primary, secondary and tertiary sectors of employments. The literacy rate of the Dalits or Scheduled Castes of the East Champaran district was 20.60 percent (male 30.25% and female 9.66%), which was the lowest literacy rate compared to the other districts in the state, according to 2001 census.

Selection of Samples

The present study has been carried out in the Chakia Sub-division of the East Champaran District in North Bihar. In the Chakia Sub-Division, the total population, according to 2001 census, is 1,71,273 persons (89,099 males and 82,174 females) in which 31,416 persons (16,331 males and 15,085 females) are Scheduled Castes. For the purpose of the data collection, the sample of respondents consists of 250 persons of which 125 respondents have been selected from a village and 125 respondents from the town-the Chakia Sub-division headquarters. More precisely, the respondents have randomly been selected. The data has been collected through the semi-structured Interview Schedule administered separately on both the rural and urban respondents.

Sources of Data Collection

The study is based on both the primary and secondary sources of data or information. The primary sources of data consist of the interviews with the respondents and also observation of their attitudes and behaviour. Similarly, the secondary sources of data are books, articles, magazines, Census data, Government documents, journals, etc. The government documents include reports of the Ministry of Rural Development, Planning Commission and reports of the State Directorate of Economics and Statistics. The Census data have been used with regards to population of Dalits, their literacy rate, occupational pursuits, and caste composition and so on. The data collected from both the sources have been processed and analyzed in accordance with the stated objectives, and a few hypotheses verified in course of pursuing the study.

The Relevance

The present study is relevant from theoretical as well as applied points of view. The study is conducted on social exclusion and status formation among Dalits due to their socio-economic vulnerability and low social status in both caste and class hierarchy. As we know that social exclusion is a process by which an individual or a group gets excluded from socio-economic, educational, political sphere on the basis of their group attributes than individual one. In this way an individual is somehow included in the social system while a group or community is socially excluded from the social process. In this situation, it is significant to analyze natures and forms of exclusion of Dalits or Scheduled Castes in Indian society in general and the this study in particular. On the other hand, we would look at hierarchical structure of caste system where it has been observed that the given status i.e., ascribed (caste status) always plays key role in determining the socio-economic status of the person in Hindu caste system after achieving the highest position in the secular domain. Therefore, dependent and independent variables have been taken for the examination of social exclusion and formation of status among the Dalits in the this study from the conceptual and theoretical points of view.

From the applied point of view, it would be significant to know their expectation about the change in both caste and class structure. The study also observes that what the Scheduled Castes or Dalits perceive change about themselves and what other castes look at change in their social status. In this situation, some indicators have been taken for measuring their exclusion as well as social status in the Hindu caste system. We have also taken constitutional provisions and some reference group model by which we will be able to enquire into whether these kinds of models have contributed bringing change in their social status in both in rural and urban areas or not. Apart from that it is also relevance to examine their aspirations or expectations about what they have perceived change in their social status in terms of other caste groups in both rural and urban areas.

Notes

1. Referred in Sen, Amartya (2004). *Social Exclusion, Concept, Application, Security,* Critical Quest, New Delhi.
2. De Haan, Arjan (1997). "*Poverty and Social Exclusion: A Comparison of Debates on Deprivation*", Working Paper No, 2, Poverty Unit, Sussex University, Brighton.
3. Silver, Hilary (1995). Social Exclusion and Social Solidarity: Three Paradigms, *International Labour Review,* Vol.133,1994/5-6.
4. Johnson, Harry M. (1960). *Sociology: A Systematic Introduction*, Allied Publisher, New Delhi.
5. Davis, Kingsley (1949). *Human Society,* The Macmillan Company, New Delhi.
6. Referred in Horton, Paul B. and Chester Hunt (1964). *Sociology*, The McGraw-Hill Companies, New York.
7. Ram, Nandu (1988). *The Mobile Scheduled Castes, Rise of a New Middle Class,* Hindustan Publishing Corporation, Delhi, p.78.
8. Thorat, Sukhdeo (2008). "Social Exclusion in the Indian Context: Theoretical Basis of Inclusive Policies", *Indian Journal of Human Development*, Vol. 2, No.1.
9. Ram, Nandu (2008). *Caste System and Untouchability in South India*, Manak Publication, New Delhi, pp.18-19.
10. Dumont, Louis (1966). *Homo Hierarchicus: The Caste System and its Implications*, Oxford University Press, New Delhi.
11. Linton, Ralf (1936). *The Study of Man: An Introduction*, New York, Appleton-Century-Crofts.
12. Weber, Max (1961). *From Max Weber: Essays in Sociology*, Routlegde and Kegan Paul, London. (translated by H.B. Gerth and C.W Mills) .
13. Referred in Bendix, R and S.M. Lipset (eds.) (1966). *Class, Status and Power*, London Routledge and Kegan Paul, p. 24.
14. Merton, R.K. (1968). *Social Theory and Social Structure*, American Publishing Co. Pvt, New Delhi, Bombay, Calcutta, New York.

15. Dumont, Louis (1966). *Homo Hierarchicus: The Caste System and its Implications*, Oxford University Press, New Delhi.
16. Saberwal, Satish (1972). *Mobile Men: Limit to Social Change in Urban Punjab*, Indian Institute of Advanced Study, Shimla, in Associated with Manohar Publications, New Delhi.
17. De Haan, Arjan (1997). "*Poverty and Social Exclusion: A Comparison of Debates on Deprivation*", Working Paper No. 2, Poverty Unit, Sussex University, Brighton.
18. Silver, Hilary (1995). Social Exclusion and Social Solidarity: Three Paradigms, *International Labour Review*, Vol.133, 1994/5-6.
19. Byrne, David (2005). *Social Exclusion*, Rawat Publications, Jaipur and New Delhi.
20. Sen, Amartya (2004). *Social Exclusion: Concept, Application and Scrutiny*, Critical Quest, New Delhi.
21. Kabeer, Naila (2008). "Social Exclusion, Poverty and Discrimination towards an Analytical Framework", *Critical Quest*, New Delhi, p. 24.
22. Louis, Prakash (2002). "*Social Exclusion of Dalits: Agony and Assertion of an Outcasted Community in Social Exclusion: Essays in Honour of Dr. Bindeshwar Pathak*" (ed.) by A.K. Lal, Concept Publishing Company, New Delhi.
23. Thorat, Sukhdeo (2008). "Social Exclusion in the Indian Context: Theoretical Basis of Inclusive Policies", *Indian Journal of Human Development*, Vol. 2, No.1.
24. Massey, James (1995). *Dalits in India*, Manohar Publishers and Distributers, New Delhi.
25. Lynch, Owen M. (1974). *The Politics of Untouchability*, National Publishing House, New Delhi.
26. Vidyarthy, L.P. & N. Mishra (1977). *Harijan Today*, Classical Publications, New Delhi.
27. Kumar, Rabindra (2002). *Impact of Rural Development on Scheduled Castes*, Anmol Publications, New Delhi.
28. Isaacs, Harold R. (1965). *India's Ex-untouchables*, Asian Publishing House, Bombay.
29. Cohn, Bernard S.(1955). "The Changing Status of a Depressed Caste", in *Village India* (ed.) by McKim Marriott, Asia Publishing House, Bombay.
30. Patwarthan, S. (1973). *Change among India's Harijans: Maharashtra: A Case Study,* Orient Longman Ltd, New Delhi.
31. Beteille, Andre (1966). *Caste, Class and Power*, Oxford University Press, Bombay.
32. Mishra, Narayan (2004). *Exploitation and Atrocities on the Dalits in India,* Kalpaz, Publications, New Delhi.

33. Bailey, F.G. (1958). *Caste and Economic Frontier,* Oxford University Press, Bombay.
34. Saberwal, Satish (1990). *Mobile Men: Limit to Social Change in Urban Punjab, Indian Institute of Advanced Study*, Shimla in Association with Manohar Publication, New Delhi.
35. Sinha, Arvind and Indu Sinha (1996). "State, Class and 'Sena' Nexus", *Economic and Political Weekly,* No. 2.
36. Sachchidananda (1977). *The Harijan Elite*, Thomson Press Ltd., Faridabad, India.
37. Rowe, William. L. (1968). "The New Cauhans: A Caste Mobility Movement in North India", in *Social Mobility in the Caste System in India* (ed.) by James Silverberg, Houton The Hague.
38. Ramashray, Roy (1999). *Dalits, Development and Democracy*, Shipra Publication, New Delhi.
39. Lal, A.K. (2008). "Dalits of Bihar" in "*Dalits in Contemporary India: Discrimination and Discontent*" (ed.) by Nandu Ram, Vol.1, Siddhant Publications, New Delhi.
40. Bharti, Indu (1990). "Dalits Gain New Izzat", *Economic and Political Weekly*, May 5-12.
41. Sahay, Gaurang Ranjan (1998). "Caste System in Contemporary Bihar: A Case Study of Selected Villages", *Sociological Bulletin*, 47(2), September.
42. Shyamlal (2006). *Untouchable Castes in India*, Rawat Publications, Jaipur and New Delhi.
43. Sharma, Alakh N. (1995-96). "Caste and Class in Rural Bihar", *Journal of Social and Economic Studies*, Vol. 12-13, p. 61.
44. Diwakar, R.R. (1959). *Bihar through the Ages,* Orient Longman, New Delhi.

Chapter - 2

The Conceptual and Theoretical Framework

Introduction

We have already stated, in the previous chapter, that the social exclusion or inclusion of person in Indian society in general and caste system in particular as well as in the secular domains of life is intrinsically related to his/her group or caste or community affiliation which, in itself, excluded from or included in the commensal and other close relationships. We have also mentioned that one's achieved status is greatly influenced by his/her ascribed status, which is inevitably assigned to him/her on the basis of birth in a particular caste or community placed in the hierarchy of castes or communities. A fact may, however, be explicated her that one's achieved status or status achieved in the secular domains does influence, if not fully then at least to some extent, one's ascribed status. Then, the question remains as to how such influence of the achieved status over the ascribed status or the relationship between the achieved status and ascribed statuses can be analyzed in a theoretical framework. So also, how the impact of such relationship on one's social exclusion or inclusion could theoretically be explained. In other words, an attempt will be made in this chapter to formulate an integrated theoretical framework to analyze our data on social exclusion of and status formation among the Dalits or Scheduled Castes located both in rural and urban areas particularly in a backward state of Bihar. But before doing that, we shall look briefly, at some theoretical-analytical frameworks, on the issues available in social sciences, especially in Sociological and Social Anthropological studies.

Social Exclusion: Some Conceptual and Theoretical Perspectives

The concept of Social exclusion is a global phenomenon, which affects adversely individuals, groups and communities. Being accepted as a multi-dimensional concept in social sciences, social exclusion basically explains the institutionalised attempt to keep a few segments of population away from their participation in the various aspects of life in a given society. It is a way of segregating a group of people from the social, political, economic and cultural domains of social life. Such segregation may be in the form of social distancing, expressed both in physical and social separation, and from the institutional functioning, as stated in Chapter 1. Thus, the process of social exclusion deals with deprivation, discrimination, marginalisation, exploitation and oppression of an individual or social group in a society. In this regard, it has been said that inequality in any country is rising due to exclusion of many social groups from their access to the available opportunities.

More specifically, the term 'social exclusion' is relatively of recent origin in the mid-1970s in Western Europe mainly through the work of the International Institute of Labour Studies (IILS) at the International Labour Organisation (ILO), and it implies to the deprivation of the poor and the marginalised section of people in the world. Rene Lenoir (1974) is the first initiator of the concept of social exclusion in the study of excluded people such as mentally and physically handicapped, suicidal people or people with the suicidal tendency, aged people who remain invalid with regard to performing actively the productive role, abused children and the abusers, delinquents, single parents, multi-problem households, marginals, asocial persons and other socially 'misfits' in France before the 1970s[1], as mentioned in Chapter 1.

There is also an official French definition of the concept, which explains social exclusion as a *rupture of social bonds* which deals with a French emphasis on the organic and solidaristic nature of society. More broadly, social exclusion has been defined as the process through which individuals or groups are wholly or partially excluded from their full participation in the society within which they live[2]. The concept of social exclusion has two main defining characteristics. First, it is a multi-dimensional concept. People may be excluded, e.g., from earning livelihoods, getting employment, owning, property, housing minimum consumption of goods achieving, education, citizenship, personal contacts or respect, etc. But the concept focuses on the multidimensionality of deprivation due to the fact that the people are often deprived of one thing or the other at the same time. It also refers to exclusion (deprivation) in the economic, social and political spheres. Second, the concept has been less discussed and analyzed in the literature but is perhaps more relevant for the theoretical contribution which implies a focus on the relations and processes that cause deprivation. People can be excluded by many different sorts of groups, often at the same time: landlords exclude others from their access to land or housing; political elite groups exclude others from legal rights; priest in India may exclude Scheduled Castes from access to temple; minority may be excluded from expressing freely their identity; labour market, but also some trade unions exclude people (non-members) from getting job; and so on. Exclusion happens at each level of society. Group formation is fundamental of human society and this is accompanied by exclusion of others. The concept takes us beyond mere descriptions of deprivation, and focuses attention on social relations, the processes and institutions that underlie and are part and parcel of deprivation.[3]

On the other hand, Silver[4] focuses on definitions of the term indicating numerous connotations and distinguishes three paradigms, i.e., solidarity, specialisation and monopoly within which the concept of social exclusion is embedded. According to her, each paradigm has a different notion of social integration, explaining social exclusion to a different cause and is based on different political philosophy. These provide explanations for multiple forms of disadvantage- economic, social, political and cultural, and encompass theories of citizenship, racial-ethnic inequalities, poverty and long-term unemployment. These paradigms are only schematic representations of different traditions and in practice these overlap; and analysts are influenced by aspects of different traditions. Now, we would discuss these theoretical paradigms in the context of social exclusion in particular.

In the *solidarity paradigm*, dominant in France, exclusion is defined as the rapture of social cultural and moral bonds between the individuals or group rather than the economic bond. This interpretation draws on Rousseau, especially the Durkheimian notion of social solidarity and order. The dualistic categories of ordering the world define the poor, unemployment and ethnic minorities as outsiders. The inverse of exclusion is integration to be achieved by insertion, which implies in a Durkheimian sense assimilation into the dominant culture.[5] Thus, solidarity paradigm implies political rights and duties.

In the *specialisation paradigm*, exclusion reflects discrimination that is the drawing of group distinctions that denies to individual full access or participation in exchange or interaction. This paradigm draws on Anglo-American liberalism tradition, especially those of Lock and Unitarianism, according to which individuals are or should be able to move across boundaries of social differentiation and division of labour. Liberal models of citizenship emphasize the contractual exchange of rights and obligations. Exclusion is often a consequence of unenforced rights and market failure, and the focus here is on exclusion of individuals and of not groups[6].

The *monopoly paradigm*, drawing on the work on Weber and, to some extent, Marx and Marshal, views social order as coercive and imposed through hierarchical power relations. It defines exclusion as a consequence of the formation of group monopolies. Powerful groups restrict the access of outsiders to valued resources through social closure. Unlike in the specialisation paradigm, group distinctions and inequality overlap in the monopoly paradigm. Inequality is mitigated by social democratic citizenship, which entails full participation in the country. This paradigm is influential, especially in Britain and many North European countries.

Further, social exclusion for Sen[7] is a relational root of deprivation. He draws attention to various meanings and dimensions of the concept of social exclusion. Sen explains by distinguishing the 'constitutive relevance' of exclusion (exclusion or deprivation is of intrinsic importance in its own rights) from its 'instrumental importance' (exclusion itself is not impoverishing but it can lead to the impoverishment of human life). These two constitutive and instrumental importance can overlap like landlessness that can be responsible for generating deprivation (instrumental) but also have value in itself in cases where being without land is like "being without a limb of one's own" (constitutive). He also differentiates between 'unfavourable exclusion' and 'unfavourable inclusion' and between active and passive exclusion. Active exclusion for him is a result of deliberate policy or law, for example, when immigrants are not given full political status or citizenship; while passive exclusion occurs through social process in which there is no deliberate attempt to exclude as in the case of poverty that is generated by sluggish economy and not a consequence of any deliberate policy or law. This simply means that there is a relational root of deprivation of an individual or group.

Contrary to this, Naila Kabeer[8] argues that social exclusion is embedded in institutional rules and norms, which are the processes of exclusion structured in the relationship between macro-economic change and the pattern of economic growth and changing life circumstances of individuals, households and groups. According to her, "disadvantage results in social exclusion when the various institutional mechanisms through which resources are allocated and values assigned operated in such a way as to systematically deny particular group of people, the resources and recognition which would allow them to participate fully in the life of that society. The analysis of exclusion can, therefore, be seen as particular aspect of institutional analysis, one centrally concerned with the dual processes of entitlement and disentitlement". She explains that "such institutions are as the 'rules of game' which distributes resources, both symbolic and material, so that institutional rules are, among other things, rules about membership and access. She further states that principles of membership, and the forms of the access they imply, are also simultaneously principles of exclusion, since they distinguish between those who can enjoy the benefits of belonging and those who cannot".

In the term of socially disadvantaged group, Room[9] explores the notion of social exclusion by consolidating and integrating five key elements in the definition and study of disadvantage which are as follows.

1. From financial to multi-dimensional disadvantage;
2. From a static to a dynamic analysis;

3. From a focus on the resources of the individual or household to a concern also with those of the local community;
4. From distributional to relational dimensions of stratification and disadvantage;
5. From a continuum of inequality to catastrophic rupture.

He describes primarily a degree of multi-dimensional disadvantage of deprivation of the excluded ones and reinforced by material and cultural degradation of the neighbourhoods in which they live. He also states that their relational links with the wider society are ruptured to a degree which is to some considerable degree irreversible.[10]

Apart from that, Gore[11] focuses on social exclusion which is embedded in the emergence of the term in French political rhetoric and the specific institutional history of the European Union in Western Europe. He argues that social exclusion is not equated with poverty. It rather referred to a process of social disintegration in the sense of a progressive rupture of the relationship between the individual and society, which was occurring because of increasing long-term unemployment particularly focused on unskilled workers and immigrants, the inability of young people to enter the labour market for the first time, greater family instability and isolated single-member households, increasing numbers of homeless people and rising tension and periodic violence in the low-cost housing settlement on the periphery of cities (*banlieues*). This tearing of the social fabric of society, in his opinion seemed to be occurring as the result of long-term transformations in the structure and organisation of economic life.

Paugam's and Prelis research on social exclusion in France is a fascinating example of kinds of insights this type of analysis can provide. They describe the 'spiral of precariousness'-how in France's deprived neighbourhoods loss of unemployment tends to be accompanied not only by loss of income, but also by social and psychological forms of deprivation resulting into such as marital problems and loss of 'social capital'. Paugam and Prelis quantitative analysis of the correlations between elements of deprivation helps to characterise the specific vulnerable groups.[12]

From the view of Dave Muddiman[13], the theories of social exclusion stress its multi-dimensional nature. He argues that social exclusion relates not simply to a lack of material resources, but also to the matters like inadequate social participation, lack of cultural and educational capital, inadequate access to services and lack of power. In other words, the idea of social exclusion attempts to capture the complexity of powerlessness in modern society rather than simply focusing on its outcome. Thus, in practical terms, the UK government Social Exclusion Unit defines exclusion in terms of a combination of "linked problems such as unemployment, poor skills, low income, poor housing, high crime environment, bad health and family breakdown (Social Exclusion Unit, 1998 cited in Dave Muddiman)". Muddiman refers to cites that social exclusion is a broader concept than poverty, encompassing not only low material means but the inability to participate effectively in economic, social, political and cultural life and, in some characterisations it leads to alienation and distance from the mainstream society.

On the other hand, Dominic Abrams and his colleagues[14] deal with social psychological perspective of social inclusion and exclusion. In general term, they characterize targets and source of exclusion as either individuals or groups; the relationship contexts as raging from transnational to intrapersonal; and the dynamics as involving degrees of interdependence; material or symbolic resources; a temporal dimension and as involving motives that center on opportunities. Such exclusion happens in several forms or modes raging from the ideological to the physical communicative and purely cognitive. They also explore the experience of exclusion on the basis of social stigma. The stigmatisation in their opinion is dependent on the specific societal contexts rather than inherent quality of the stigmatized groups or individuals. Thus, exclusion is based on a social identity rather a personal identity.

In Indian context, Prakash Louis[15] looks into a theoretical framework of social exclusion by mentioning that social exclusion is the process and outcome of excluding, casting out, depriving and denying equal space to some of the citizens of a country or members of a society. This is the denial of space in all senses and in all sectors, which are closely associated with relative deprivation. In this regard, it has been stated that the rising inequality in various country has contributed to the exclusion of many social groups from their access to the opportunities available in whatsoever forms therein.

Social Status: Some Theoretical Explanations

Another issue to be analyzed in the present study is of the status or social status and its formation among the Dalits or the Scheduled Castes both in rural and urban areas. For the purpose we shall first look into a few theoretical explanations on status and social status provided by a number of sociologists and social anthropologists. The concept of status simply means a socially defined position of a person in a group or a social system or society such as female, student, teacher, child, mother, father, etc. A status occupant is expected by others to behave in a socially prescribed specific way in the given situation. For instance, the relation of a father and a child is reciprocal and gives to each other a position in the family or group. In other words, position is always relative, whereas status implies a group or a society. It is in this sense certain privileges, rights and duties are associated with every status. Most of the sociologists have used the terms position and status synonymously, but some have also made distinction between them. Position, however, denotes one's situation placed in the role-structure, which is subjective, while 'status' refers to the evaluative aspect of the position wherein others see it as 'high' or 'low' in an objective term. For instance, Harry M. Johnson[16] has distinguished the three related terms role, status and position. He has defined a social position as something filled in by an individual member of a social group or community. The position consists of two main elements, i.e., (1) expectations and obligations, held by other members of the group or community and the concerning behaviour of the incumbent, and (2) right or the legitimate expectations of the incumbent and the concerning behaviour of other members. Johnson calls the first element as the role of a position, while the second element as the status of a person. It actually denotes the prestige of a position of an individual.

Further, according to Kingsley Davis,[17] status is a position in the general institutional system, recognised and supported by the entire society. Similarly for Horton and Hunt[18] status is the rank or position of the individual in a group whereas status in Weber's analysis refers to the esteem or social honour given to individuals or groups. Again, there are a bit difference between the two terms- status and social status, though these terms are generally used synonymously. The term status simply indicates the position a person occupies in a group, whereas social status is the amount of honour and prestige his/her receives from members of the community and from the large society in a stratification system. It denotes not only the position but relative social 'standing'[19] of a person on publicly recognised scale or hierarchy of social worth. In this sense, it embraces his/her particular statuses based on the general roles that determine his/her social standing in a society. Social statuses may be very general in nature (such as those associated with gender roles) or may be much more specific (as in the case of occupational positions). Social status of a person is determined by a wide range of facts factors, and conditions such as original nature and physical characteristics, accidental conditions, physique, mentality and temperament. Similarly, sex, age, race, caste, class, economic position, etc. are also important factors that affect the social standing of a person in a society or the community he lives.

Linton also makes distinction between status and role performed by individuals in a society. By status he means a position in a social system occupied by the designated individual and by role he means his/her behaviour of him or her enacted in the patterned expectation attributed to that position. Thus, status and role are to connect the culturally defined expectations with the patterned behaviour and relationship which comprise the social structure. Linton further observes that each person in society inevitably occupies multiple statuses and that for each of these statuses, there is an associated role.[20] He has also noted two types of status: one is ascribed status and the other is achieved status: The status which is given to a person at birth like age, sex, kinship, race, caste, etc. is known as his/her ascribed status. These are "assigned" to a person by the society without taking into account the person's unique talents or characteristics. Such ascribed characteristics cannot be changed by individual effort. These are, more or less, determined by the cultural situation over which he or she has no control initially. For example, position or status of a boy or a girl in a family is ascribed in terms of both sex and age. Likewise, Negro or Harijan is ascribed status of a black person in the western society and of a lower caste or untouchable person in India respectively. Generally, ascribed statuses are determined on four bases: (a) sex dichotomy (male-female), (b) age difference (child, youth, adult), (c) kinship (brother, sister uncle, aunt, in-laws, etc.) and (d) marital status (married, divorcee, widow, widower). In a traditional or developing society, most of statuses are ascribed with one's birth in caste or a community and the prescribed or assigned occupation. An ascribed status however, does not have the same social meaning in every society. For instance, the term old man is viewed as more of an insult in somc societies, while respect for the elderly person is an important cultural norm in India and other Asian countries or society. Yet, these statuses often confer privileges to some and deprivations to others.

On the other hand, the achieved status, according to Oxford Dictionary of Sociology[21], means any social position held by an individual due to his or her personal accomplishments in an open formal or market competition with others. Thus, it is a position or social position which a person attains through his or her own efforts, individual choice and competition. It is secured through one's ability, performance and possibility by good or ill fortune. The collector, policeman, college graduate, teacher, etc. are examples of the achieved status. An achieved status requires the individual to make choice not only of occupation, but also of friend, marital partner, and place of residence, school, college and social organisations (recreational clubs). The main bases of achieved status are: Property (Jagirdar, Zamindar, etc.), occupation (doctor, engineer), education (college graduate. illiterate), specialisation and division of labour (foreman, machine), political power (Prime-minister, President, etc.), marital relations (husband, wife, sister-in-law), and achievements (good sportsman, musician, etc.).

Weber[22] has also developed the sociological concept of status, which he called 'honor'. In contrast to classes, status groups are normally amorphous kind of communities the economically class situation leads to status situation and is atypical component of the life of men that is determined by a specific, positive or negative, social estimation of honor. This honour may be connected with quality shared by a plurality and, of course, it can be linked, in the most varied ways with status distinction. In content, status is normally expressed by the fact that, above all, a specific life style can be expressed from all those who wish to belong to the circle. Weber connects this expectation to restriction on social intercourse (that is, intercourse which is not subservient to economic or any other of business's functional purposes). This restriction may continue on normal marriage within the status circle to completely endogamous closure. As soon as there is not a mere individual and socially irrelevant an agreed- upon communal action of this closing character, the status development is underway.[23] Further, in Weber's analysis status of a person invariably is endowed with certain privileges, though contrary is equally true where it goes along with deprivation. For all practical purposes, status goes hand in hand with a monopolisation of ideal and material goods or opportunities. Beside the specific status honour or honorific status, it may also be full of material monopolies. Such honorific preference may consist of the privilege of wearing special costumes, of eating specific dishes and exhibiting life style in many ways, of course, material monopolies provide the most effective motive for the exclusiveness of a status group.

A somewhat similar explanation has been given by T. H. Marshall[24] who refers to status as the position of an individual relative to other individuals which he acquires along several dimensions such as intellect, culture, social standing, personal look, etc. In that way, one may achieve high status in one dimension and low in the other. Marshall has also analyzed the term social status in terms of superiority and inferiority of an individual. Thus, he has examined the factors which produce differences in status, as well as different types of status-personal, positional, etc. In the other words of Ram,[25] "by social status, we mean a man's general standing vis-à-vis the other members of society or some section of it. It is based on both the subjective and objective aspects of evaluation; the term social status carries an idea of inferior and superior and is a position accorded in the terms of social values current in the society. Thus, in a social system like that in India and even in the urban setting, where the primordial loyalty are still continuing in one form or other, a person's social status is to be measured on the basis of subjective, composite and corporate criteria of status evaluation". Further, Bottomore[26] has argued that there has been a shift from class organisation to status organisation or as he terms it, from multi-bonded but uni-dimensional groups to multidimensional and uni-bonded groups.

Besides Weber and Marshall, Homans[27] also has theoretically analyzed status of an individual as the complex set of stimuli presented to others which are evaluated by others as better or worse, higher or lower. The particular kind of such stimuli is defined by him as status factors. A person's status achieved in two different situations may or may not be congruent to each other. Hence, according to Homans, status congruence is realised when all the stimuli presented by a man rank better or higher than the corresponding stimuli presented by another, or when all the stimuli presented by both rank as equal.[28] According to such definition, the status of the same individual may be congruent in relation to certain people and incongruent in relation to others. The incongruence of the status factors is, thus, treated here as the characteristic of a relationship between two types of status achieved by an individual.

The concept of incongruence of status factors can be useful for at least two purposes. First, it may be serviceable in an analysis of society as a system and in an enquiry concerning, for example, the problem of relationships between the congruence of status factors in particular strata, on the hand, and the sharpness of social divisions, the isolation of certain strata from others and the formation of class consciousness on the other. Secondly, the term may be used in the analysis of differences in the behaviour of the different categories of individuals and differences in their relations, depending on the degree of congruence of their statuses.[29] Thus, according to Homans both status and status incongruence, which distinguishes one individual from others, may become a status factor. The status factors may be of these types. In the first type are various characteristics of the individual himself, such as skin, colour, age, education, caste, religion, sex, income, property, home, different kinds of behavours, name, etc. In the second type, there are characteristics connected with the relationship of the given individuals with group, organisation, communities, duration of membership, seniority at work, authority, degree of independence, social origin, marital status, circle of acquaintances, etc. And in the third type, there are the characteristics which are the result of the attitude of others to the given individual, e.g. the approval of esteem he enjoys.[30] Homans further says that the behaviour of a person with others is governed by the congruence or incongruence of his or her status. The incongruence of status implies that the individual presents some contradictory stimuli to others. This is only so when the incongruent status factors are perceived by the same people. In other words, the incongruence of status is to give inconsistent stimuli in which the incongruent status factors should be perceived by the same people. Further, "the stimuli presented by the individual to others affect their reactions towards that individual. If the individual simultaneously presents two conflicting stimuli of which the first causes respect and the second contempt, other people may react to the second type of stimuli and show their contempt for the individual, although this is not justified in the light of the reasoning leads to the formulation of the following two propositions.

The greater the incongruence of simultaneously perceived status factors of the given individual, the more insecure is his status. This means that others are likely to react to that individual as if he had a lower status than the one he really enjoys.

The incongruence of status factors simultaneously perceived by other people brings punishments and the elimination of that incongruence is a source of reward".

From proposition 2, one should not conclude that people will always avoid an incongruence of status factors. Status incongruence is a source of punishments and its elimination a source of rewards, but it is not the only kind if punishment and reward. A sharpening of the incongruence of status factors may at the same time raise the general status of the individual.

In the case of Indian society, especially in the caste system, the term **s**tatu**s** has diverse meanings. For Instance, Dumont[31] reverses the term status for religious status, i.e., rank of caste in caste hierarchy. According to Beteille[32], "In traditional India, in Dumont terms, the ideology of caste system that stresses on purity and pollution encompassed the dimensions of power and wealth and several scholars tell us that the three kinds of inequality tended to coincide. Thus, in Sripuram, membership in one or another (caste group) was the basis of the individual's identity, not only in ritual contexts, but also in the economic and political spheres". In other words, an individual's status is assigned to him by others in the caste system and is a part of 'corporate' or group status sanctioned to his caste.[33] This is equally assigned to a person irrespective of his living in rural or urban areas, though in the latter caste his status is also influenced by his material achievement. According to Saberwal,[34] "For one thing, the unit of social appraisal in urban India is increasingly not the corporate group but the individual; and the determinants of this appraisal include education, economic resources, political influence, general knowledgeability, etc, besides religious status. This composite evaluation of one's social standing[35] by others and one's awareness of this evaluation by them will here designate status with a capital S".

Further, status of a person in caste system is necessarily to be seen in the context of caste-hierarchy. Dumont[36] defines hierarchy in terms of the superiority of the pure over the impure. He writes that the castes teach us a fundamental social principle of hierarchy. He also argues that the opposite of equality is hierarchy and not inequality. According to Dumont, hierarchy is an indispensable element of social life everywhere, but it is more so in the case of India as it is very well affirmed. He further explains that caste system is a system of ideas and values, a formal, comprehensive rational system, a system in the intellectual sense of the term. The foremost aim is to understand this intellectual system an ideology where castes are related through a system of oppositions and its structure in terms of opposition between the pure and impure. Thus, Dumont introduces the notion of 'system' and 'structure' in terms of ideology of and relations between the pure and impure castes. Sharma further says that "Dumont clearly states that religion is supreme, and politico-economic domain is subordinate and further economics remains undifferentiated within politics. He uses *dharma* (ideology) becomes subordinate to *artha* (power) and if the formal is upheld as subordinate. The ruler becomes subservient to the priestly order. Finally, he upholds ritual or religious power (hierarchy) super ordinate to politico-economic power".[37]

We have already stated that a person occupies different statuses in different situations. Merton[38] has termed these statuses of a person as his or her status sets. He explains the concept of role-sets and status-sets in terms of social structure at a particular time. He considers these status-sets as changing in the course of time and the succession of statuses occurs with sufficient frequency as to be socially patterned. It will be designated as a status sequences. According to Merton,[39] the Status-set refers to the complex of distinct positions assigned to individuals both within and among social systems. Status-sets plainly provide one basic form of interdependence between the institutions and subsystem of a society. "This stems from the familiar fact that the same persons are engaged in the distinct social system. It should be noted that just a group and society differ in the number and complexity of social statuses comprising part of their structure, so individual people differ in their number and complexity of the statuses comprising their status-sets. Complex status-sets not only make for some form of liaison between subsystems in a society, they confront the occupant of these statuses with distinctly different degree of difficulty in organising their role-activities".

Merton further mentions that social structure is not without power of learned adaptation that transmits through changed cultural mandates. This helps to mitigate the frequency and intensity of conflict in the status-set. Because of multiple statuses, conflict occurs in an assigned situation. This means that each individual caught up in these stressful situations that need not improvise new adjustments. Social mechanisms for reducing each conflict can also be considered in terms of status-sequences, i.e., the succession of statuses through which an appreciable proportion of people move.[40]

An Integrated Theoretical Framework on Social Exclusion and Status Formation

After analyzing the conceptual and theoretical explanations of both social exclusion and status or formation of social status, we may attempt here to formulate an integrated theoretical framework to enquire into the social exclusion and formation of social status among the Scheduled Castes or Dalits both in rural and urban areas in India in general and in the state of Bihar in particular. In the first set of the framework, Arjan De Haan's two conceptual understandings, i.e., multi-dimensional and relational root of deprivation have been adopted to examine exclusion or social exclusion of the Dalits from the social, economic, political and cultural spheres of their life in the Hindu social system. Similarly, Silver's three paradigms of exclusion, i.e., solidarity paradigm, specialisation paradigm and monopoly paradigm shall be applied to analyze the multiple disadvantages of exclusion faced by the Dalits in the society.

Another issue examined in the present study is of status formation among the Dalits in both rural and urban areas. In this connection, we have analyzed our data Linton's theory of Ascribed and Achieved statuses related to status formation among the Dalits in the caste system and class structure, existing in rural and urban areas. This theory is relevant to examine the ascribed status of Dalits in terms of their low evaluation by people of the higher and middle level castes even after achieving the higher or highest social position in the class or socio-economic status hierarchy. Finally, within the given theoretical frameworks on social exclusion and status formation, we have also enquired into how social exclusion affects adversely the status formation among the Dalits of our study locales.

Conclusion

This chapter highlights the conceptual and theoretical perspectives and dimensions of social exclusion as well as types of statuses, i.e., ascribed and achieved from sociological perspective. It also focuses on how the concept of 'social exclusion' was developed by many social scientists, scholars and policy makers in the mid-1970s and after in the Western Europe. After analyzing the various approaches, it shows the social exclusion as a global phenomenon primarily dealing with the institutionalised attempt to keep a few segments of population away from their participation from the social, economic, educational, political and cultural spheres of social life. Apart from that, the chapter due highlights conceptually and theoretically the term status or social status. Finally, an attempt has been made to evolve an integrated theoretical framework for analyzing empirical data collected from the study locales.

Notes

1. Referred in Sen, Amartya (2004). *Social Exclusion, Concept, Application, Security,* Critical Quest, New Delhi.
2. De Haan, Arjan (2008). *Social exclusion: Two Essays*, Critical Quest, New Delhi.
3. De Haan, Arjan (2008). *Social Exclusion: Two Essays*, Critical Quest, New Delhi, pp.7-8.
4. Silver, Hilary (1995). Social Exclusion and Social Solidarity: Three Paradigms, *International Labour Review,* Vol. 133, pp. 532-43.
5. Silver, Hilary (1995). "Reconceptualizing Social Disadvantage: Three Paradigms of Social Exclusion" in *Social Exclusion: Rhetoric, Reality, Responses* (eds.) by Rodgers, Gerry, and et. al., International Institute

of Labour Studies, United Nations Development Programme, Geneva, pp. 66-67.

6. *Ibid.,* pp. 67-68.
7. Sen, Amartya (2004). *Social Exclusion: Concept, Application and Scrutiny*, Critical Quest, New Delhi.
8. Kabeer, Naila (2008). "Social Exclusion, Poverty and Discrimination towards an Analytical Framework", *Critical Quest*, New Delhi, p. 24.
9. Room, G.J. (1999). Social Exclusion, Solidarity and the challenge of Globalisation, *International Journal of Social Welfare*, p. 167.
10. Room, G.J. (1999). Social Exclusion, Solidarity and the challenge of Globalisation, *International Journal of Social Welfare*, p. 172.
11. Gore, Charles, Jose B. Figueiredo, & Garry Rodgers, (1995). "Introduction: Market, Citizenship and Social Exclusion", in *Social Exclusion: Rhetoric, Reality, Responses*, (eds.) by Rodgers, G. C. Gore, and Jose B. Figueiredo, International Institute for Labour Studies, Geneva, pp. 1-2.
12. Evans, Martin Serge Paugam, and Joseph S. Prelis, (1995). "Chunnel Vision: Poverty, Social exclusion and the Debate on Social Welfare in France and Britain", London School of Economics, Welfare State Programmme, Discussion Paper WSP 115.
13. Muddiman, Dave (1999). "Theories of Social Exclusion and the Public Library', Working Paper, 1, p. 2.
14. Abrams, Dominic, M.A. Hogg, J.M. Marques, (eds.) (2005). *The Social Psychology of Inclusion and Exclusion*, Psychological Press, New York, p. 3.
15. Louis, Prakash (2008). "Social Exclusion: A Conceptual and Theoretical Framework", Working Paper, p. 4.
16. Johnson, Harry M. (1960). *Sociology: A Systematic Introduction*, Allied Publishers, New Delhi.
17. David, Kinsley (1949). *Human Society*, The Macmillan Company, New York.
18. Horton, Paul B. and Chester Hunt (1964). *Sociology*, The McGraw-Hill Companies, New York.
19. This term 'standing' is different from David Pocock. For him, a person, a family, or a group of family has standing…within the caste as opposed to status which they may have in their relationship with other castes (1972:65).
20. Linton, Ralf (1936). *The Study of Man*, Appleton-Century-Crofts, Inc., New York.
21. Marshall, Gordon, J. Scott (1995). *Oxford Dictionary of Sociology*, Oxford University Press.
22. Weber, Max (1991). "Class, Status and Party" in *Social Stratification*, (ed.) by Dipankar Gupta, Oxford University Press, New Delhi, pp. 462-63.

23. *Ibid.,* 463.
24. Marshal, T.H. (1963). *Sociology at the Cross Roads*, London, Heinemannn.
25. Ram, Nandu (1988). *The Mobile Scheduled Castes, Rise of a New Middle Class*, Hindustan Publishing Corporation Delhi, pp. 86-7.
26. Bottomore, T.B. (1962). *Sociology, A Guide to Problems and Literature*, Blackie & Son (India) Ltd, pp. 195-6.
27. Homans, G. C. (1961). Social Behavior, New York, Harcourt, p. 149.
28. *Ibid.,* 248.
29. *Ibid.,* 149.
30. *Ibid.,* 150.
31. Dumont, Louis (1966). "A fundamental Problem in the Sociology of Caste", *Contributions to Indian Sociology*, No. 9.
32. Beteille, Andre (1966). *Caste, Class and Power*, Oxford University Press, New Delhi, p. 223.
33. Ram, Nandu (1988). *The Mobile Scheduled Castes, Rise of a New Middle Class,* Hindustan Publishing Corporation Delhi, p. 86.
34. Saberwal, Satish (ed.), (1972). *Beyond the Village: Sociological Explorations*, Indian Institute of Advanced Study, Shimla, p. 114.
35. Saberwal uses the term "standing" to refer to one's social position in one's society at large, not within one's caste alone.
36. Dumont, Louis (1988). *Homo Hierarchicus: The Caste System and its Implications*, Oxford University Press, New Delhi, p. 66.
37. Sharma, K. L. (1994). *Social Stratification and Mobility*, Rawat Publications, Jaipur &New Delhi, p.105.
38. Merton, R.K. (1968). *Social Theory and Social Structure*, American Publishing Co. PVT.
39. *Ibid.,* 434-35.
40. *Ibid.,* 436.

Chapter - 3

The Research Setting

Introduction

We have already mentioned briefly, in Chapter 1, that Bihar is one of the most backward states in the country and the north Bihar is more backward than the south Bihar. However, all the regions in the north Bihar are not equally backward. Rural areas, for instance, are more backward than the urban areas. Since our study is located both in a village and a town in north Bihar, we shall briefly analyze, in this chapter, their social structure or social system and demographic and socio-political structure or composition. Besides, we would elaborately elucidate social composition of the Dalits, their literacy and educational level and economic profile, compared to that of the non-Dalits in the respective study locales. Finally, we shall describe briefly the socio-personal background of the respondents, selected from a village and a town, to situate empirically the various issues examined in the present study. But before doing that, we shall cursory look at the socio-demographic and politico-economic features of the state of Bihar as a whole.

The Socio-Political Geography of Bihar

Bihar, the ancient land of the Lord Buddha, has witnessed golden period in Indian history. It is the same land where the seeds of the first republic were sown, which cultivated the first crop of democracy. It has such a fertile soil that has given birth to innumerous intellectuals who spread the light of knowledge and wisdom not only in the country, but also in the whole world. Patna is its capital, which is situated on the bank of the holy river Ganga. The state has witnessed partition thrice: from the province of Bengal in 1911, from the province of Orissa in 1935, and most recently, from the tribal southern region in 2000, which is now called Jharkhand. The word 'Bihar' has originated from 'vihara,' meaning Buddhist monastery. In the ancient time, Bihar was known as Magadh.[1] At one time in the epoch of history, these viharas bore all strewn over the landscape of Bihar around villages and cities alike. On the other hand, it is also said that the name of Bihar is derived from the Sanskrit word vihara, meaning the abode. It is, however, said that in the ancient and medieval periods, vihara was the abode of the Buddhist monks.

Bihar is situated between 22° 00' North to 27° 31' North and 83° 20' East to 88° 17' East. Its length from north to south is about 605 kms and from east to west about 483 kms, covering about 5 percent of the total area of India's geographical territory.[2] It is bounded in the north by the Kingdom of Nepal, in the south by Jharkhand, in the east by West Bengal and in the west by Uttar Pradesh. Bihar's geographical location in the map of India is on the upper half and slightly to the left of the tropical cancer. "This can be termed as the heart of India … and being the fountain head of its previous history, little is known about the state's remote past. This point of departure for the most recent historiography expedition into Bihar's past has been the Mugadhan empires".[3] Bihar is traditionally divided into North Gangetic and South Gangetic plains. The northern portion is almost entirely a plain, while large areas of the southern Bihar are hilly and covered with thick forests (a large part of it has gone as Jharkhand State). North Bihar has extremely fertile land, being watered by the three rivers-Sarajug, Gandak and Ganga. The southern Bihar is thickly wooded, and consists of hills and mountain ranges[4]. Bihar is the birth place of several religions, including Buddhism and Jainism. The Buddha attained his Enlightenment at Bodh Gaya, a town located in the present district of Gaya. Mahavira, the 24th and the last Tirthankara of Jainism, was born in Vaishali. The tenth Guru of Sikhism, Guru Govind Singh, was born in the present day city of Patna.

Socio-Demographic Profile

The present Bihar, which constitutes of about 5 percent of the geographical area of India and about 8 percent of its population (8.29 crore as per 2001Census), is the most populous state of the country[5]. After Independence in 1947, Bihar province formed the state of Bihar as a part of the Republic of India. On 14th November 2000, the southern half of Bihar became the state of Jharkhand, as mentioned above. Bihar lost approximately 45 percent of its territory, with its mineral resources in its southern part, to the new State of Jharkhand. At present, the total area of the state is 94163 square kilometers, out of which rural area is 92358 sq. km. and urban area covers 1805 sq. km. only. The population density is 800 persons per sq. km. It is heavily inclined towards the urban area, i.e., 809 persons per sq. km., compared to rural areas in which it stands as 803 persons per sq. km. The average size of agriculture operation holding is 0.93 hectares, whereas the national average is 1.57 hectares.[6]

Source: www.mapsofindian.com

Figure 1: Map showing the studied District

The social structure of Bihar in terms of social composition of its population consists of Hindus, Muslims, Christians and others. According to 1981 Census, the social composition of Hindus in Bihar can broadly be classified into six categories of Brahmins, Bhumihars, Rajputs and Kayasthas belonging to the first category that constitutes 12.7 percent of the total population of the state. These upper castes are called twice-born and are dominant in all domains of social life. The second major social category is known as backward classes or castes, who constitute nearly half of the population (48.9) of the state. This category can be divided into upper backwards and lower backwards, constituting 18.7 percent and 31.2 percent respectively of the total population. The cultivating castes like Yadav, Kurmi and Koeri belong to the upper backward class and people of Kahar, Lohar, Hajjam, Teli, Kumhar, etc., considered to be the lower backward category, do mainly some specified occupations and are artisan of different types. The Banias, who are also considered broadly to be the backward class or caste, have traditionally been following the trading and merchandise occupation. The category of the Scheduled Castes consists of 14.5 percent of the total population of Bihar[7], according to 1991 Census, which was increased 15.7 percent in 2001 Census. The composition of different castes in Bihar, as per the 1931 Census (since 1931 the enumeration of all castes, except the Scheduled Castes was stopped). See Table3.1 below.

Table 3.1: Showing Caste Composition among Hindus in Bihar

Caste Category	Name of Caste	Percentage Population
1. Upper Castes	1. Brahmins	04.6
	2. Bhumihars	02.8
	3. Rajputs	04.1
	4. Kayasthas	01.2
	Total	**12.7**

2. (a) Upper Backwards (b) Lower Backwards	1. Banias	00.6
	2. Yadavs	10.7
	3. Kurmis	03.5
	4. Koeris	04.0
	Total	**18.7**
	1. Barhis	01.0
	2. Dhanuk	01.8
	3. Hajjam	01.4
	4. Kahar	01.7
	5. Kander	01.6
	6. Kumhar	01.3
	7. Lohar	01.3
	8. Mallah	01.5
	9. Talwa	01.5
	10. Teli	02.5
	Total	**15.6**
	11. Other Backward Castes	35.7
3.	Scheduled Castes	14.5
4.	Bengali and Others	02.8
	Grand Total	17.3

Note: Total population of Hindus was 79.0 percent and the remaining 21.0 percent was of the Sikh, Christians, Buddhists, Tribals, etc.

Source: Calculated from 1931 Census by Blair, Harry W. (1980). "Rising Kulaks and Backward Classes in Bihar", *Economic and Political Weekly*, Vol. 15. No. 2, January. 2, p. 65.

Since 1931 Census the caste-wise enumeration of population has been stopped, except in the case of the Scheduled Castes and Tribes, it is difficult to ascertain the number or percentage of population of each caste or community in the recent years. Yet, it can easily be said that there would have not been radical growth or decline of population of any caste or community in the state.

Bihar is one of those states where the upper castes, although numerically very small, have traditionally enjoyed ritual superiority and social prestige. Their limited numerical strength is compensated by their ritual status, social prestige and politico-economic power and dominance.[8] Hence, their dominance in the state has been much greater than their number. In ritual matters, the Brahmins enjoy the predominant position, followed by the Bhumihars, Rajputs and Kayasthas. In the second group of castes, the backward castes (both lower and upper) are considered as intermediary castes between the upper castes and the Scheduled Castes.

With regards to agrarian social structure, the backward castes consist of tenants and agricultural labourers. Two-third of the agricultural tenants in the state belongs to the upper backward castes like Yadava, Kurmi and Koeri. Interestingly, a sizeable number of the upper backward castes have become land owners after abolition of the zamindari system and implementation of other land reform policies after Independence in the state. The Scheduled Castes or the Dalits constitute the third category of castes groups in the state. The status of Dalits in Bihar is, by and large, not different from the Dalits in other states of the country. They continue to be the marginalised sections and subjected to exploitation and humiliation. They form a large labour-force for the land owning upper and upper-middle level backward castes. There are twenty-three castes in this group. The Chamar, Dusadh, Musahar, Bhuiya, Pasi and Dhobi are 87.67 percent of the total Scheduled Castes population in the state.[9] But according to 2001 Census, the Chamar and Dusadh castes constitute 31.3 and 30.9 percent of the total Scheduled Castes population in the state. Thus, the Chamar and Dusadh, along with Musahar, Pasi, Dhobi and Bhuiya, constitute 93.2 percent of the total Scheduled Castes population in the state, according to 2001 census.

The Socio-Political and Administrative Structure of Bihar

Bihar is considered to be a caste and faction-ridden state. Factions have existed within and across each caste and community to establish its or of its few members' dominance, or to settle the score(s) against other(s), or to get certain favour/work done which might not be possible otherwise. Such faction could also be found in the political arena in which every political party is faction-ridden. It was founded by Zamindars who also wanted a little change in the colour of the skin of the rulers.[10] After the Independence of India, the Congress Party being the oldest and largest in terms of its membership and support looked to the men, who were already enjoying power in the society, for support, and did nothing to disturb the established order. During the early years, there was upper caste domination in the politics where most of the MLAs, from the non-reserved seats, belonged mainly to the four upper castes. This pattern was maintained in 1967 and 1969 elections till the period of emergency. Of the total MLAs for the general seats 54.9 percent came from the forward castes.[11] There was also the upper castes' domination in the ruling party at the ministerial level in State. But in the post-Mandal era, the situation had changed and the upper backward castes' representation at all levels (local and the state) has drastically changed the political scenario in the state. Now, the Yadavs, Kurmis, and Koeris are enjoying power with the support of Scheduled Castes or Dalits in the state.

The people in Bihar have been regarded to be notorious for casteism, corruption, inefficiency and criminalisation of politics and administration. Money and the short-term gains, related to politics, have become the guiding factors. The growing tension, between the upper and upper backward castes, with the ethos of the Brahminical culture for domination over the Dalits and the lower backward castes with their growing socio-cultural awareness in both rural and urban areas, is another significant trend in the state[12].

The administrative set-up in Bihar, like other states in India, is such in which the Chief Secretary among the administrators is the head of the Secretariat located in the city of Patna. The secretariat consists of Secretary, Principal Secretary, and Deputy Secretary, Under Secretary, and other supporting staff. The local administration is of four tier; Commissionary, District, Sub-division and Block. Every Commissionary has a Commissioner. The District is headed by the Collector who is also called District Magistrate and whose office consists of an Additional Collector, District Development Commissioner, Deputy Collector, District Welfare Officer, District Panchayat Officers, District Public Relation Officer, Land Acquisition Officer, District Statistical Officer, District Account Officer, Treasury Officer, Assistant Mining Officer, District Industries Officers, Special Officer for the Package Programme, District Rationing Officer and Assistant Rationing Officers. The staff posted at the sub-divisional Headquarters mainly consist of Sub-Divisional Officer, Deputy Collector-In charge-Land Reforms, Deputy Collectors, and Assistant District Supply Officers. And at the Block level, there are Block Development Officers (B.D.O) and Anchal Adhikaris (C.O). Incidentally, most of these officers are from the upper castes and a few from the upper level backward class or castes in the state.

Agrarian structure of Bihar

The society and economy of Bihar is primarily an agrarian in its pursuit. Nearly 87 percent of its population lives in rural areas, while 90.97 percent of the Dalits living in villages. In the rural areas, 80 percent of its population is directly dependent on agriculture, but a majority of the Dalits is landless labourers. Even few of them hold land; it is often in small quantity, infertile, unirrigated and economically unenviable. Prasad also has explained the agrarian structure of Bihar as the exploitative one and has termed it as semi-feudal[13]. In terms of social indices like literacy and mortality rates, employment, per capita income, agricultural productivity, status of women, etc., Bihar ranks almost at the bottom of the scale from the all-India point of view.

In North Bihar, 94.8 percent of the people live in rural areas and there is landlordism, exploitation, sharecropping, and oral leases in 40 percent of the cultivated area. The landlords and the rich peasants have found ways and means of circulating their own laws relating to land ceiling, share-cropping and agricultural wages. That is why, the North Bihar is one the poorest, most backward and feudal regions in India. It is also known as 'Bihar fatigue' which tells the story of horror, economic backwardness, social inequality, electoral banditry, political cupidity, caste riots and cultural degradation which is structured in semi-feudalism.[14] Such a situation has compelled a large number of landless workers to look for work as manual labourers in different states of the county.[15] The economy of the North Bihar is "severally disturbed, causing immense suffering to the people on account of flood and drought because the density of population is very high and the pressure on the cultivated land are very heavy. The average density of population in North Bihar works out to be 855 persons per square mile...about 86 percent of the population depends upon agriculture (against all-India average of 69.84 per cent), and in the rural areas more than 90 percent are agricultural labourers; they are thrown out of employment whenever agriculture is dislocated either by flood or drought".[16]

The Dalits or the Scheduled Castes have historically constituted to be the poorest and socially most disadvantaged groups in India in general and Bihar in particular. They have been integral part of its social and economic structure since the time immemorial.

The economic relation among the people in rural Bihar is fundamentally represented in terms of '*Malik'* (upper castes landlords) and '*Praja'* (lower castes without any control over land). The maliks consist of the Brahmins, Rajputs, Bhumihars and Kayashas who control the means of production both in rural and urban areas. "The maliks have been accepted in the past and it continues, in one form or the other, even today by the prajas as their *sarkar* (law incarnate), *deobhagwan* (God incarnate) and *maibap* (Parents). The parajas have been subordinated to the maliks for the benefit from the land and the livelihood. However, land owners are arranged hierarchically in the caste system, like high and low, superior and inferior in terms of purity and pollution and ritual status".[17]

Historically speaking, the Permanent Land Settlement in 1793, the other situation that existed prior to the abolition of the Zamindari System in 1950 and the complicated stratified system of relationship of the people to the land[18] was heavily in favour of the upper castes in Bihar. In fact, the numerical weakness of the upper castes did not come in their way of enjoying their ritual status, social prestige and economic power. This is true even today in Bihar as well as in other states in the country. For instance, in ritual matter, the Brahmins enjoy the first position, followed by the Bhumihar, Brahmins and the Rajputs. The Kayasthas, although low on scale of the ritual status, have rivaled the Brahmins in everything connected with the pen.[19] Thus, the upper castes, consisting of Brahmins, Bhumihar Brahmins and the Rajputs, have acquired a major part of land and thereby dominate the economic field, as mentioned above. This is due mainly to historical facts as observed by Mishra, who states that, "Before coming of the British, the influence which dominated the village community was that of a particular kind especially of Brahmins and Rajputs, who owned most villages either as village zamindar in the Upper Province and parts of Bihar or as Taluqdar in Bengal, as Mirasdar in the South or Inamdar in the West and the other occupation groups remained in subservience to the dominant landed interest of the village".[20]

Thus, Vidyarthi and Mishra[21] have dealt with the permanent settlement of land, which was settled in favour of cultivators, zamindars and the persons who put in claims for land. At that time, Dalits did not have any desire for the land, because they were quite happy with their traditional occupations. However, many of them acquired a few patches of land. According to Lal[22], the life of Dalits in rural Bihar at present "is reduced to total dependency on the landlord, since in most places semi-bonded agricultural labour is the only source of livelihood so also their political life is often reduced to the status of being vote banks for those who control their life". Thus, the most deprived and downtrodden among the Dalits of Bihar are the Musahars who are placed at the margin of subsistence surviving on rats, snails or anything of that sort. Therefore, it is true that the landownership is positively related to caste. High status castes possess most of the land, while the upper crust among the intermediary castes constitutes the middle peasant. Those without land are from lower middle castes and Scheduled Castes. Of the four elite castes in Bihar, the Rajputs and Bhumihars own the most substantial land and are dominant in the rural areas.

Looking at the growing population of Dalits, we find that most of them are landless labourers and are now crying for land. They have been agricultural labourers and cultivators, and a sizeable number of them as unskilled, semi-skilled and skilled manual workers in industry. Their small numbers are also placed in a few professions, administration, and trade and commerce. Besides, a sizeable member of them has also become educationally better off than before, but their majority are still lacking of benefits of the required professional qualification to occupy the positions at the highest levels.[23] Anyway, it is quite evident that the landownership plays very crucial role in the rural areas and contributes to form a separate 'social class's in the state of Bihar.

Class (Socio-economic status) Structure in Bihar

The term class or class structure in the Indian context, unlike in the western societies, is not completely devoid of the primordial linkeages (such as caste, tribe, religion, gender, etc.) of its members. This is equally true in the case of both urban and rural areas, although a number of social scientists have attempted to situate class in Indian context and classified the population in terms of class structure. They have accepted and interpreted class both in Marxian and Weberian senses. For instance, Desai (1948) and Mukherjee (1957) have analyzed class in Marxian sense-control over means of production, whereas Mishra

(1961), Beteille (1966), Bhatt (1975), Sharma (1991), Ram (1988), etc. have studied it in terms of socio-cultural distinctiveness, besides that of economic one, and classified the population accordingly. Such attempt has been made by a few scholars in the case of Bihar also, which is predominantly a rural society, as stated earlier. In their opinion, class or social class in Bihar is to be studied differently for both rural and urban areas as the different types of classes, with different characteristics, are found in both the areas. Besides, the landlord class, with landholding, upper caste lineages, ritual purity and the enormous amount of prestige as well dominance, as well as class of landless agricultural labbourers, with low caste origin and ritual impurity and low prestige, there are merchant and artisan class in rural Bihar. For instance, Max Harcourt has distinguished class in the Muslim population as *ashraf* (landlord), *bakal* (village shopkeepers), *Pawania* (artisans), *jatiya* (small peasants directly cultivating their land), and a class of low castes at the local level.[24] There are a large number of small and marginal farmers also in Bihar, like in the other states in the country. They usually possess not more than five acres of land. They have sufficient surplus labour and tools of production. They also work as share-croppers. They mainly employ what is called family labour on their own farms. They are essentially self-producers without hired labour. They have considerable control over labour power as occasional employers of hired labour. Because they have little land and they cultivate others' lands, they are called tenants.[25] There are also agricultural labourers who possess little or no land. Despite this, there are unskilled manual labourers. Most of these classes of people are poor, and socially and educationally backward. They all have specific roles, and positions within the system such as casual and unskilled labourers, tenants, share-croppers, artisans, etc.[26]

The upper and upper middle classes in Bihar are comparatively small in number or size of its members. The upper middle class includes big businessmen and industrialists, senior bureaucrats, and the *Zamindars,* although the zamindari has largely been abolished. The *Zamindars* are certainly Bihari in origin, but most of the industrialists are from Gujarat, Rajasthan and the Punjab.[27] The people of this class are not active in any political party, though they extend their support to it from outside and enjoy power as a ruling class in Bihar. On the other hand, Sharma[28] has mentioned about seven classes existing in Bihar, which may be regarded as descriptive categories. They have been identified on the basis of generation of surplus value in agriculture and its appropriation through the labour processes. According to him, these classes are:

(i) *The tied agricultural wage labour*- those households who are hired out as agriculture wage labour and are tied to an employer land owner-cultivator through loan and or patch of land, regardless of other activities rendered or performed by him.

(ii) *Untied Agricultural wage labour*- those households who are hired out as agricultural wage labour, but are not tied with any employer or cultivator, regardless of other activities performed by them.

(iii) *Poor-Middle Peasants*- those who are cultivating their own land, but do not hire in or out agricultural wage, nor do they *lease* out their land to others.

(iv) *Middle Peasants*-Cultivating, not hiring-out but occasionally hiring-in of wage labour, not leasing out their land, both males and females working on own land.

(v) *Big Peasants*-Cultivating, not hiring-out but hiring-in of wage labour, not leasing-out their land, only male household members working on own land.

Landlords (including gentlemen farmers)- Landlords are those leasing-out land, and gentlemen farmers are those who are cultivating land by themselves but supervisory works only, not hiring out but hiring-in wage labour, no leasing out land.

Non-agriculturalists-all remaining households who are not dependent on agriculture; mostly include artisan castes.

Here, it may be pointed out that this classification of population into various classes, in rural areas, does not depend solely on land owned or cultivated by them, and is also not totally free from their primordial-caste, religion, etc. linkages. This means, the rich peasants and the big landlords in rural areas, and the upper and upper middle classes in urban areas, are mostly from the upper castes, besides a few Muslims. Similarly, the middle level peasants are from the middle level or backward castes, and the wage labours are mostly from the lower or the Dalits castes.[29] This supports our points, mentioned at the outset of this section.

The Dalits or Scheduled Castes

As stated earlier, there are 23 castes which have been included in the list of the Scheduled Castes in Bihar. The Dalits or Scheduled Castes do not comprise of the homogeneous groups. Being heterogeneous in nature, they are scattered in all the districts in the state. Some of the Scheduled Castes in Bihar are Bantar, Bauri, Bhogta, Bhuiya, Bhumij, Chamar, Chaupal, Dabgar, Dhobi, Dom or Dhangar, Dusadh, Ghasi, Halalkhor, Mehtar, Kanjar, Kurian, Lalbegi, Musahar, Nat, Pan, Pasi, Rajwar, Turi, etc. We shall explain below the location or placement of the Dalit castes in the traditional caste system and the hierarchical arrangement of their occupations in the state of Bihar. The Dalits or Scheduled Castes in Bihar are considered to be at the bottom of hierarchy of the caste system and the most backward Scheduled Castes, compared to those found in the other states in India. Bihar has the greater concentration of the Dalit population than that in most of the states in the country. In fact, it ranks third in India with regard to Dalit population in the country.

Presently, the Scheduled Castes population has gone up by 4,76,908 persons, which accounts for 3.79 percent growth rate. The Scheduled Castes constitute a sizeable section (about 8 million) of population of the state. According to 2001 Census, their population stood at 1.30 crore, which accounted for 15.7 percent of total population of the state, as stated earlier. About 46 percent of the SC population is located in the north Bihar. The Chamars, Dusadhs and Musahars constitute more than a million each, and comprise of about 71 percent of the total Scheduled Castes population in the state. The Scheduled Castes are scattered throughout the state, as mentioned earlier. Yet, the bulk of them are located in south Bihar. The density of their population varies from district to district. They have a high concentration in the districts of Gaya (29%), Vaishali (20.7%), and Nalanda (20%).

The Scheduled Castes constitute as one of the most disadvantaged groups in Indian society as well as in the state of Bihar, as mentioned above. They are stigmatized and suffer from the numerous disabilities, which are regulated through religious beliefs and practices. The majority of them have low economic status, segregation, lack of political power and low level of literacy and social mobility, as discussed below.

Literacy and Educational Level of the Dalits

The Scheduled Castes or the Dalits have educationally been deprived for centuries. The general condition of education among them in India as well as in Bihar has remained pitiable after about 66 years of Independence. During the British period, education was only for the upper sections of the society. Only they were allowed to take education in society and the untouchables or Scheduled Castes were totally deprived of such facility in the traditional Hindu society. But after Independence in 1947, a little change has occurred in the domain of Dalit education in Bihar.

In Bihar, the state government passed the Bihar Harijans (Removal of Civil Disabilities) Act in 1947 and set up a Welfare Department, having a District Welfare Officer (DWO) in each district along with 22 Welfare Inspectors, in 1948, for spreading education among the SCs and STs. This was done by opening schools, giving stipends to students from these castes and communities and for making available to them loans, subsidies, medical aids, etc.[30] Due to this, there was some progress recorded in respect of education among them. For instance, by 1960, there were six Harijan Kalyan Hostels and 26 Harijan Lower Primary Schools in the district of Saran.[31] Similarly, by 1958-59, the number of schools for Harijan children was twenty-one, and the number of Harijan students attending different institutions of education was six thousand five hundred twenty one in Palamu district. Thus, by 1960, there seemed to be some progress in education among children of the Dalits in the state of Bihar. Yet, looking at the literacy rates among the people in general and the Scheduled Castes in particular both in rural and urban areas in the state and comparing that in the country as whole, we find that Bihar is recorded with the lowest literacy rate both in the case of males and females. The same may be seen in the Table 3.1 in Appendix-A and Table 3.2 given below.

Compared to 21.95 percent general people (35.85% males and 8.11% females) and 5.95 percent Dalits (11.2% males and 0.9% females) were literate in 1961. But by 2001, there were 47.53 percent general (60.32% males and 33.57% females) and 28.5 percent

Dalits (40.2% males and 15.6% females) literates (see Table 3.1 in Appendix-A). This shows that there has been slight increase in the literacy rate among the Dalits, compared to the general population from 1961 to 2001 in India.

Table 3.2: Literacy Rates among the Scheduled Castes in Bihar during 1961-2001

Decades	Gen			SC		
	Male	Female	Total	Male	Female	Total
1961	35.85	8.11	21.95	11.2	0.9	5.95
1971	35.86	9.86	23.17	11.9	1.00	6.53
1981	47.11	16.61	32.32	18.02	2.51	10.40
1991	51.37	21.99	37.49	23.97	5.44	15.12
2001	60.32	33.57	47.53	40.2	15.6	28.5

Source: *Education of Scheduled Castes and Scheduled Tribes 1997-98,* Department of Secondary and Higher Education, Ministry of Human Resource Development, Government of India, New Delhi.

Before looking at increase in the literacy rates and the levels of education among the people in general and the Dalits or Scheduled Castes in particular between 1961 and 2001, it is necessary to briefly explain some of reasons or facts responsible for that. In fact, there has been gradual increase in the literacy rates among the people, including Scheduled Castes, in the country during the decades 1961-1971. But such increase became faster during the subsequent decades perhaps due to major emphasis on the level of literacy and education of the people in general. In other words, the challenge of illiteracy of the people, particularly the poor and deprived ones, was taken as a mission by the government in which the voluntary organisations, a few philanthropic agencies and the needy people themselves had contributed significantly in one way or the other. It is also clear that the increase in literacy rate is higher in the case of general population, compared to that of the Scheduled Castes- both among males and females. The literacy rate among Scheduled Castes in the country, according to the 1991 Census, was only 37.41 percent (49.91% males and 23.76% females) as against 52.21 percent of the general population. According to 2001 Census, the literacy rate among the Dalits has been 54.69 percent (66.64% males and 41.90% females), compared to 64.80 percent (75.30% males and 53.70% females) of the general population in the country (see in Appendix-A Table 3.1). Thus, the literacy literates among the people in general and the scheduled castes in particular in Bihar has been less than that in the country as whole, as a stated earlier.

The reason for such wide gap between the two could be manyfold. One, there has been a general trend among the people, both males and females of the upper castes, Muslims, Christians, etc. to become literate and have at least some education right from the beginning. Hence, the literacy rates among them have always been higher, compared to that among the Dalits and other backward castes in both rural and urban areas. Two, in view of the first reason, the literacy among the Dalits and even backward castes has remained a recent phenomenon. Three, the Dalits including their women and children have always been engaged as manual labour in the productive works where literacy has hardly been needed. And four, Dalits have always suffered from subordination as well as untouchability and other forms of discrimination of the upper castes, backward castes and other religious communities. As a result, any effort made by them to become literate and achieve even the minimum level of education has been discouraged by the people of these castes and communities. In many cases in the past, the Dalits were socially boycotted and severely punished-both physically and financially by imposing fines, especially in the rural areas, if they dared to become literate and achieve even the minimum level of education. The same was applied in the case of Dalits in Bihar also till recently.

Retrospectively, literacy rate among the Dalits or Scheduled Castes in Bihar is only 28.5 percent, according to 2001 Census, which happens to be the lowest in India. Their literacy rates, both in rural and urban areas, are also very low, compared to the other castes groups (see Table 3.3). Even increase in the female literacy rate among the Scheduled Castes has dismally been low. This shows that the gap between literacy rate of the Scheduled Castes at the national level and at the level of Bihar state is quite glaring. In the case of female literacy rate among the Scheduled Castes, the national average is nearly five times more than that of the state in Bihar.

Table 3.3: Caste-wise population of Scheduled Castes in Bihar, 2001

Sl. No.	Caste	Rural			Urban			Total		
		P	M	F	P	M	F	P	M	F
1.	Bantar	100992	524034	48820	231	134	97	101223	53403	48820
2.	Bauri	1746	898	848	350	177	173	2096	1075	1021
3.	Bhogta	12607	6681	5926	52	31	21	12659	6712	5947
4.	Bhuiya	532498	284696	267802	15905	8331	7574	56803	293027	2753
5.	Bhumij	2289	1175	1114	44	22	22	2333	1197	1114
6.	Chamar	3882782	2011625	871157	207288	111167	96181	4090070	2122732	1967338
7.	Chaupal	95982	49867	46115	4129	2154	1975	100111	52021	4809
8.	Dabgar	1943	967	976	1647	846	801	3590	1813	1777
9.	Dhobi	573080	296842	276238	74411	40038	3437	647491	336880	310611
10.	Dom	123257	64048	59209	32126	16867	15319	155383	80855	74528
11.	Dusadh	3758129	1962049	1796080	271282	145486	125796	4029411	2107535	1921876
12.	Ghasi	462	245	217	212	120	92	674	365	309
13.	Halalkhor	3259	1689	1570	701	380	321	3960	2069	1891
14.	Mehtar	127187	65526	61661	54561	2809	26052	181748	94035	8771
15.	Kanjar	914	488	426	706	372	334	1620	960	760
16.	Kurarian	5972	3084	2888	595	282	313	6567	3366	3201
17.	Lalbegi	785	431	354	24	14	10	808	445	364
18.	Musahar	2052971	1061927	991044	5916	31150	20015	2112136	1093077	1019059
19.	Nat	34594	17920	16674	4021	2056	1965	38615	19976	18639
20.	Pan	1879	976	903s	1774	983	791	3653	1559	1694
21.	Pasi	584991	303748	281243	126398	6658	59547	11389	370599	340790
22.	Rajwar	206506	106060	100446	7289	3771	3518	213795	109831	103964
23.	Turi	30703	15829	14880	2935	1521	1414	33638	17344	16294

Source: Calculated from A-10 State Bihar Primary Census Abstract for individual Scheduled Castes, 2001, pp.1-12.

Since the data for the purpose of present study has been collected from the respondents of the Chamar, Dhobi, Dusadh, and Musahar castes, it is necessary to provide below a brief profile of these castes in the state as well as in the East Champaran district of north Bihar and also of the study locales- the village and the town.

The Chamar

The Chamars are one of the most important segments among the Scheduled Castes or Dalits in Bihar as well as in other Indian states in north India. They constitute 31.3 percent of the total Scheduled Castes population in the state, according to 2001 Census. They comprise of 2122732 males and 1967338 females of the Dalit population.[32] They are widely distributed group in the state. The Chamar in the state of Bihar is the largest caste group due to the fact that as many as 1156 Chamar sub-castes were reported in the Census of India, 1891.[33] However, the Chamars in Bihar are presently divided into a number of endogamous sub-castes in Bihar. These are known as *Dhuria, Kanaujia, Jaiswal, Gawali (Mochi), Kulaha, Dhar, Chamar, Tatwa, Dakhinaha, Dabagar, Jhogh, Lakikaur, Kular* and *Farikaur.*[34] Among them, Kanoujia sub-caste is considered superior to all the sub-castes while the Dhar and the Tatwa are regarded as the lowest ones. Earlier, the inter-caste or inter-sub-caste marriages were strictly prohibited among the Chamars. They had been practicing child marriages, but now they go mostly for the adult marriages and also follow the custom of dowry. The marriages are usually arranged with the help of a mediator. Earlier, men and women from amongst the Chamar caste were not allowed to practice the second marriage, but, now, it is permitted among them and the divorce takes place on the basis of barrenness, impotence and unfaithfulness. The marriage rituals among the Chamars are primarily an imitation of the marriage rituals of the Hindu castes. Earlier, Brahmins did not recite *mantra* (the hymns) in the marriage ceremony of the Chamars, but now, they fix up the auspicious date and time of marriage and perform the rituals at the Chamar's house. They accept only the *kachcha* food as *Sidha* (kind-rice and pulses or fruits).

They were traditionally dealing with hides and skins, besides being landless agricultural labourers. They had also been engaged in making and repairing shoes and chappals. The nature of their occupation made it necessary for them to come into contact with dead animals. They either took off the hide of the dead animals and sold it in the market or used it for making shoes and chappals. Due to this practice, their occupations have been regarded as impure and polluting ones. The Chamar women were considered as experts in midwifery and they supplemented their family income by acting as midwives. It is significant to note that in most the villages, they are still considered to be the only specialist available for delivery of the child. They are called, in villages, as *Chamein* or *Daii* or *Doctor Daii* and their male counterparts as *Chamar*. The Chamars are closely related with the other communities of their village through the *Jajmani system* (system of the patron-client relations). They supply shoes chappals and provide other services to their *jajmans* (clients) on certain occasions.

The Chamars cremate their dead and the burial happens in cases of death because of some contagious diseases. The death ritual is observed by the family members for 10 days. At the end of the period, they perform the usual *Shradha* ceremony. The Chamars believe in all the Hindu gods and goddesses and celebrate all the Hindu festivals like *Chhath*, *Dusehra*, *Holi*, *Diwali*, *Karma-Dharma*, *Jwitiya, Magh Sankranti*, etc. They also believe in magic cures. They believe that *malaria* and *cholera* are caused by an evil spirit. The Chamars are terribly afraid of *churail* (a witch female evil spirit), which generally attacks either the pregnant women or women with just after the child birth. They also have faith in *Bhoot* and *Pisach* (evil spirit of a dead man). They have among them *ojhas* or sprit doctors. The Chamars have their caste councils (caste Panchayat) headed by the 'Sardar'.[35]

The Dusadh

Dusadh is the second largest caste group among the Scheduled Castes in Bihar, with their 30.9 percent of the total SC population, according to 2001 Census. They comprise of 2107535 males and 1921876 females of the Dalit population in the state.[36] The Dusadhs are known by different names like *Darh* and *Darhi*. "Their caste titles are *Hazra*, *Paswan*, *Bhagat* and *Manjhi*. The Dusadhs are largely concentrated in Muzaffarpur and Darbhanga districts in the north Bihar as well as in a few districts in the south Bihar".[37] They are considered as good agricultural labourers, and also work as the watchmen or *chowkidars* and the henchmen of the landlord. They actually rear cattle along with pigs but due to the impact of sanskritisation, they have given up the practice of rearing pigs.

The Dusadhs are regarded as the endogamous groups and do not share cooked food from hands of the other groups (sub-castes) of their caste. They are divided into a number of sub-castes like *Kanoujia*,

Magahia, *Silhotia*, *Darhi*, *Darh*, *Manjhi* and *Pariva*[38]. Although they practice child marriage, they do not take dowry among them. Their marriage rituals are mainly an imitation of the Hindu marriage rituals. The Brahmins fix the date and time of marriagc among them and perform the rituals, but they do not accept *kachcha* food in their marriage ceremony. They accept only *kachcha* grains as '*sidha'*. It is a fact that certain changes have occurred among people of the Dusadh caste, and now they prefer the priest from their own caste or community to perform their marriage ceremony in some parts of Bihar. They generally burn their dead and perform *shradh* or death ceremony. They eat pork and consume drinks, but now-a-days, they are giving up such habits because of the impact of sanskritisation. Yet, their occupational status has not changed substantially and the bulks of them remain as agricultural labourers.

They worship a number of deities and the chief among them is known as Rahu. The deities they worship are *Goraya*, *Manusdeva*, *Sokha*, *Sahlesh*, *Bhairawa*, *Jagdamba Mai* and *Kali Chauharmal Baba*[39]. Besides, they also worship a number of Hindu deities. During the festivals, they offer animals sacrifices and fruits to the deities. Besides, they sort out any dispute occurred among them through their own caste council.

The Musahar

The fourth largest caste group among the Scheduled Castes in Bihar is Musahar.[40] They constitute 16.22 percent (2109307 males and 1019059 females) of the Dalit population in the state.[41] The Musahars trace their origin from the legendary Sabri who served berries (a kind of fruit from the forest) to Lord Rama. They are largely concentrated in Darbhanga, Saharsa, Purnea, Munghyr districts in the state of Bihar. Their surnames are *Bhogta*, *Chharidar*, *Kopat*, *Mahton*, *Naik* and *Manjhi*. They are predominantly rural and landless, and rear pigs and poultry. They also consume rats and snails[42], as stated earlier.

They are divided into six sub-castes namely *Mahatwar*, *Dharwar*, *Bhogta*, *Ghatwar*, *Soutar* and *Tirwar*[43]. The social and territorial location of people of the Musahar caste is different from those of the other caste groups. "They follow endogamy among them, but divorce, desertion and remarriage are permissible among them. They worship many deities including *Diwali*, *Bir*, *Bhairon*, *Mado Bir*, *Tulisini Bir*, *Dudhi Bir*, *Bansahiya*, *Parmeshwar*, *Fulang*, *Maldano*, *Ganga Ram*, *Masan* and *Devi*, and also believe in the Hindu gods and goddesses"[44]. They also practice child marriage, and in the marriage Brahmins are called for the ritual performance. Like other Dalits castes, they celebrate the festivals with their own caste members. During the celebrations of festivals or any other religious ceremonies, they invite their own caste *Bhagat* or priest who performs *Puja* at the 'Deviasthal'- their installed in home in the tolas. In their tolas, they also have their own caste Panchayats where adult or elderly males among them are selected as the tola or village head called 'Choudhary'. The Panchayat head maintains caste norms, and any infringement of the caste code gets punished. The Musahars have alliance with people of the other castes groups for their socio-economic supports in the village.

The Dhobi

The Dhobi is considered to be one of the important Scheduled Castes or Dalits of the state and is treated differently such as washerman, unclean, polluted one, etc. They constitute 4.97 percent (336880 males and 310611 females) of the Dali population in the state.[45] The Dhobis are regarded unclean due to their low caste status as well as their low occupation in the caste hierarchy. They take help from the donkey for carrying their bag of others' dirty or unclean clothes for washing to the river bank or pond. It has also been seen that some of them have shifted from their traditional occupation in the urban areas and have opened laundries as their occupation, but bulk of them are still associated with cleaning the dirty clothes of others in the rural areas.

The Dhobis are found in almost all the villages as well as in the towns. Their caste surnames are *Baitha* and *Rajak.* The Dhobis are also divided into many sub-castes such as *Ajodhabasi*, *Belwar*, *Jaiswar*, *Kannaujia*, and *Magahiya* on the basis of their regional origins. In villages, they are still paid in kind, while in towns or cities they get their wages in cash. They are also provided customary gifts at birth, marriage, funerals and other religious and ritual ceremonies of their *Jajman* of other castes and communities. In rural areas, some of their caste members work as agricultural labourers. It is said that they are considered to be advanced among the Scheduled Castes or Dalits due to their contact with people of the higher castes.

Child marriage as well as the custom of dowry is practiced among them. Their marriage rituals are generally imitation of the Hindu-marriage rituals. The remarriage and divorce are common among them. They also worship the Hindu gods and goddesses, and celebrate almost all the Hindu festivals like Holi, Dussehra, Diwali, etc., and the goddess Kali is the most popularly revered deity among them.

They have their own caste Panchayat, like other Scheduled Castes or Dalits. The head of the Panchayat is known as *Manjan*. He is considered as the chief judge and also the chief executive of the Panchayat. After inviting suggestions or advices of elders of the locality he takes appropriate decisions on the issues pertaining to a guilty person of the caste or the caste as a whole.

Profile of the East Champaran District

The Champaran district was first created in 1866. But on 1st of December 1971 the district was split into two districts, i.e., Purbi (east) Champaran and Paschim (west) Champaran[46]. The Purbi or East Champaran is one of the important districts of north Bihar. The word Champaran is derived from champa-aranya or champkatanys, meaning forests of magnolia (champa) trees, and as it is located at the purbi or the eastern side, it is called East Champaran. The district of East Champaran is a part of the Tirhut division. It is an administrative unit of Bihar and the district headquarter is located at Motihari. The East Champaran district comprises of an area of 3,968 sq. kms. Presently, the district consists of six sub-divisions and twenty seven blocks. These sub-divisions are Motihari Sadar, Chakia, Areraj, Raxaul, Sikarahna and Pakridayal. The district is bounded on the north by Nepal, on the south by Muzaffarpur district, on the east by Sheohar and Sitamarhi districts and on the west by the West Champaran (Bettiah) district. According to 2001 Census, the district has a population of 3933636 persons (2072350 males and 1861286 females). The rural population consists of 3688687 persons (1941681 males and 1747006 females), whereas the urban population consists of only 251086 (6.31%) persons. The sex ratio of population of the district is 898 females per 1000 males. The density of population of the district is 991 persons per sq. km.

The literacy rate of the East Champaran district was 27.59 percent (39.65% males and 13.69% females) according to 1991 census, which was increased to 38.14 percent (50.14% males and 24.65% females) in 2001. It shows that the literacy rate has increased not only among males, but also among female between 1991 and 2001 Censuses. Yet, it is still lower, compared to that in the other districts in the state. Similarly, the literacy rate among the Dalits or Scheduled Castes in the district was 20.60 percent (30.25% among males and 9.66% among females), which was the lowest, compared to that in other districts in the state, according to 2001 Census. There were 36.40 percent (51.38% males and 19.97% females) main workers engaged in the primary, secondary and tertiary sectors of employment in Bihar. In the case of the East Champaran district, there were 38.24 percent Dalits or Scheduled Castes (56.15% males and 17.93% females) who were engaged in the primary, secondary and tertiary sectors of employments. The total number of workers, including those of the Scheduled castes in the East Champaran district engaged in different occupations is given in Table 3.5 below.

It is clear that the cultivators (350295 persons) and agricultural labours (704768 persons) were more in number than those engaged in the other occupations, according to 2001 Census. There were 35935 persons who were employed in the household industries, while other workers were 195848 persons in the district. On the other hand, the main workers or those who were full-time workers were 1025654 persons and marginal workers 261189 persons, and the non-workers were 2652930 persons. Thus, agriculture happened and continues to happen a way of life of people of the district.

Table 3.4: Distribution of Workers of the East Champaran District

Total Workers	**1,286,843 (Persons)**	**1,013,185 (Males)**	**273,658 (Females)**
Cultivators	350,295	301,019	49,276
Agri-Labourers	704,768	508,977	195,791
Household Industry	35,932	24,398	11,534
Other Workers	195,848	178,791	17,057
Main Workers	1,025,654	890,069	135,585
Marginal Workers	261,189	123,116	138,073
Non-Workers	2,652,930	1,063,862	1,589,068

Source: Prasad, Jagdish (2007). *Bihar: Dynamics of Development*, Mittal Publications, New Delhi, p. 139.

Besides the people's participation in the State and Centre levels political activities, mainly during the elections periods, they remain active in the political activities at the local level also. There are 18 Panchayats in the Chakia Block, consisting of 76 villages and the village Bara Govind, selected for the present study, is located in the Baisaha Panchayat. The other two villages located in the Panchayat are Taraniya and Baisaha.

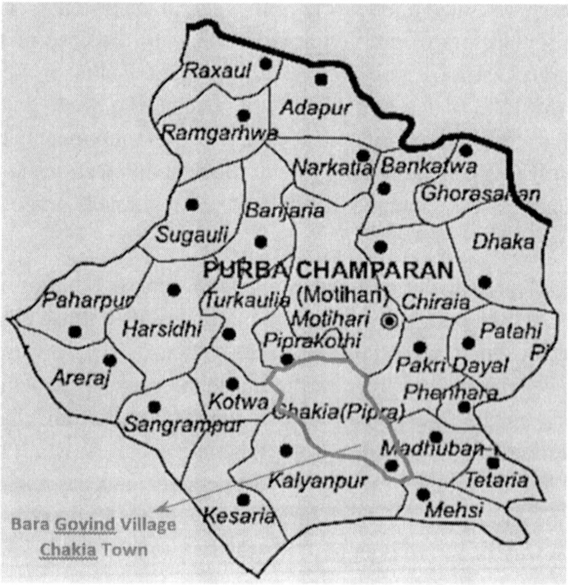

Source: www.mapsofindia.com

Figure 2: Map showing the studied locales

Bara Govind Village

The Bara Govind village is located in the Baisaha Panchayat of the Chakia Sub-division in the East Champaran district, as mentioned above. The village is situated on the bank of the Budhi Gandak River. The term 'Bara' means the place where only upper strata live in, according to one of the respondents, who explained during the field work. The village is a part of the Bhojpuri speaking belt. It is about three kms north of the Chakia town and is completely separated from the town by the river. Before 2005, the village was totally cut off from the main town because there was no proper means of transportation and people used to commute to the town either through the *Pipa Pool* or by the boat. But now, a bridge has been constructed over this river by the government. The village is affected by flood every a year. There is no proper metalled road connecting the village, except the *kachcha* or unmetalled road. During the rainy season, the road deteriorates quite rapidly and it becomes difficult for the traffic to move. Due to the bad road condition, there is no regular bus or auto service from the village to the town. People generally use to go to the local market for buying groceries. Now, it has relatively better connectivity than earlier after making a bridge over the river, which connects the village to the local markets as well as the main town to the National Highway 28.

Anyway, the total population of the Bara Govind village is 3362 persons, while the Taraniya village has 1883 persons and the Baisaha village has 4257 persons. The village under study has been more backward in the socio-economic, educational and political spheres, compared to other two villages. The Bara Govind village consists of Brahmins, Bumihars, Yadavs, Kurmis, Baniyas, Dalits or Scheduled Castes, etc. The upper and backward castes are numerically less in number, but socially and economically dominant, compared to the Dalits in the village. The literacy rate of the village is 21.87 percent, compared to the literacy rate of state (47%), according to Census 2001. The female literacy rate is 16.22 percent, while the male literacy rate is 27.38 percent. The total working population is 48.48 percent out of which working population of the men is 65.48 percent, while of women 31.05 percent. Further, the main working population of the total population is 42.2 percent out of which men are 59.47 percent, whereas women are 24.49 percent. Similarly, the total population in the village, the marginal working population is only 6.28 percent, of which men are 6.01 percent, while women are 6.55 percent. The total non-working population of the total population is 51.52 percent of which men are 34.52 percent and women are 68.95 percent, according to Census 2001.

Demographically, the Scheduled Castes or Dalits are concentrated in the isolated area called *Tola* of the village. A tola specifies a fixed area of the village, which is physically or spatially separated from the main village where the people of upper castes live. The tola remains worst effected due to lack of proper approach road or passage, electricity and sanitation. Beteille [47] has rightly observed, "The physical structure of the village has not meanwhile undergone any substantial change; it continues to reflect the primary cleavages of its traditional social structure". J.P Singh[48] also says that "the notion of purity and pollution has segregated the village community into several pockets or *tolas* on the basis of caste in rural Bihar. Each caste is separated from other by a greater or lesser distance. A few castes may live in houses situated side by side but live apart for all practical purposes". Thus, the Bara Govind village is presently divided into many *tolas* like Chamar *Tola*, Dusadh *Tola*, Musahar *Tola,* etc., where people of the Dalit communities reside.

Most of the Dalits belonging to Chamar, Dusadh and Musahar castes do not have *pacca* houses and electricity facilities. They either live in *kachcha* or mixed houses or in huts. Caste as an institution and as a group plays a very crucial role in the day-to-day life of people in the village. The hierarchy of caste is also observed in the village where the upper castes inherently feel superior to the lower castes. They also keep distance in social relations or interactions with people of the Dalit castes due to low rank of their caste in the caste hierarchy. Traditionally, the village remained under the *Zamindari* system during the British period. But now, there are three local zamindars- each belonging to Bhumihar, Brahmin and Yadav castes, who control the village. In addition, the Brahmins, Bhumihars and Yadavs, even being less in numerical strength, hold most of the land in the village. On the other hand, most of the Dalits are economically poor and landless daily wage labourers. The Dalits are completely deprived of rights of possessing land in the village. As far as education is concerned, most of Dalits of the village are illiterate and only a handful of them are educated. Thus, the Scheduled Castes or Dalits, i.e., the Chamars, Dusadhs and Musahars, from whom we have selected our respondents for the purpose of data collection, are the most deprived of their social, economic, educational, political and cultural rights due to hegemony of the upper and middle level castes. Not only that, but they also experience the highest level of exclusion from their social rights of access to all the spheres mentioned above.

Chakia Town

The Chakia Town, another locale of our study, is located at 26°

42' N 85° 05' E of the Tropical Cancer. It has an average elevation of 52 metre (170 feet) from above the sea level and is one of the important commercial towns in the Purvi Champaran district in the state of Bihar. The river Budhi Gangak flows nearby it. The Chakia town is a sub-divisional headquarter as well as of the block headquarter and a broad gauge railway line, with a railway station at Chakia, passes through it directly, connecting it to Calcutta, Delhi and rest of the country. The railway station is also nearest to the Kesaria Stupa, a Buddhist pilgrimage site. It has a sugarcane mill, which is closed now.

According to Census 2001, Chakia town had a population of 16,618 persons of which males constituted 53 percent and females 47 percent. As per the 2011 Census, the population of the town would have been increased, but the figures are not yet available. The town has literacy rate of 51 percent, which is lower than the national average of 59.5 percent. Nearly, 18 percent of population in the town is under 6 years of age. The total working population is 33.07 percent of which 35.68 percent are men whereas 9.41 percent are women. Further, the main working population in the town is 30.55 percent of which 51.18 percent are men and 6.87 percent are women. Similarly, out of 66.93 percent, the total non-working population 46.32 percent is men and 90.59 percent are women.[49]

The people living in the town are Hindus, Muslims and others. The Hindus belonging to the Brahmin, Bhumihar, Rajput and Kayastha castes are dominant in all domains of social life. The second major category of the Hindu is of the backward classes or castes, constituting Yadav, Baniya, Marwari and Kurmi castes. The third category of the Hindus is of the Scheduled Castes- Chamar, Dusadh, Dhobi, Mehtar, Dom and other castes who are ranked lowest in the caste-hierarchy prevailing even in the town. We have selected our respondents from the Chamar, Dusadh and Dhobi castes as people of the Musahar caste are not found in the town like, Dhobi caste not found in the selected village.

Socio-Personal Background of the Respondents

We shall briefly look at, in this section, the socio-personal background, i.e., caste, age, educational level, occupation, and monthly income of the respondents from the village as well as the town under study. Such an examination will help us to view their present social status and the status formation taking place among them in both the village and the town as well as in the surrounding areas. The number of respondents selected from the different Scheduled Castes or Dalits of the village and the town is given in the following table.

Table 3.5: Caste of the Respondents from the Village and the Town

Caste	Caste of the Respondents			
	Bara Govind Village		Chakia Town	
	Frequency	Percentage	Frequency	Percentage
Chamar	42	33.6	42	33.6
Dhobi*	-	-	47	37.6
Dusadh	38	30.4	36	28.8
Musahar**	45	36.0	-	-
Total	**125**	**100.0**	**125**	**100.0**

*Dhobis are not found in the village; hence, respondents from the Musahar caste have been selected.

**Musahars are not found in the Chakia Town; hence, respondents from the Dhobi caste have been selected.

The Chamars are in large number, followed by the Musahars and Dusadhs in the village; and number of the Dhobis is more, followed by Chamars and Dusadhs in the town. Since the Musahars are still predominantly rural in their habitation, they are absent in the town. Similarly, Dhobis are not found in the Bara Govind village, and the residents are dependent on services of the Dhobis residing in the neighbouring village.

Table 3.6: Age of the Respondents from the Village and the Town

Age (Years)	Age of the Respondents			
	Bara Govind Village		Chakia Town	
	Frequency	Percentage	Frequency	Percentage
20-30	35	28.0	31	24.8
30-40	32	25.6	58	56.4
40-50	28	22.4	17	13.6
50 Above	30	24.0	19	15.2
Total	**125**	**100.0**	**125**	**100.0**

It is evident from the table that more than 50 percent respondents are young and middle-aged and the rest are from the younger and the elder age group in the village. So also, respondents from the Town are, more or less, from the similar age-groups. A point may be noted here that as the young generation of Dalits, in both rural and urban areas, are more conscious and aware of their rights, subordination and super ordination and are familiar with the outside world, their responses to various issues examined in the present study would be both quantitatively and qualitatively different from those of the elderly respondents.

Education is one of the most important indicators of the socio-economic development. Historically, the Scheduled Castes or the Dalits have been educationally deprived for centuries, as stated earlier in this chapter. The general condition of education among them in India as well as in the state of Bihar is pitiable even after 66 years of Independence. It is a matter of common knowledge that the Scheduled Castes have lagged behind in the field of education not only in Bihar, but also in other states because of their being late starter and ever the existed socio-economic barriers. This is also evident from the fact that more than half of the total (54.4%) respondents from the village are illiterate, followed by 15.2 percent respondents who have achieved the primary level education and 10.4 percent respondents with middle level education. Apart from that, only 14.4 percent respondents have high school education, only 4 percent respondent are intermediate pass, out followed by 1.6 percent respondents who are graduate (see Table 3.7 given below).

Table 3.7: Educational Qualification of the Respondents from the Village and the Town

Educational Level	Educational Qualification of the Respondents			
	Bara Govind Village		Chakia Town	
	Frequency	Percentage	Frequency	Percentage
Illiterate	68	54.4	-	-
Primary	19	15.2	-	-
Middle School	13	10.4	11	8.8
High School	18	14.4	38	30.4
Intermediate	5	4.0	31	24.8
Graduation	2	1.6	38	30.4
Post-Graduation	-	-	7	5.6
Total	**125**	**100.0**	**125**	**100.0**

As far as educational status of the respondents from the town is concerned, it is by far better than those from the village, as not a single respondent from the town is illiterate. Not only that, but more than one-third respondents from the town is graduate and post graduate, compared to only 2 respondents from the village with such educational background.

Table 3.8: Present Occupation of the Respondents from the Village and the Town

Occupation	Occupations of the Respondents			
	Bara Govind Village		Chakia Town	
	Frequency	Percentage	Frequency	
Traditional Caste Occupation	6	4.8	-	-
Agricultural Labourer	96	76.8	-	-
Non-agricultural labourer	7	5.6	4	3.2
Govt. Job	3	2.4	47	40.8
Private	4	3.2	24	19.2
Petty-Business	-	-	19	15.2
Unemployed	9	7.2	31	24.8
Total	**125**	**100.0**	**125**	**100.0**

In terms of occupation, 4.8 percent respondents are engaged in their traditional occupations like making or repairing shoes/chappals (the Chamar respondents) and toddy tapping (respondents from the Dusadh castes), while 76.8 percent (respondents from the Chamar, Dusadh and Musahar castes) are agricultural labourers. Only a few respondents, from the village, are employed as peons, helpers, etc. in both the government (2.4%) offices and private factories (3.2%), located in the urban areas, while some respondents are engaged in non-agricultural (5.6%) works like road and house construction and still a few (7.2%) are engaged in other works like rickshaw and *thela* pulling. Interestingly, there are 40 respondents, i.e., 9 from the village and 31 from the town are pursuing their higher education and thereby are unemployed.

Similarly, most of the respondents from the town are employed in government and private jobs and some of them are pursuing their petty-businesses like having own medical shop, garment shop, Kirana (grocery) shop, electronic shop, Pan Shop, dealership, etc. Some respondents are also engaged in other works as auto driving, painting, paldari, salesmen, tailoring, laundry, etc., followed by 12 percent respondents being unemployed.

To ascertain the monthly or even annual income of the people in general and of the respondents from the village is not an easy proposition due to the fact that their employment is not regular throughout the month or year, and in most of the cases their wages are paid not in cash but in kind. There are 12.8 percent Chamar, 10.4 percent Dusadh and 17.6 percent Musahar respondents who get grain in their wages. Secondly, the income of those respondents is not regular who are employed as labourer in house construction as well as in transporting river sand and truck loading and unloading. In fact, they receive less than Rs 1000 a month. There are 18.4 percent respondents who earn more than Rs 1000. They are either in government or private jobs, but their number is very dismal. They are doing the fourth grade jobs, as stated earlier. They are economically poor and unable to maintain their daily basic needs. Even they do not have land, which is the main source of income in rural areas in Bihar as well as in other states and their main source of income is agricultural labour, rickshaw and *thela* pulling in the nearby town and returning to their home every day. Contrary to that, the respondents from the town are economically better-off. For instance, 60.8 percent (Chamar 21.6%, Dusadh 18.4% and Dhobi 20.8%) respondents earn more than Rs 3000 and are employed in both government and in private jobs, and the rest 39.2 percent (Chamar 12%, Dusadh 10.4% and Dhobi 16.8%) earn less than Rs 3000 per month.

Table 3.9: Monthly income of the Respondents from the Village and the Town

Income (Rs)	Income of the Respondents	
	Bara Govind Village	Chakia Town
In Kind	51(40.8)	-
Less than1000	51(40.8)	-
1001-2000	23(18.4)	-
2001-3000	-	49(39.2)
More than 3000	-	76(60.8)
Total	125	125

Conclusion

The above discussion, in the present chapter, explores certain explanations. Out of the three Dalit or Scheduled Castes-Chamar, Dusadh and Musahar living in the studied village, the Chamars and Musahars are more in number. The people of these two castes have comparatively high level of illiteracy and are daily wage labourers. A large number of the respondents from both the village and the town belonging to young and middle-aged groups, while a few respondents are from the old age group. Some of the respondents from the village are still engaged in their traditional occupations like shoes/chappals repairing and making, toddy tapping, etc. Most of the respondents are landless agricultural labourers, and they are socially, economically, educationally, politically and culturally discriminated and deprived of their rights by people of the upper and middle level castes. On the other hand, most of the respondents living in Chakia town are Chamars and Dhobis and a sizeable of them have received education up to graduate and post graduate levels and so also a comparatively better socio-economic status. They are not engaged in any traditional occupations but in petty- business, and jobs in both government and private sectors. We shall examine, in the next chapter, the views of the respondents about the nature and forms of discrimination practiced against them, and that of their exploitation and exclusion from their access to the various spheres of life both in the village and the town.

Notes

1. Benjamin, Joseph (1989). *Scheduled Castes in Indian Politics and Society*, ESS ESS Publications, New Delhi, p. 93.
2. Jha, Hetukar (2000). "Promises and Lapses: Understanding the Experiences of Scheduled Castes in Bihar in Historical Perspective", *Journal of Indian School of Political Economy*, July-December, Vol. 12, No. 342, p. 423.
3. See Das, A. N. (19992). *The Republic of Bihar*, Penguin Books, New Delhi, p. 18.
4. Diwakar, R. R. (1959). *Bihar Through the Ages,* Orient Longman, New Delhi.
5. Sharma, Alakh N. (2005). "Agrarian Relation and Socio-Economic Change in Bihar", *Economic and Political Weekly*, Vol. 40, No.10, March 5-11, pp. 960-72.
6. Yadav, Ramendra and Ravi Kumar (2004). *Bihar: Myth and Reality*, Hope Publications, India.

7. Benjamin, Joseph (1989). *Scheduled Caste in Indian Politics and Society*, ESS ESS Publications, New Delhi, p. 95.

8. Roy, Ramashray (1970). "Caste and Political Recruitment in Bihar", in Rajni Kothari (ed.), *Caste in Indian Politics*, Orient Longman, New Delhi, p. 229.

9. Kumar, Rabindra (2002). *Impact of Rural Development on Scheduled Castes*, Anmol Publications, New Delhi, pp. 41-45.

10. Sinha, Arun, "Caste and Factions in Bihar Politics", *Times of India* (July 9, 1986).

11. Blair, Harry W. (1980). "Rising Kulaks and Backward Classes in Bihar", *Economic and Political Weekly*, Vol. 15(2) January, p. 67.

12. Kumar, Rabindra (2002). *Impact of Rural Development on Scheduled Castes*, Anmol Publications, New Delhi, p. 54.

13. Prasad, Pradhan H. (1975). "Agrarian Unrest and Economic Change in Rural Bihar: Three Case Studies", *Economic and Political Weekly*, June, 14, p. 1979.

14 Das, Arvind, N. (1992). *The Republic of Bihar*, Penguin Books, New Delhi, p. 11.

15. Singh, Shyama Nand (1990). *Reservation: Problems and Prospects*, Uppal Publishing House, New Delhi, p. 43.

16. Ojha, K.P. (1959-60). *Bihar: Facts and Figure*, Directorate of Public Relations, Bihar.

17. Kumar, Rabindra (2002). *Impact of Rural Development on Scheduled Castes*, Anmol Publications, New Delhi, p. 47.

18. Jannuzi, Tomasson F. (1974). *Agrarian Crisis in India: The Case of Bihar*, University of Taxes Press, California, p. 25.

19. Mishra, B. B. (1961). *The Indian Middle Class: Their Growth in Modern Times*, Oxford University Press, London, p. 54.

20. Kothari, Rajni (ed.) (1970). *Caste in Indian Politics*, Orient Longman, New Delhi, pp. 230-31.

21 Vidyarthi, L P & N. Mishra (1977). *Harijan Today,* Classical Publications, New Delhi, p. 26.

22. Lal, A.K. (1997). "Bihar: Old and New", *Seminar*, 450, February, pp. 19-20.

23. Beteille, Andre (2000). "The Scheduled Castes: An Inter-Regional Perspective", *Journal of Indian School of Political Economy*, Vol. 12, July- December, p. 372.

24. Harcourt, Max (1977). "Kisan Population and Revolution in Rural India, in D.V. Low, (ed.), *Congress and the Raj,* South Asia Books, Colombia, p. 324.

25. Singh, Shyama Nand (1990). *Reservation, Problems and Prospects*, Uppal Publishing House, New Delhi, pp. 55-56.
26. Joshi, P.C. (1978). "Organizing Rural Poor: Some Basic Issues", *Mainstream*, 12August, New Delhi, p. 7.
27. Ibid, pp. 58-59.
28. Sharma, Alakh N. (1996). "Caste and Class in Rural Bihar", *Journal of Social and Economic Studies*, Vol. 12-13, pp. 62-63.
29. There are some anomalies in the classification. For instance, those who are forced to lease out their land because of age or illness and this prevents them from cultivating it, will be classified as landlords-correct up to appoint but only half the story. Households with no female members of working age cannot, by definition, be classified as middle peasants.
30. Roy Chaudhury, P.C. (1964). *Bihar District Gazetteers*, Darbhanga Secretariat Press, Patna, p. 654.
31. Roy Chaudhury, P.C. (1960). *Bihar District Gazatteers,* Saran Secretariat Press, Patna, p. 449.
32. Economic Survey 2008-09, Bihar.
33. Kamble, N.D. (1982). *The Scheduled Castes*, Ashish Publishing House, New Delhi, p. 2.
34. Sachchidananda (1977). *The Harijan Elite,* Thomson Press (India) Limited, p. 17.
35. Sachchidananda (1977). *The Harijan Elite,* Thomson Press (India) Limited, pp. 17-18.
36 Economic Survey 2008-09, Bihar.
37. *Ibid.,* 19.
38. *Ibid.,* 19.
39. Sachchidananda, *Ibid.,* 20.
40. They are also known as *Bhuiya* in some parts of the state.
41. Economic Survey 2008-09, Bihar.
42. *Ibid.,* 21.
43. *Ibid.,* 22.
44. *Ibid.,* 22-23.
45. Economic Survey 2008-09, Bihar.
46. www.bihar.com or www.eastchamparan.com
47. Beteille, Andre (1966). *Caste, Class and Power*, Oxford University Press, New Delhi, p. 44.
48. Singh, J.P. (2001). "Caste and Morphology of Rural Settlement", *The Eastern Anthropology*, Vol. 54, No. 2 April-June, p. 159.
49. www.bihar.com or www.eastchamparan.com

Chapter - 4

Discrimination, Exploitation and Social Exclusion of Dalits

Introduction

The Dalits have been facing, even today, the discrimination as well as deprivation, exploitation and exclusion of various types within the Hindu social structure and in the social structure as a whole in the Indian society. It is a known fact that they have historically been excluded and remained deprived, for centuries, from their socio-cultural, economic, educational and political rights. The present chapter, based on our field data collected from both rural and urban areas in Bihar, focuses mainly on the existing discrimination vis-à-vis deprivation and exploitation as well as social exclusion of Dalits, which are deeply rooted in the Hindu caste system, besides in the present socio-economic and political system. But before doing that, it is necessary to briefly explain the concepts of discrimination and deprivation, exploitation and social exclusion in general and in the Indian society in particular.

We have explained briefly, in Chapter 1, the concept of discrimination and deprivation as analyzed in social sciences, particularly in Sociology and Social Anthropology. Before analyzing the social interaction and relations, socio-cultural dimension of deprivation, exploitation and exclusion of the Dalits in the Indian society in general and Dalits in particular, it is significant to discuss here about the nature and extent of discrimination practiced against them even today. According to Prakash Louis[1], discrimination is the most dominant form of social exclusion which deals with the denial of opportunities and rights to certain groups of people on the basis of race or caste or community, sex, ethnicity, age and physical disability. In the common parlance, discrimination is defined as prejudice transformed into action. He further states that discrimination also carries a derogatory or negative perception about a group of people and, thus, promotes the behaviour or creates conditions that adhere to the thought and behaviour.

Nature and forms of discrimination have been analyzed conceptually and theoretically by many scholars. For instance, according to Ram[2], "Dalits face discrimination, at two levels, in both the public and private sectors organisations. One, at the time of recruitment itself when the recruiters or selectors remain non-Dalits who are invariably guided by their traditional prejudices against the Dalits. Secondly, the discrimination rather social discrimination against Dalits comes from their fellow employees and superiors in the work organisations". Townsend (1993) also defines the concept of deprivation (a consequence of discrimination) in terms of social dimension. In his view, people are deprived, if they lack the resources to participate in the normal social life of their community. In his own words, "people are relatively deprived if they cannot obtain, at all or sufficient, the conditions of life-that is, the diets, amenities, standards and services-which allow them to play the roles, participate in the relationships and follow the customary behaviour which is expected of them by virtue of their membership of society" (cited in Baily, Spratt and others).[3] This definition is important because it deals with two issues which need to be taken into account when measuring discrimination and deprivation, i.e., it is being *relative* and *multi-dimensional* as explained by Townsend also. Further, social discrimination vis-à-vis deprivation may be correlated with or it may contribute to social exclusion, when a member in particular society is ostracized by other members. Thus, the excluded member is discriminated as well as denied access to the resources that allow his/her for healthy social, economic and political interaction with other persons. It is, then, very obvious that the discrimination or deprivation is a multi-dimensional concept which deals with the nature of exclusion of people from their social rights. Apart from that, Oommen[4] explores the sources of deprivation of the Dalits of India, which were (and still are) three: low ritual status, appalling poverty and powerlessness. He links the protest with deprivation by explaining that Dalits' protests in India first crystallised against their socio-cultural oppression, particularly untouchability. This was followed by their mobilisation for political enfranchisement. Finally, their protest against economic exploitation gradually emerged which might be linked to the hierarchy of deprivations as perceived by the Dalits.

A point may be mentioned here that the deprivation is all along preceded by discrimination, wherein one is discriminated in not getting/allowing to participate in certain activities including inter-personal relationship with others. Even if one is allowed to participate, certain amount of both physical and social distance vis-à-vis discrimination might be maintained against him or her, and, thus, depriving him/her from his/her full participation in such activities. Hence, both discrimination and deprivation get full reinforcement, if these are deeply rooted in the given traditional social structure or extended, in one form or the other, even in the emergent social structure. The deprivation, though being independent conceptual and substantive entity, is being imbedded or well-entrenched in the social discrimination of one type or the other in Indian society and elsewhere. However, a fact cannot be denied that the traditional social structure has undergone both quantitatively and qualitatively changes, more in urban than in rural areas. Accordingly, changes are visible both in attitude and behaviour of people, more in some and less in other domains of life which in themselves are the intrinsic components of the given social structure.

Further, the term exploitation is popularly used in the economic domain of life. So also, it is used for taking undue advantages in the socio-cultural, political and emotional domains of one's life. Anyway, the term 'exploitation' may be defined as the utilisation of service of any persons for selfish purpose. It is concerned with at least two persons: one is the exploiter and the other is exploitee or the exploited one. In this way, the exploiter exploits the exploitee for his/her selfish purpose. Marx uses the term exploitation in economic sense, wherein he argues that the domination or ownership of private property is the major source of human exploitation. According to Marx[5], people's position in society is determined by their relationship to the means of production, i.e., the factory, the machines and anything apart from labour that is needed to produce goods. The workers produce the commodities, but they do not get the proper wage of their labour. Gail Omvedt[6] also has dealt with the discrimination and exploitation and stated that "in the traditional Indian system, hierarchy and inequality among the exploited stands out clearly. Such inequality existed among all feudal societies (it has been estimated, for instance, that in medieval Europe nearly one-third of all peasant families were landless); but in India, it was institutionalised in the caste system. Cultivating peasants with firm rights to the 'lower share' or to supervising the village distribution of the 'grainheap' were at the top of the village hierarchy; artisans and subordinate tenants had rights that were both institutionalised and secondary; herders and forest dwelling hunters and gatherers exchanges sometimes on a basis of inferiority, sometimes with more independence; but everywhere the lowest castes of Dalits/untouchables performed their most menial labour and were fundamentally differential from the others in being classed as 'impure'".

On the other hand, Social exclusion is a process by which individuals or groups are wholly or partially excluded from their participation in the society in which they live[7], as stated earlier. In Indian society, social exclusion deals with the form of segregating a group of people from the social, economic, educational, political, cultural and religious domains of their social life, as mentioned in Chapter 2. Thus, the process of social exclusion describes deprivation, discrimination, marginalisation, exploitation and oppression of an individual or social group (caste or primordial collectivity) in a society. In other words, discrimination or deprivation, exploitation and exclusion are interconnected and interrelated, in some ways or other.

In view of the above conceptual explanations, we shall examine below the views of the respondents, from both the village and the town, on various aspects of discrimination vis-à-vis deprivation, exploitation and exclusion or social exclusion of Dalits from the different spheres of their day-to-day life. This would, in turn, reflect on the existing discrimination, deprivation, exploitation and social exclusion of the Dalits both in the rural and urban areas in state like Bihar and elsewhere in the country.

We shall analyze briefly below the views of the respondents from both the village and the town on social discrimination, exploitation and social exclusion of the Dalits in both the studied areas respectively. In doing so, we shall look on views of the respondents on discrimination or social discrimination against, followed by exploitation and social exclusion of the Dalits in the various spheres of life-social interaction and relations, commensal relations, educational pursuit, socio-cultural participation and participation in elected political organisations.

Forms and Extent of Social Discrimination

Social interaction and Relations

Social interaction refers to a particular form of externalities or external behaviour of a person with the other person. Besides carrying one's personal likes and dislikes against the other, it also carries one's socio-cultural moorings rooted in one's family neighbourhood, peer group and over and above one's caste or community affiliation from where one gets socialised. Over and above, nature and form of social interaction and relation depends on the context or the issue (s) on which it takes place. Social interactions are sometimes purposive (similar to market situation) and sometimes non-purposive called non-market interactions which is not regulated by the price mechanism). Situating interaction in the caste system or a system of birth-ascribed statuses, Berreman[8] argues that any interaction or social interaction between two persons occurs within the maximum limits of status-equal interaction and, thus, interaction is consistently hierarchical. Such an interaction includes social intercourse to marriage, occupation, economic, political, ritual, friendships and so on. But beyond that, social interaction between two persons of two different castes or communities remains unequal, though the possibility of equal or non-hierarchical social interaction between two persons of the same achieved status, but from two different castes or communities, cannot be ruled out.

Anyway, when we look with the above mentioned framework at social discrimination of Dalits in terms of their social interaction and relations with people of the different caste groups in the studied village and the town, we find that in the Bara Govind village the pattern of social relationship between the Dalits, though being is in more number than those of other castes people, is hierarchically arranged. In the village, people of the upper castes, known as *Uchcha jati ke log* (people of high castes) do not have regular social interaction and relationship with the *Neech jati ke log* (people of the low castes). Thus, caste as an ascribed status or social status in the village plays the key role in deciding the mode and level of social interaction or relationship with people of the different castes and in such social interaction and relationships, the Dalits are completely segregated and discriminated due to their low caste status in the local caste-hierarchy. They are unequally treated by the upper and middle level castes, in day-to-day interaction, in terms of their being considered inferior because of their caste location in the caste hierarchy, which we can be seen from the Table 4.1 given below. As we know, social interaction is a process by which social status of a person gets changed in the society. But if such a process takes place with Dalits in the village, it takes another shape.

Table 4.1: Caste-wise views of the Respondents on Pattern of Interaction of Dalits with other castes

Caste	Pattern of Interaction					
	Bara Govind Village			Chakia Town		
	Superior	Inferior*	Equal#	Superior	Inferior	Equal
Chamar	-	39(31.2)	3(2.4)	-	15(12)	27(21.6)
Dhobi	-	-	-	-	19(15.2)	28(22.4)
Dusadh	-	36(28.8)	2(1.6)	-	10(8)	26(20.8)
Musahar	-	44(35.2)	1(0.8)	-	-	-
Total		**119(95.2)**	**6(4.8)**		**44(35.2)**	**81(64.8)**

*Respondents are socially, economically and educationally not better off.

#Respondents are socially, economically and educationally better off.

As stated, in Chapter 3, the Chamars of the village have already given up their traditional occupations due to their being treated low by people of the upper and middle level castes and most of them are now landless agricultural labourers. They have unfavourable social interaction and relationship with different caste groups including Bhumihars, Brahmins, Yadavs, etc. Most of the respondents of this caste have stated that their relationship with the other castes people is not permanent but a temporary or purposive one wherein if they have certain works to be completed by them, the relationship occurs; otherwise, it is absent. So also is the case of their interaction, which, of course, remains unequal one. A point may be mentioned here that the social interaction of Dalits with non-Dalits in the village takes place apparently not with the groups or caste as such but only with individuals or members of these groups or castes. Then, the group or caste gets excluded, while individual gets included. But in reality, this does not happen as an individual member of a caste community cannot and does not forego his/her caste or community identity and interacts with other entirely as a being.

Further, in their day-to-day social interaction, Dalits of the village address the upper caste people with regards. If the latter are elder or similar in age, the Dalits address them either as *Babu Saheb* or *Malik*. And if the non-Dalits are younger in age, the Dalit address them as *Babua ji* or *Babua Saheb.* This connotes affection as well as due respect to the addressee because of his higher caste status (and also economic and political dominance, if that is there) in the caste hierarchy. In reverse, the upper caste people neither pay any respect or regard to the Dalits nor consider about that even if the latter are senior in ages. They invariably insult them publicly by addressing them with their caste surnames as *Ram*, *Paswan*, *Baitha* and *Manjhi.* Thus, most of the respondents have stated that they are called not by their personal name but by their caste name or surname by people of the upper castes. Sometimes, people of the upper castes also address the Dalits of the village by using derogatory term like *Rey or Aray*. They even humiliate or abuse them in public due to their low caste background. For example, Bhagirath Ram, a Chamar by caste, a priest in the Hanuman temple in the village since 2003. People of the upper caste of the village do not give respect or prestige to him because of his low caste background and always pass vulgar comments on him while passing through the Chamar *Tola* or *Muhallah*. During the weekly or monthly or annual coronation of the idol, people of the upper castes in the village do not accept *Prashad* from him and state that "*Chandan lagane se koi uchcha jati nahi banta*" (applying *chandan* on forehead and wearing sacred thread a person (of the lower caste), cannot be member of an upper caste Brahman, Bhumihar, Rajput) they also say that your social status cannot be improved. Therefore, you cannot compare yourself with the upper caste people and stop all these dramas".

Similar is the condition of the Dusadhs who do not practice any traditional occupation in the village and are mostly agricultural labourers, as stated earlier. According to Awadh Paswan, an illiterate Dusadh respondent, caste system plays a very crucial role in determining social relationship of a person with others in the village which determine with whom such relationship and interaction occurs whether with a Dalit individual or with Dalit caste of individuals. He further says that the caste background (or even economic position) of a person is important in establishing the social interaction and relationship with people of the upper or middle level castes in the village. He says, "It is humiliating and is with hatred. They also treat us unequally in day-to-day interaction. Their attitudes and behaviour are discriminatory and oppressive towards the Dalits. They do not give any respect or social prestige to the people of Dalit castes. They do not sit on the same *chouki* (wooden cot) or *khatiya* (the knitten cot) with them. People of the Bhumihar caste even do not let the Dalits touch their personal things in the house. Whenever the latter go to meet the former, they put off their chappals outside the entrance of the house and then enter their *Baranda* or *Chouwutra* (pedestrian). Most of them address the Bhumihars or Brahmins by calling them *Malik* in the village. Thus, social interaction of the Dalits is uneven or lopsided with Bhumihars, Brahmins and other middle level castes in terms of latter being considered as *Malik* (master) and the Dalits as *Noukar* (servant). If they do not practice it, they are humiliated and discriminated by them. For example, a Dalit boy was insulted for saying *pranam* to the village landlord, instead of bowing low, from a distance, to say *salam malik,* which is the accepted form of greeting by a low caste person to an upper caste elder, especially someone who is landlord (malik) in the village.[9]

Finally, in the case of social interaction and relations of Musahars, the most sufferer compared to the other Dalit castes, with people of the upper and middle level caste, we find that they are not allowed to fetch water from the well, used by members of dominant castes in the locality, although they do not have any traditional occupation and most of them work as daily wage labourers but are placed at the bottom after the Chamars and Dusadhs in the local caste hierarchy. The respondent named Tutu Manjhi has stated that the people of Bhumihar and Brahmin castes do not interact regularly with Musahars but only when they have their works to be done by them. In the village, they are the most discriminated ones socially, economically and educationally. As such, the relationship of Dalits with the Bhumihars and Brahmans are insulting, because of the latter not giving any respect to them and address them by their caste name or surname whether they are elder or younger in ages. Thus, untouchability and discrimination are observed by the upper and middle level caste against the Dalits. Members of the upper and middle level castes have discriminatory and humiliating attitudes and behaviour towards the Dalits and they treat them unequally in their day-to-day social interaction with them by practicing the caste system.

It is generally accepted that the social interaction and relationship between the Dalits and other castes and communities would be somewhat better in urban than in rural areas. With such a hypothesis in mind, when we enquired into the nature and forms of social interaction between the Dalits and non-Dalits in the Chakia town, we have found that it is almost purposive and depends on their needs and requirements (see Table 4.1). Dalits living in the town have already given up their caste-based traditional occupations and adopted new ones like jobs in public and private sectors organisations and in petty-business, besides the manual laboure as stated earlier. The secular employment position has created somewhat congenial atmosphere where most of them are in a better social position today than that in the villages. The respondent Awadhesh Ram, a Chamar by caste and a teacher in the government primary school and a follower of Jai Gurudeo sect, has expressed his view by stating that he has achieved 'equal' status with people of the upper and middle level castes in both his work-place and neighbourhood in the town. A point may be mentioned here that the term 'equal' is to be taken not in absolute but in relative sense wherein he necessary compares his interaction and social relation as well as of his caste people with those of the upper and middle level castes in rural areas with that in the town. In his social interaction with people of the other castes, he does not think that it is a short term or purposive; rather a long term social interaction and relation with them. It is a matter of fact that such social interaction happens with an individual rather than with people of an upper or middle level caste. In the whole interacting pattern, the respondent does not find any offensive language used against him by people of the upper castes. They equally give the regard to each other's caste where they reside. Therefore, neither the respondent nor people of the upper castes address each other by their caste name or caste surname in the town. That is why, he never experiences any discrimination related to his caste in his social relationship or social interaction with them due to his present socio-economic status. He is equally treated by people of both the upper and middle level castes in the social relationship. Similarly, another respondent Satya Narayan Ram, of the same caste and presently engaged, along with his family members, in the petty-business in the town, has stated that he also does not face any sort of caste discrimination and has a good social relationship with people of the different castes. Being from a low caste status in the caste-hierarchy, he receives almost equal respect or prestige from people of the upper and middle level castes. In the town, the notion of caste discrimination is not as rigid as it is in the rural areas, according to the respondent.

Further, a number of people of the Dusadh castes have adopted new occupations like jobs in the public and private sectors organisations and the petty-business in the town. As a consequence, their social relationship with other castes people has improved considerably, despite their low caste background. The people belonging to other castes generally do not care for the (Dusadhs) caste background and look at their present social position in the locality. The respondent Sujeet Paswan has described that most of his caste members have social interaction with people of different castes on the basis of their present social positions in the town. They do not think that their interaction with them is either a short term or purposive one. Like the respondents from the Chamar castes, most of the respondents from this caste also are of the view that they have continued their social interaction and relationship with the individuals and not with group of individuals of other castes for a long period of time. In the process of interaction, people of either groups or castes give respect or prestige to each other publically and do not find any discrimination in their social relationship. Another respondent, Prabhu Bhaitha, a Dhobi by caste and a Branch Manager in the Gramin Bank, and his family members are highly educated and most of them are either in the government jobs or pursuing petty-business in the town. He has described that the personal relationship of Dalits is improving nowadays with people of the other castes. It is in the sense that today they are giving up their caste-based traditional occupations and adopting the new ones. On the basis of that, the social interaction of an egalitarian type is taking place today between them and people of the different caste groups. He has further stated that it is a positive sign which happens both as a short-term and purposive with people of the other castes. In the process of social interaction, it happens with an individual of a particular caste on the basis of individual attributes where an individual and not his/her group or caste is included in the social system. On the other hand, another respondent named Jagdish Bhaitha who deals with the same thing by saying that people of the upper and middle level castes treat people of the lower castes equally in such a relationship. As far as the social interaction with people of the lower castes is concerned, people of the upper and middle level castes do not behave discriminatory and humiliating attitudes towards them on the basis of their caste background.

Thus, a majority of the respondents have ascertained that both the lower and upper and middle level castes people address each other with regards and the former do not find any discrimination in their social interaction and social relation in the locality. Such Dalits are not looked down upon and, humiliated by people of the upper and middle level castes because of their present economic and educational statuses (see Tables 4.1 and 4.2 in Appendix-A). They do not think that people of the upper and middle level castes keep discriminatory and humiliating attitudes towards them in the locality where they live in on the basis of their earlier practice of traditional occupations. Most of the respondents have stated that the relationship of Dalits with the other castes groups has presently changed due to their improved economic as well as education position, as mentioned above. Thus, it is clear that most of the respondents are socially conscious and aware about their rights and are not victim of any sort of discrimination in the public domain. The Dalits residing in the town have both long as well as short-term social interaction with people of the upper and middle level castes. Due to their better socio-economic and educational status, most of the respondents from the town have an equal social interaction or relationship with people of other caste groups. In interacting with people of the different caste groups, they do not find any kind of discriminatory and humiliating attitudes and behaviour towards them in the town. Now, most people of the lower castes have established their commensal relationship with people of the upper and middle level castes in the locality.

Commensal Relations or Taking food Together

Before going into details of data, it is pertinent to see what Ram[10] talks of unequal placing of the numerous castes in the caste-hierarchy, operating in different parts of the country. The lower castes or the Dalits are everywhere placed at the bottom in such hierarchy. Besides, they have also been deprived of their commensal relations with the people of other castes and communities, sharing common culture (s), participating on equal terms in decision-making, etc. Not only are they kept deprived in all such spheres but they are also treated socially unequal to others.

Keeping the above statement in mind, we may explain briefly about the meaning of commensal relations and then discuss about such relations of Dalits with people of different caste groups in the studied locales. Commensal relation simply means all men (and women also separately) of a caste taking food, cooked in a common hearth, together by seating in a single row, or drinking water fetched from the common source, or smoking from the same smoking stem pipe. But more than that, the commensal relation promotes the unity or oneness among all members of a particular caste against those of the other caste. Thus, in the villages, people of each caste have all along been maintaining their commensal relations as well as entertaining or feeding separately the members of other castes on both the auspicious and inauspicious occasions for showing 'fraternity' of people of the village as unit. Mayer[11] also mentioned that the status of caste of a person is reflected by his position in the commensal or dietary hierarchy, which "can be assessed on the principle that eating food cooked or served by another caste denotes equality". On the other hand, Sachchidananda[12] has explained that "due to the secular order, rigid restriction on eating with Harijan is gradually losing its force. And the age-old prohibition on commensal relations between the Harijan and caste Hindu is only slightly altered". This has been attributed to the democratic in situations in Independent India as it has been said that, "now-a-day a man belonging to a higher caste may be seen eating in the house of Scheduled Caste due to the enforcement of the Indian Constitution and the Untouchability Act"[13]. However, over a period of time, the village people have also gone for feeding their own caste men and women, besides people of other clean castes, but people of the lower strata are fed separately due to their low caste rank or status in the hierarchy of the caste system. This has been so as they believe in the notion of purity and pollution, according to most of the respondents, people of the upper and middle level castes in the village are very rigid about the practice of the caste system. They do not eat the *kachcha* food (cooked with water) or even *pucca* (cooked in oil or ghee-butter) food at the house of a Dalit due to their belief in the notion of purity and pollution. Only a handful people of the lower backward castes only take *pucca* food from the hand of people of the lower castes, though they do not have commensality or an inter-dinning relationship with them in the village. Although people of the upper and middle level castes invite the Dalits for ceremonial dinner but they are served meal separately. They are not allowed to sit together with people of the higher and middle level castes in the same *patt* or line, and are served meals when other castes members would have had finished their dinner. Even they have to throw away the plates (banana leaves) on which they have eaten their meal. Interestingly, only the educated Dalits are invited through the invitation letters or cards during the marriage ceremony in the houses of the upper and middle level castes, but even they cannot have their meals with people of the non-Dalit castes. They are also served meals separately and are treated unequally.

Amongst people of the Dalit Castes, the Musahars are treated badly by people of the upper and middle level castes in their commensal relationship or taking food together in the village. Most of the Musahars live in an absolute poverty and do not have inter-caste or intra-caste relationship. People belonging to both the upper and middle level castes practice untouchability against them in the rudest manner and do not accept water from hands of the Musahars. Thcy think that if they take water from them, they will get polluted; and, their caste members would look them down upon in the village. Thus, most of the Musahar respondents are excluded by people of the upper and middle level castes from their commensal relationship or from relation of taking food together in the village. Thus, in the era of even 21th century, where people talk of modernity or modernisation of the social systems, no qualitative as well as quantitative changes have occurred in commensal or even inter-personal relationships between the non-Scheduled Castes and the Scheduled Castes or Dalits in the village under study. In fact, the social relations of a person with other person (s) continue to be based on his/her caste background rather than his/her achieved quality or attributes. This can be seen from Table 4.2 given below.

Table 4.2: Caste–wise views of the Respondents on taking *Kachcha* and *Pucca* foods by people of other castes

Caste	Types of food					
	Bara Govind Village			Chakia Town		
	Kachcha	Pucca	None	Kachcha	Pucca	None
Chamar	-	14(11.2)	28(22.4)	23(18.4)	17(13.6)	2(1.6)
Dhobi	-	-	-	21(16.8)	24(19.2)	2(1.6)
Dusadh	-	9(7.2)	29(23.2)	16(12.8)	19(15.2)	1(0.8)
Musahar	-	-	45(36)	-	-	-
Total	**-**	**23(18.4)**	**102(81.6)**	**60(48)**	**60(48)**	**5(4)**

As far as the town is concerned, the situation seems to be somewhat better as some people of the Dalit castes do take their food with people of the different castes including Brahmins, Bhumihars, Rajputs, Yadavs, etc. This can be seen from the above table. In fact, according to the respondent Awadhesh Ram, a teacher in the government primary school, some people of the upper castes do not hesitate in taking *kachcha* or *pucca* or cooked food in the Dalits' house, who are friendly to them. Even they invite Dalit friends, through invitation card, in their celebrations and they are served meals with people of the higher castes in a single uniform row in the same *pandal*. The respondent, Kundan Paswan has also stated that the people belonging to the lower castes have inter-dining relationship with people of the higher castes in the town and the latter now accept water and even cooked food from the Dalits. Occasionally, the Dalits are even invited by people of the upper and middle level castes for taking meals in their houses. Meals are also served to them along with people of the upper and middle level castes in the locality. Sometimes, they are also invited by people of the upper and middle level castes for taking meals together either in the market or at their home, and they share occasionally the same *dish* or *thali* with them in the hotel as well as their home. This has been supported by the respondents from the Dhobi caste also. A point may, however, be mentioned here that such changes in the dining relationship of a few Dalits with people of the other castes groups have occurred in the town because of their present socio-economic and educational status.

Socio-Cultural Domain: Religious Ceremonies and Festivals, Temple Entry, etc.

Quite a few literature available on the Dalit issues reveal as how the Dalits, with their low caste status in the society, have been discriminated and deprived from their participation, along with others, in the socio-cultural life in the locality and elsewhere. Dalits were not allowed to worship deities in temples and pilgrimage centres. They did not celebrate festivals together with people of the other castes and communities. They were not allowed to hear any religious *Katha* (mythological stories). No Brahmin priest visited their houses to perform any ritual or religious ceremony. The milk and *ghee* (butter) from their houses were not accepted by others for performing any religious ceremony. Although some of them were ritual specialists, like the Dom being the ritual specialist of cremation, the Dhobi being the ritual specialist of the 10th day of the death and the *chathi* or the 6th day celebration of birth of a child and the Chamar, the specialist of some marriage ritual, but they were not enjoying high religious status in the society.[14] On the other hand, Berreman[15] has argued that ones being the high as well as low castes reveal the effects of their status in the attitudes as well as in their values, beliefs, and behaviour. According to him, members of the higher castes consistently exhibit their feelings of superiority of their greater intrinsic "worth expressed in terms of such attributes as purity, honour, morality and intelligence.

On the basis of such attributes, the social interaction with different caste groups takes place in a society".

Being part of the Hindu caste system, the Scheduled Castes or Dalits also, are religious minded in rural areas. Religion plays a very crucial role in regulating their social life. They have strong believes in the Hindu gods and goddesses. They also believe in their family deities (gods and goddesses) concerning to their own caste, as stated earlier in Chapter 3. Most of the Dalits are economically poor and landless, they celebrate it with their own caste members. We would analyze below the views of the respondents about participation of the Dalits in various socio-cultural activities organised at the community level both in rural and urban areas. The Scheduled Castes or Dalits of the Bara Govind village generally celebrate almost all the Hindu festivals like *Chhath*, *Dewali*, *Holi*, *Durga Puja*, *Ram Nawami*, *Jitiya*, *Makar Sankranti*, etc., as already mentioned in Chapter 3. Some of them also celebrate birth and death anniversaries of Guru *Ravidas* and Dr. *Ambedkar* in the village. They are educationally a little better off and know about their emancipators who fought against untouchability and the caste system. Therefore, they remember them through the celebrations of their birth and death anniversaries, according to some respondents.

The Dalits worship some benevolent deities or spirits, particularly concerning to their caste. For instance, the Chamars believe in *Suraj* or *Surajahi Bhagwan* (Sun God) who is said to be the creator and the supreme source of energy in the universe. Like the Chamars, other Dalits such as Dusadh, Dhobi and Musahar also revere the Sun god and worship it. However, according to Bhagirath Ram, a respondent, the notion of untouchability is observed by people of the upper and middle level castes during the worship or celebration in the village. For instance, whenever the upper caste females go to worship the Devi Mai, the Dalit females are not allowed to go with them. They think that if they go along with the females of lower castes, their homely made *prashad* would be polluted due to their physical touch. Therefore, they generally try to avoid going with the latter.

There is a Hindu temple in the village where members of all caste, including Dalits, are allowed to worship. Although they are allowed to worship in the temple, they do not go along with people of the upper castes. First, the members of the upper castes enter the temple and go out after worshipping the deity, and then the Dalits enter the temple and worship the deity. According to Bachchan Paswan, the Dusadhs are also not allowed to enter the temple with them. The people belonging to upper and middle level castes practice discrimination with the Dalits on the basis of their low caste background. There is clear cut restriction on them in entering the temple along with people of the upper castes. To avoid the ritual inferiority of the Dalits, people of the upper castes have constructed another temple in their locality where people only of the upper and middle level castes are allowed to worship, according to most of the respondents. The *Musahar Tola* is situated by the side of the old temple, which is constructed on the land of a person of Bhumihar caste. Whenever Musahars go to worship the idol in the temple, the priest of the temple closes the gate and does not allow them to enter the temple, according to Bhuta Manjhi. During the festival, Musahars offer water at the gate of the temple because of strict prohibition for them. This may also be due to the fact that the Musahar are economically handicapped and educationally most backward group among the Dalits in the village. They are extremely vulnerable caste to face the strict social segregation. Even the location of their *Tola* is separated from the main village.

Further, on the occasion of marriage ceremony or any other social functions, are not invited by people of the upper and middle level castes through invitation card in the village. They are only asked to clean the *Pandal,* at the end of the function and whatever remains left in the *Bhoj* or dinner, it is distributed among them. People of the upper castes also do not participate in their marriage ceremony. They celebrate their ceremonies or rituals with their own caste members. They are badly treated by upper and middle level castes and even by the other Dalit castes in their social relationships in the village. Table 4.3 shows the restriction on Dalits on their entry in the Hindu temples situated in the village and the town.

Table 4.3: Caste-wise views of the Respondents on Dalits' entry in Temples in the village and in the town

Caste	Temple Entry of the Dalits			
	Bara Govind Village		Chakia Town	
	Permitted	Not Permitted	Permitted	Not permitted
Chamar	12(9.6)	30(24)	42(33.6)	-
Dhobi	-	-	47(37.6)	-
Dusadh	9(7.2)	29(23.2)	36(28.8)	-
Musahar	8(6.4)	37(29.6)	-	-
Total	**29(23.2)**	**96(76.8)**	**125(100)**	-

Table 4.3 reveals that most of the respondents are of the view that the Dalits in the village are still prohibited from their entry in the Hindu temple due to the notion of purity and pollution. Only 23.2 percent of the respondents have affirmed the Dalits' entry in the Hindu temple, while 76.8 percent respondents have replied in negative. Most of the respondents have stated that the Dalits cannot enter the Hindu Temple along with people of the upper and even middle level castes during the festivals, but they visit the same after them.

The socio-cultural life of people in the town is different from that of the village, where people of the Dalit communities do have different opinion about the Hindu festivals. Today, quite a few Dalits living in the town are either *Ambedkarite* or believe in the sects like *Kabir Panth* and *Jai Gurudeo*. Most of them do not celebrate any Hindu ceremonies and festivals. Only those who are the hardcore followers of the Hindu belief system and gods and goddesses in the town, they celebrate the Hindu festivals and ceremonies. Like many *Jai Gurudeo* followers, the respondent Awadhesh Ram believes in Jai Gurudeo sect and does not celebrate any Hindu festival but only *Guru Purnima* once in a year. Yet, whenever people of the upper castes invite him during their celebration of any festival, he goes there and does not find any practice of discrimination against him during celebration. He takes meal with them in their houses. Also, during the marriage ceremony or any other social functions of the caste Hindus, he is invited by people of the upper and other backward castes to participate in their celebrations and, in reverse, they also participate in the social functions organised by him. Although most of the respondents of the better socio-economic status find the congenial atmosphere in such social gatherings, but the same may not be true in the case of other Dalits living in the town.

As far as the temple entry is concerned, the Paswans are allowed to enter the temple. There is no restriction on them for entering the temple with people of the upper castes. On the occasion of marriage ceremony or other social function, they are also invited by the upper and other backward castes through invitation cards and, in turn, they also do the same thing. During the occasion, people of the upper and other castes do not practice any discrimination and take their meals at their houses.

One of the respondents, Prabhu Bhaitha of the Dhobi castes, says that today there is no restriction for the Dalits in the temple entry, especially in the town. If they wish to enter the temple, they may do so and worship and the deity any time. Due to their improving socio-economic and educational status, they are invited by people of the upper and middle level castes in their marriage ceremony or on other social function where they are treated equally by them in the town. In reverse, people of the upper castes do participate in the Dalits' ceremonies or functions. It is, thus, obvious that the earlier pattern of relationship among people of the different castes has changed in a positive way in the town. Thus, in the town, the Dalits respondents are allowed to enter in the Hindu temple along with people of the upper and middle level castes due to their socio-educational status and social consciousness among Dalit castes.

Like people of other castes, the Scheduled Castes or Dalits also celebrate different religious festivals in the village as well as in the town. One of the most important festivals of Bihar is *Chhath Puja* (celebration) celebrated by all the Hindus and where discrimination and untouchability is observed by the upper and middle level castes towards the Dalits. We may also see how the Dalits are kept separated by people of other castes from their physical touch during the celebration. The *Chhath Puja* also known as the *Surya Shashti,* celebrated to worship Sun (Surya) God. It is performed in order to thank Surya for sustaining life on earth and fulfilling all wishes of the worshippers. The Sun is considered the god of energy and of the life force, and is worshipped during the Chhath Puja to promote well-being, prosperity and progress. The Puja is performed on the *Kartika*

Shukla Shashti, which is the six day of the month of Kartika of the Hindu calendar. This falls in the month of October or November in the Gregorian calendar. It is also celebrated in the summer (March-April) on the *Chaitra Shashti*, a few days after the Holi and is called the *Chaiti Chhath*. This festival starts with *Naha-Kha-* taking meal after bath by the worshipper either male or female. The devotees strictly retrain from taking non-vegetarian meal and also abstain from eating garlic, onion, etc.

The Puja is celebrated either on the bank of a river or *Pokra* (pond). All the members of a family go to the *Ghat* with a *Doura* (basket) filled with sugarcane, fruits, home-made sweets, *dhup* and other puja materials, where they worship the Sun and celebrate the festival with their family members, neighbours and relatives. People of the upper castes do not allow members of Dalit community, in villages, to celebrate it along with them at the same Ghat. Most of the respondents from the village have reported that the notion of discrimination and untouchability is observed in such celebration by people of the upper and middle level castes. Being from the Chamar, Dusadh and Musahar castes, they have stated that people of the upper and middle level castes celebrate the *Chhath Puja* in a separate Ghat located at a distance, in the ascending direction (from which water flows), from the one where the Dalit communities celebrate. Due to the notion of purity and pollution, people of the upper and middle level castes make the separate *ghat* keeping distance from the one of Dalits. Thus, it clearly seems a spatial separation of the ghat of people of the upper and middle level castes and that of the Dalits during the Chhath celebrations. When people of the upper caste make offerings (Aragh) to the setting and the rising Sun, they go to that side from where the stream of the river flows. They first occupy that place so as no Dalits could go there. If they touch the running water, it would get polluted and, therefore, the *prashad* or *aragh* they offer to the Sun also be polluted one. Due to the escape of polluting aragh, people of the upper castes first and the foremost start offerings to the Sun, then members of the other castes follow it. Even the upper castes do not accept home-made *Prashad* of the Dalits during the Puja. In the whole picture, people belonging to upper and middle level castes practice untouchability against the Dalits living in the village, has mentioned above.

But as far as the town is concerned, people belonging to all castes and communities celebrate this festival with their neighbours in the locality. The Dalits also do not experience the rigid form of caste discrimination as they do in the village. In the town, there is a possibility to mix up with people of the other castes during the celebration. Therefore, some of the respondents belonging to the *Jai Gurudeo sect* and *Kabir panth* sects and even the *Ambedkarites* do not celebrate any Hindu festivals in the town because they do not believe in the Hindu religious gods and goddesses, as stated earlier.

So is the case of celebration of the 'Holi' festival both in the village and the town. Holi is celebrated on the 1st day of the Chaitra month (March-April) by all the Hindus. It is considered the festival of colour and is related with the *Khaliyans* (threshing-ground), full of the Rabi crops, of the peasants as well as those of the agricultural labourers. People, especially children, to all castes, including Dalits collect woods and cow dung cakes at the fire place and lit the fire in the night. On the next day, Holi with colour, is celebrated. It also reveals the discriminatory attitudes and practices followed by different castes groups. Lal[16] argues that the Holi festival means humiliation to the Dalits and their females. In the celebration of the festival, famous for its vulgarity, the Dalit women have to bear the brunt of obscenities hurled at them by people of the upper and middle level castes in the villages. He quotes, "In the manner in which it is used to be observed in Bihar, Holi represented very directly the subjugation of the lower castes, of the lower caste women in particular. While the sexuality explicit songs would be sung in all *bastis* of the village, it was only in the lower caste *bastis* that particular women would be named in the songs. The lower castes also had their houses splashed with dirt".[17]

According to the respondents, the Dalits celebrate it freely with their caste members but when they celebrate it with people of the upper and middle level castes, they feel fear of their adverse reaction in applying *gulal* or colour on their faces. In the evening, the festival starts with *gulal* or colour by rubbing on the face of one another. Generally, the Scheduled Castes or Dalits do not rub *gulal* on the face of the upper castes, if they are in similar or senior in age; instead, some of them put *gulal* on the feet of people of the upper castes. They cannot colour the face of women of the upper castes, but, in reverse, people of the upper castes colour the face of Dalit women in the village. Also in the evening, when people of the upper castes visit the *Tola* of the lower caste, they use abusive language for Dalit women; but the Dalit males do not use such type of language for women of the upper castes during the *Chayata* as well as *Fagua* songs. In this way, the joking relationship is established with the Dalit women but not with the upper caste women. During this festival, the untouchability is observed by people of the upper and middle level castes, according to most of the respondents. People of the upper and middle level castes do not share cooked food and even drink with the Dalit men prepared in the Dalit houses in the village. In fact, the former do not visit the Dalit houses during the religious celebrations due to their ritual superiority.

Bihar is one of those states where the upper castes, although numerically very small, have traditionally enjoyed ritual superiority and social prestige, as stated earlier in this chapter.[18] Yet, most of the respondents from the town have stated that they celebrate Holi with members of the other castes. They are not discriminated by people of the upper and middle level castes on the basis of their caste background. But this does not apply with all the Dalits living in the town. It is also a fact that a few of the upper castes still make distance from the Dalits in the celebration of religious functions even in the town. Although they celebrate the Holi festival with them, but they hesitate to eat cooked food in the Dalit houses.

Education and Discrimination

Education is one of the agents of human development which bring social change among the people. It is a light of understanding by which people express their opinion in the public. It is also considered as the equaliser that equalises inequality existing among the people in the society. In this context, role of the teacher is very important who plays as the catalyst in the school or an educational institution. According to Durkheim[19], education is "the action exercised by the older generations upon those who are not ready for social life. Its object is to awaken and develop in the child those physical, intellectual and moral states which are required of him both by his society as a whole and by the milieu for which he is specially destined". Wankhede[20] has stated that the root of educational deprivation vis-à-vis discrimination of the Scheduled Castes communities can be traced back to their position as untouchables in the caste structure of traditional Hindu society. The present educational system in India although modern in character, is alien to the Indian tradition and culture and caters only to a section of the society (always upper castes and classes). Secondly, although education being highly subsidized, most of the lower strata cannot afford it. Finally, due to socio-religious prejudice, entry to and substance of their educational achievement is very poor. Further, it is also a fact that the real socio-economic and intellectual power lies in those who get educated through English medium in the urban metropolitan centers. Students from the weaker sections who manage to reach to the higher level often fail to meet the required standards in the face of no help from the teachers and peer group students due to social prejudice; and hence, they perform badly or drop out altogether. Moreover, education gives to the people a light of understanding, a sense of feeling and social awareness. Then, in the light of this, we shall analyze below the educational status of Dalits in Bihar in general and of our respondents in particular from the village as well as town, under study. It also includes the views of the respondents from both the village and the town about hurdles, in availing of it faced by them and the Dalits in general.

As a matter of fact, Bihar is one of the most educationally backward states in the country. As per the 2001 Census, the literacy rate among the Dalits or Scheduled Castes in Bihar is only 15.12 percent which happens to be the lowest in India. Their literacy rates, both in rural and urban areas, are also very low, compared to the other castes and communities in the state. Even the increase in female literacy rate among the Scheduled Castes has been dismally low in Bihar, as per the recent censuses. The national literacy rate of the Scheduled Castes, according to 2001 Census, is 54.69 percent (males 66.64 percent and females 41.90 per cent). But in Bihar, the literacy rate of the Scheduled Castes population is 28.5 percent (males 40.2 percent and females 15.6 per cent), according to the Census of 2001. This shows that the gap between literacy rate of the Scheduled Castes at the national level and in the Bihar state is quite glaring. In the case of female literacy rate among the Scheduled Castes, the national average is nearly five times more than of that the state in Bihar.

Since the literacy rate is not the true indicator of one's being educated, we shall look into respondents' views about the educational status of the Dalits, along with the discrimination, if any practiced against them both in Bara Govind village and the Chakia town to substantiate that, in a way, of the Dalits in the state. The hindrances faced by the Dalit children in availing of education in schools in villages have been analyzed by other studies also. For example, Jeebanlata Salam[21] focuses on the root of educational deprivation of Scheduled Castes located fundamentally in their exclusion from the larger socio-economic, political and cultural processes maneuvered by insignificant powerful social groups. Anyway, the village, under the study is educationally backward, compared to the other neighbouring villages of *Tarania*, *Baisaha*, etc. In the village, there is a government school located in the mixed castes locality. The children of all castes are allowed to go to the school. But, children of the Dalit communities experience social discrimination in the school because of their caste background. The teachers belonging to the upper castes also do not pay equal attention on the Dalit children in the class.

The central government has provided a numbers of facilities, to be implemented by the state government, for promotion of education among the Dalits children, especially in rural areas. Some of these facilities or provisions are freeship and free books and stationary, school uniform, mid-day meal, etc., though these have not been properly implemented. For instance, according to the respondent Huseni Ram, the Dalit children do not get free books in the school. Although the Government provides stipend and free books to those Dalit children whose parents are economically poor, but these children do not get such facilities adequately in the school. This is so due to misuse of the government fund by the schools. When the stipend is distributed among them, the teachers of the school get assured of their commission from the amount to be distributed among the Dalit children; otherwise, in absence of that, they do delay to distribute the amount. If some of the Dalit children miss to collect the amount then the same is channelised among the teachers and the officials. Similarly, the government is running the free Mid-day meal (lunch)

Table 4.4: Caste-wise views of the Respondents on Discrimination faced by Dalit Children in the school

Educational Level	Degree of Discrimination																							
	Bara Govind Village												Chakia Town											
	Chamar				Dusadh				Musahar				Chamar				Dhobi				Dusadh			
	M	**L**	**L**	**N**	**M**	**L**	**L**	**N**	**M**	**L**	**L**	**N**	**M**	**L**	**L**	**N**	**M**	**L**	**L**	**N**	**M**	**L**	**L**	**N**
Illiterate	17	2	1	-	11	2	1	-	42	-	-	-	-	-	-	-	-	-	-	-	-	-	-	-
Primary School	4	1	1	-	3	2	1	-	2	-	-	-	-	-	-	-	-	-	-	-	-	-	-	-
Middle School	3	2	1	-	2	3	1	-	-	1	-	-	2	1	-	-	1	2	2	-	1	1	1	
High School	3	2	2	-	3	3	2	-	-	-	-	-	6	4	3	-	5	4	6	-	5	4	2	
Intermediate	1	1	-	-	1	2	-	-	-	-	-	-	1	2	2	7	-	1	2	8	-	1	1	9
Graduation	-	1	-	-	-	1	-	-	-	-	-	-	-		-	12	-	-	-	13	-	-	-	10
Post-Graduation	-	-	-	-	-	-	-	-	-	-	-	-	-	-	-	2	-	-	-	3	-	-	-	1
Total	**28**	**9**	**5**		**20**	**13**	**5**		**44**	**1**			**9**	**7**	**5**	**21**	**6**	**7**	**10**	**24**	**6**	**6**	**4**	**20**

Note: M-Most Discriminated, **L**-Less Discriminated, **L**-Least Discriminated, **No**-No Discriminated.

scheme for school children of all castes in the school. But the mid-day meals are not served to the Dalits children along with of children of the upper and middle level castes. Instead, they are served meals by making them sit separately. The views of the respondents on the degree of discrimination practiced against the Dalit education in the school can be seen in the Table 4.4.

The table clearly shows that the degree or level of discrimination in educational domain is highest among the children of the Musahar caste, compared to those of the Chamar and Dusadh castes in the village school. In fact, the Musahar children are discriminated a lot in the school. In fact, all the three Dalit castes are educationally backward, but the Musahars are the most educationally backward, compared to the Chamars and Dusadhs in the village. The number of illiterates is also very high among them due to their absolute poverty. A respondents of the Chamar caste has said that, "One of the upper caste students had abused him on his caste line, by asking him- *Re Chamar pad kar kya karoge* (what will you Chamar do after study), when he was in 8th class. He complained the class teacher about the student, but the teacher of the school did not pay proper attention on his complain. Then, he returned home with such a humiliation. He was totally upset after this incidence and when his father asked about his sadness, he did not disclose it. After this humiliation, he left the school and now working as a wage labourer". Abdulraheem[22] rightly explains that discrimination in education is a facet of schooling and manifests itself in a spectrum of social and psychological inequalities. Further, an educated respondent has stated that Dalit children face multiple social discriminations in the village school. The village is dominated mainly by the upper castes, particularly the Bhumihar and the middle level castes like Yadavs, where Dalits experience more social discrimination in day-to-day life. Being low or lowest by their castes, the Dalits are humiliated, discriminated and deprived from their access to all the resources. Secondly, because of their poverty and illiteracy, they are harassed and exploited by people of the upper castes. It is also observed that those who are educated amongst the Dalit communities, they also face discrimination by people of the upper and middle level castes, but their discrimination is of less degree than of the uneducated ones.

Another respondent of the Musahar caste, working as daily wage labourer on the land of an upper caste is extremely poor and unable to provide neat and clean clothes to his children. Whenever his children go to the school with their dirty dress, teachers do not let them to enter in the class and sit with other students. They were to be allowed they wore clean clothes. Almost all children of this caste face the similar social boycott and are not paid equal attention by teachers in the school due to their dirty dress. It is also true that the behaviour and attitude of the teachers play negative impact on the Dalit children and that is why, their drop out ratio is very high among them in the village.

On the contrary, the Dalits living in the towns are educationally better off than those in the villages. There is both government as well as private schools in the urban areas where children of all castes are allowed to go to the school. In the town, there is a lot of opportunity for the education of these children. Today, most children not only of the respondents but of the other Dalits in Chakia town, study not only in the government, but also in the private schools and do not face any discrimination in availing of education. It is also true that those children who are unable to get the required economic support from their parents, they get free books, stipend and freeship from the government through their schools. They also do not face any discrimination in availing of such facilities there. In this context, the town has created a better educational opportunity for the Dalit children.

The Government is also running the mid-day meal scheme in the schools where children of all castes take free meal together and the Dalit children do not find any discrimination in taking meals along with children of the upper and middle level castes in the school. Further, most of the respondents from the Dusadh castes have stated that educated Dalits are more socially aware than the non-educated ones. There is the least possibility of discrimination against the educated ones than the non-educated ones. Therefore, the level of discrimination against the Dalit communities in the urban areas has decreased because of their socio-economic and educational achievements.

On the other hand, the respondents from the Dhobi caste in the town are educationally better off than those of the Chamar caste. Being highly qualified among the Dalits in the town, the majority among them are not attached nowadays with any traditional occupation. Our respondent Bhola Bhaitha, who is running a medical shop in the town, sends his children in the private school where children of each and every caste study. His children in the school do not face any caste discrimination. Not only he, but most of his caste members send their children either to the private or the government school. In both the types of schools, neither the children nor the teachers of other caste have discriminatory attitudes and behaviour towards the Dalit children. The teachers of the school equally behave with the students of each and every caste in the town. Despite all these, it is also true that a hierarchy, even in the educational domain, is taking place among the Dalits themselves. The educated Dalits enjoy more privileges than the non-educated ones, and accordingly the social discrimination of a subtle form occur with them whereas in the non-educated Dalits face more crude form of social discrimination.

Table 4.5: Education-wise views of the Respondents on Discrimination faced by Dalit Children in the school

Educational Level	Degree of Discrimination							
	Most	Less	Least	No	Most	Less	Least	No
	Bara Govind Village				Chakia Town			
Illiterate	68	-	-	-	-	-	-	-
Primary	15	3	1	-	-	-	-	-
Middle	9	3	1	-	5	3	3	-
High	13	3	2	-	6	7	13	12
Intermediate	1	2	2	-	3	5	9	14
Graduation	-	1	1	-	-	6	13	19
Post-Graduation	-	-	-	-	-	-	1	6
Total	**106**	**12**	**7**		**14**	**21**	**39**	**51**

Social Discrimination and Power and Authority

Before going into the detailed analysis of our data, it is essential to see how Weber[23] defines the term 'power'. According to him,

"In general, we understand by power the chance of a man or a number of men to realise their own will in a communal action even against the resistance of others who are participating in the action". On the other hand, Beteille[24] deals with the location of power in formal structures like *panchayat* and political *parties,* and also the informal groupings which do not have boundaries. He states that an understanding of power also requires the analysis of network of interpersonal relations which cut across the boundaries of *class*, *panchayat* and *party*. But Milner[25] looks at power in a different perspective by explaining that status is a form of power which is based on approvals and disapprovals known as status power. Weber uses the term 'domination' and 'authority' interchangeably in his discussion by stating that "domination or authority refers to the right of a ruler within an established order to issue commands to others and expect them to obey while power is the ability of individual to carry out their will in a given situation, despite resistance". According to him, authority is a legitimate form of domination while power is considered to be an illegitimate one.[26] Since the frame of reference of power and authority, in the present study, is the village Panchayat and the town Panchayat or Panchayat Samiti in the town, it is pertinent to note of how the panchayat or samiti functions at the village level, the local power politics of the Gram Panchayat is completely guided by the 'dominant castes', a term conceptualised by M.N. Srinivas[27] who says that, "A caste may be said to be dominant when it preponderates numerically over the other castes, and when it also welds preponderant economic and political power. A large and powerful caste group can be more easily dominant if its position in the local caste hierarchy is not too low".

Keeping the above explanations in mind, we have analyzed the nature and extent of power and authority possessed by the Dalits in general and our respondents in particular in both the studied village and town. We have already mentioned that the Bara Govind village, located three kilometers away from another village, is dominated by people of the upper and middle level castes. They are more socially and politically consciousness, compared to people of the rest of the castes. According to our respondent Huseni Ram, the elected Dalit members do not actively participate in the meetings of the Village Panchayat due to manipulation of members of the upper and middle level castes, only the higher caste people who take decision without any consent of the former. Because of that, the Gram Panchayat does not function properly for the development, particularly of the Dalits. It is because of the upper castes' political, economic and muscle power, Dalits feel threatened during the elections or any other public gatherings. It is true that the policy of political representation or reservation and its functioning has produced some positive results along all these decades after Independence. It has played a positive role in the Dalits' access to the power and authority even at the local level. It is in the sense that a handful people from the Dalit communities at least show their courage to contest the elections, through the reservation, at various levels in the dominant areas of the upper castes. But the bulk of them are still deprived of their access to such power and authority in the villages due to political hegemony of the upper and middle level castes.

Further, according to Lakhan Paswan, election is considered as a formality in the sense that the function of caste, money and muscle power factors play the crucial roles in the election. People of the upper and middle level castes easily win the election on the strength of *Lathi* (big stick), *Paisa* (money) and *Jati* (caste), if the candidates are from their castes. According another respondent of the Musahar, Dalits or the Scheduled Castes, including people of his/her own caste do not enjoy electoral rights due to upper castes money, muscle and *jati* power. They do not allow Dalits to reach to the booths and cast their votes without their consent. If the Dalits insist to cast their vote, they are either abused or beaten up publically. Therefore, due to fear of people of the upper and some even middle castes, Dalits generally do not go to the booth; and if anyone insists to cast, his/her vote he/she is abused, harassed or beaten up the publicly. Even other Dalits of the village do not cast their votes in favour of the Dalit candidates because of the upper castes fear. Thus, people only of the upper caste and middle level castes choose even the Dalit candidates for contesting elections from local to state and national levels in accordance with their own benefits.

Most of the respondents from the village of Bara Govind have stated that the Dalit elected Panchayat members in the village do not actively participate in the meetings of the Panchayat due to dominance of people of the upper or middle level caste who, in reality, control the power and regulate it accordingly. The Dalit Panchayat heads or Sarpanches of the Panchayat play their role as the nominal head, whereas the dominant upper caste people control their electoral power, and whatever they say, the elected Dalit representatives do accordingly. During the Gram Panchayat meetings, the elected Dalit member does not get respect or prestige from the upper caste members. If the member does not act according to their advice, he/she is humiliated or discriminated during the meetings. As far as the elected Dalit women members are concerned, they are badly treated in the meetings by the upper caste males. When the respondents of Dusadh caste were asked about participation of the elected Dalit women member in the meetings of the Panchayat, they have said that they do not participate equally in the meetings as men do. According to them, there are three main causes of their unequal participation in the meetings. These are: the upper caste male dominance in the local politics, the lack of their educational qualification and the gender issue. According to respondent Laxman Manjhi, if a Dalit woman wins the election for the post of Ward Member or any other post, she does not participate in the Gram Panchayat meetings. Her husband works on her behalf in the village. This is so because it has been seen that the Dalit member is often discouraged or humiliated by the elected members of the upper and middle level castes during the meetings.

Kumar[28] has explained about the social hurdles faced by the Dalits in political sphere. He has stated that due to the traditional caste hierarchy, Dalits are not allowed to have their access to the strategic positions of the authority in the public domain and to the decision-making process. We have also found similar type of hurdles where the dominant castes of the village deprive the elected Dalit members from their participation in the decision-making process. They do not allow them to participate actively even in the meetings of the Gram Panchayat and take decision and implement it for the benefits of their own people or the Dalits. Further, the elected Dalit members do not get due respect also from the upper caste members in the meetings of the Panchayat. Members of the upper and middle level castes do not even think it necessary to take suggestions from them about any issue or matter related to the village. They completely ignore the Dalit members' suggestions in the meetings. At the interview, many respondents of the Musahar caste have stated that since people of the upper castes are powerful, they regulate the power structure in the village. If any dispute occurs between the persons of an upper and a lower caste, the case is not allowed to be reported in the Thana or Police Station because people of the lower caste always live under their fear. In this way, they feel fear in approaching to any other officer.

On the contrary, most of the respondents from the town have stated that the Nagar Panchayat works effectively for the development of people, including Dalits, in event of their elected representatives. The change has been seen in the electoral system, especially in the urban areas, where people belonging to the Dalit castes do not face any trouble during the Nagar Panchayat elections and they are allowed to cast their votes freely. They also have got new *Izzat* (respect) in thier participation in the decision-making political bodies.[29] Whenever the meeting of the Nagar Panchayat is called, every elected member, including Dalit members, participates and puts his/her views there. Unlike the elected Dalit member in village Panchayat, in the Nagar Panchayat meetings, he is not discriminated and humiliated by members of the other castes and communities. But ironically, the elected Dalit women members do not participate equally and effectively in the meetings of the Nagar Panchayat. This may be so as they are sometimes discouraged, harassed or humiliated by the male elected members of the other castes. Most of the respondents have stated that the male elected members dominate in the meetings of the Nagar Panchayat.

As mentioned above, the elected Dalit members in the town also participate in the decision making process in the Nagar Panchayat. But whenever the matter of implementation of the issues comes before people of the upper and middle level castes, sometimes they take suggestions from the elected Dalit members and sometimes they do not think it necessarily to take suggestions from them. According to most of the respondents, Dalits in the town are socially aware and conscious about their rights, therefore, they do not feel any hesitation in approaching the Thanas, CO/BDO about any issues. These respondents also feed that the grievances of the Dalits are listened to properly and sorted out immediately, but sometimes the delivery or

Table 4.6: Caste-wise views of the Respondents on Political Participation of the Dalits in the village and the town

Political Participation in	Bara Govind Village												Chakia Town											
	Chamar				Dusadh				Musahar				Chamar				Dhobi				Dusadh			
	Degree of Discrimination																							
	M	L	L	N	M	L	L	N	M	L	L	N	M	L	L	N	M	L	L	N	M	L	L	N
GP	22	7	3	-	14	11	4	-	32	7	1	-	-	-	-	-	-	-	-	-	-	-	-	-
NP	-	-	-	-	-	-	-	-	-	-	-	-	5	3	2	13	3	5	5	14	4	3	2	13
PL	5	3	2	-	4	3	2	-	1	1	1	1	3	1	5	10	4	3	1	12	3	1	3	7
Total	**27**	**10**	**5**	**-**	**18**	**14**	**6**	**-**	**33**	**8**	**3**	**1**	**8**	**4**	**7**	**23**	**7**	**8**	**6**	**26**	**7**	**4**	**5**	**20**

GP-Gram Panchayat, **NP**-Nagar Panchayat, **PL**-Political Party.

M-Most, **L**-Less, **L**-Least, **N**-None.

implementation is delayed. Further, most of the respondents have also stated that the Nagar Panchayat works effectively for development of the people belonging to all the sections. In the town, the Dalits enjoy their equal electoral rights, which are enshrined in the Constitution of India. They cast their votes freely without any trouble.

As far as the discrimination with the elected Dalit women in the meetings of the Panchayat is concerned, they are less humiliated and discouraged by the elected male members of other caste and communities in the Nagar Panchayat, than that in the village. In the whole process of improvement, the protective discrimination like reservation in Panchayat and other such bodies has played the vital role in enhancing the power and authority of the Dalits in urban areas. By the policy of such reservation, the people belonging to Dalit communities are appearing in the political domain also at the local level. They also participate in the decision-making process though the other caste members try to exclude them from that. Apart from that, people of the upper and middle level castes also take and give suggestions to the elected Dalit members in the town. Thus, a handful of Dalits in the Chakia town are holding their power or authority in the political structure of the Nagar Panchayat, which copes with a positive development of the historically marginalised section of the society, although a bulk of them are still deprived of sharing power and authority in the political domain of life.

Forms and Extent of Economic Exploitation

We have already stated, in the introductory of the chapter, some conceptual explanations of the term exploitation. Here, we shall provide a little more elaboration of the term exploitation which has conventionally been deliberated upon in the discipline of Economics and very sparsely in other disciplines like Sociology and Social Anthropology. In economics also, exploitation has primarily been located in economic domain wherein a person is exploited either by another person or economic organisation on account of paying wages or return of the capital investment. But in the latter case, the organisation itself may appear to be egalitarian or a non-exploitative one. Anyway, in the case of exploitation, the fault leading to exploitation is said to be located at the level of the exploited, and not the exploiter one. One can, however, trace the root of exploitation in the very systemic arrangement itself in which the exploiter is placed in the privileged position and the exploited one remains at the bottom of the system itself. In other words, the exploited one gets exploited because of his/her social structural location at the bottom of the system or social arrangement itself. A point may be mentioned here that exploitation is both preceded and succeeded by discrimination and deprivation. One is exploited because one is discriminated and one remains deprived of due benefit because one is exploited both economically and socially. Notwithstanding further explanations of causes and consequences of both economic and social exploitation, we shall analyze briefly the views of our respondents from the rural and urban areas, on the socio-economic exploitation of the Dalits of the studied locales.

In the case of the people in rural Bihar, like in many other states of India, their power and domination, or otherwise, have been linked to their rights over land, water and other resources naturalised in the caste hierarchy. Of nearly 95 percent population living in rural Bihar, 85 percent depend on agriculture for their livelihoods (Census of India, 2001). Their differential access to land and other related resources play a significant role in underpinning the rural power relations (Kunnath, 2012).[30] Yang (1998 referred in Kunnath, 2012) also argues that land plays the key role in determining political, social and cultural relations in rural Bihar. Landownership is positively related to caste where people of the high castes possess most of the land, while the upper crusts of the intermediately lower castes or middle level castes constitute the middle level peasants, and those without land are from the lower middle castes and the Scheduled Castes, as stated earlier. Of the four elite castes in Bihar, the Rajputs and Bhumihars own the most substantial land and are dominant in the rural areas.[31]

If we see the economic status of the Scheduled Castes or Dalits in the Bara Govind Village, we find that, as matter of fact, they have historically constituted to be one of the poorest and socially most disadvantaged groups. Yet, they have been an integral part of the social and economic structure of the village, since the time immemorial. These three Scheduled Castes namely, the Chamar,

Dusadh and Musahar have remained the major labour force in the village and they still play the most significant role in the maintenance of its social and economic system. Land is the major source of income and prestige of people in the village. Those who have land are socially and economically better off those who do not have it are economically, socially and educationally the most backward groups. In the context of land, most of the Dalits are landless, as stated above, and are daily wage labourer. Sen[32] rightly states that landlessness is an instrumental of deprivation. A family without land in the peasant society may be deeply handicapped. The landlessness can also have a constitutive importance in a world that values a family's special relation with its land. Hence, to be without land may seem like being without limb of one's own. In our study of Bara Govind village, we have found the same situation where land mainly belongs to Brahmins, Bhumihars, and small section of Yadavs who are known as the Zamindars. The relationship between the Dalits and the Zamindars is of the *Malik* and *Noukar* (servant). People generally call them Malik and the Malik treat them as their *noukar* in the locality. Kumar[33] also explains the similar economic relations in Bihar which are fundamentally represented in terms of '*Malik*' (upper castes landlords) and '*Praja*' (lower castes without any control over land), as mentioned in the Chapter 3. We have found the same type of economic relations among people in the Bara Govind village, which are fundamentally represented in terms of *'Malik'* (upper castes landlords) and *'Praja'* (lower most disadvantaged groups). In such economic relations, Dalits are the most deprived from landownership, compared to people of other castes of the village.

It is evident from the above table that nearly two-third (66.4%) rural respondents from all the three Scheduled Castes or Dalits and from all income groups have stated that the Dalits are most exploited people, compared to people of the other castes in the village. Compared to this, only 14.4 (18) percent respondents from all Dalit castes from income groups have expressed their views of Dalits in the most exploited ones in the town. Interestingly, the respondents who are engaged in the manual labour like *rikshaw* and *thela* pulling, *paldari*, etc. have expressed their views on Dalits being exploited a lot, compared to others in the town. It is generally stated that people

Table 4.7: Caste and Income-wise views of the Respondents on Exploitation of Dalits

Income	Bara Govind Village												Chakia Town											
	Chamar				Dusadh				Musahar				Chamar				Dhobi				Dusadh			
	Degree of Exploitation																							
	M	**L**	**L**	**N**	**M**	**L**	**L**	**N**	**M**	**L**	**L**	**N**	**M**	**L**	**L**	**N**	**M**	**L**	**L**	**N**	**M**	**L**	**L**	**N**
In Kind	11	2	3	-	9	3	2	-	29	2	1	-	-	-	-	-	-	-	-	-	-	-	-	-
Less than 1000	13	5	3	-	7	3	2	-	5	2	1	-	-	-	-	-	-	-	-	-	-	-	-	-
1000-2000	2	1	2	-	5	5	2	-	2	2	1	-	-	-	-	-	-	-	-	-	-	-	-	-
2001-3000	-	-	-	-	-	-	-	-	-	-	-	-	3	3	3	14	4	2	2	14	3	4	2	9
More than 3000	-	-	-	-	-	-	-	-	-	-	-	-	3	-	5	11	3	2	2	18	2	3	1	12
Total	**26**	**8**	**8**	**-**	**21**	**11**	**6**	**-**	**36**	**6**	**3**	**-**	**6**	**3**	**8**	**25**	**7**	**4**	**4**	**32**	**5**	**7**	**3**	**21**

having certain level of educations are more conscious and aware of exploitation than those who remain illiterate.

As already mentioned, most of the Dalits of the village do not have land, and are economically poor and unable to maintain their daily basic needs. Such a deprivation of the minimum rights of livelihood of Dalits in the village is deeply rooted in the village social structure. Ashwani Kumar[34] explains that socio-economic exploitation as well as exclusion or social exclusion of Dalits and Shudra or backwards castes continues in the economic, political and cultural structures and institutions.

The allotment of land is also one of the major problems of the state government for improving the economic status or position of Dalits in Bihar. According to Bhagirath Ram, a respondent, a large section of the Scheduled Castes population earns their livelihood by working on the land of Bhumihars and Yadavs. There are mainly two types of land available for distribution, i.e., *Gair Mazarua Aam*, and *Gair Mazarua Khas*. The first type of land is meant for the common use such as grazing, installation of irrigation sources, graveyards, etc. The second type of land is cultivable land, but it is neither under the zamindars for self-cultivation nor under the tenants. This type of land has been captured, for a long time, under cultivation by the powerful upper castes landowners in the state. Thus, under the Land Distribution of Programme, this second type of public land is still not distributed among people of the Dalit castes. The same land distribution in the state of Bihar has been mentioned by Kumar[35] in his study. In this way, most of the Dalits in the village are landless and economically handicapped. Some of Chamars and Dusadhs are holding small pieces of land where their houses are situated. Due to unemployment in the village, most of the Dalits migrate temporary from the village to different states for their better livelihood and earnings. Most of the Musahar respondents have reported that almost 99 percent Musahars are landless and living in absolute poverty. They are the most vulnerable group among the Dalits in the village. For their livelihood, they work as labourers on the land of Bhumihars, Brahmins and Yadavs. They have still not benefited from the land reforms implemented by the government.

Another respondent, Laxman Manjhi of the same caste has explained the pathetic condition of the Dalits, particularly people of his own caste. In his opinion, people of his caste are not only *Mazdoor* (labourer), but also *Mazboor* (helpless), i.e., they are agriculture and other kind of wage labourer for the survival of their family members. And they are *Mazboor* by the needs and requirements for survival of themselves and their family members as well as are forced by others to do work on their field even at cost of threat, humiliation, abuses, less wages and thereby their exploitation. A somewhat like the similar story is mentioned by Sharma[36] which narrates that "A Brahmin was constructing his house and he asked a Musahar to come for day's work. That time, the Musahar had to go to some other village to see his relatives and, therefore, he expressed his inability to come. The Brahmins was furious and he called a meeting of all Brahmin of the village that day where three decisions were taken. Musahars will not be given any work; their cattle will not be allowed to graze on the Brahmin's field and their women will not be allowed to cut grass or to collect dry leaves from the fields of the Brahmins".

Like in other states, the state government of Bihar has also implemented the Mahatma Gandhi National Rural Employment Guarantee Act (MGNREGA) for the rural poor- mostly the Dalits or Scheduled Castes. According to many respondents from the village under the Study, some people of his Dalit castes also work under the MGNREGA sponsored by the government, but they get fewer wages and that too not on time. Houses also have been allotted to Dalit under the Indira Awas Yojna (IAY). But the Yojna or scheme has not been properly implemented and there is also mismanagement of this fund by the officers. When they sanction amount for constructing houses for the Dalits, they also cut some money out of the fund. Therefore, houses of Dalits do not get completed due to the lack of money and they are still living in such houses without roof, according to some of the respondents.

Contrary to that, the Dalits in the town are engaged in the urban industrial occupations like government or private jobs and business, skilled and semi-skilled works, etc. which are mainly sources of their income and livelihood. The urban areas are particularly open for the upward mobility where quite a few Dalits have got better socio-economic position. Ram[37] has argued that the socio-economic conditions of Dalits are relatively better in urban areas where they are free from the traditional bondages, though their majority is employed there in the menial and semi-skilled jobs in unorganised sectors. In the case of Chakia town, we have found the similar type of upward mobility among a sizable number of Dalits through their secular roles in both organised and unorganised sectors of economy. Yet, a sizeable number of respondents are of the views of that most of the Dalits, especially those employed in the menial and semi-skilled jobs, are economically and socially exploited in one way or the other. The employment-wise views of the respondents on economic and social exploitation of the Dalits in the village and the town can be seen from the Table 4.3 in Appendix-A.

Social Exclusion of Dalits

As already stated in Chapter 1, Arjan De Haan[38] has explained social exclusion in terms of denial of equal opportunities imposed by certain groups of people upon others in a society. We have also mentioned in the beginning of this chapter that social exclusion simply means deprivation of a person or group or persons from various types of socio-economic, educational, cultural and political opportunities existing in the society. Anyway, social exclusion in terms of deprivation or denial of opportunities to persons or groups of persons invariably leads to their inability to participate in the basic social, civil, political, economic and cultural functioning of a society in which they live. Thus, social exclusion is a process by which an individual or a group of people gets excluded from social, economic, educational and political domains of their life by another person or group of persons on the basis of one pretext or the other. In the whole context of social exclusion, either one or several factors play the crucial role in determining a person's exclusion from or inclusion in the existing opportunity structure or organisational arrangement of the social system.

In Indian society, Dalits or Scheduled Castes have remained the excluded or deprived groups or communities from their socio-cultural, economic, educational and political rights for centuries, as stated earlier. They have been subjected to various kinds of social deprivation or discrimination and exploitation in the local systematic arrangement in the country. In fact, the origin of their exclusion from other groups or communities in the Hindu society or social system can very well be traced from the structural-functional organisation of the caste system itself. This can also be understood from the Hindu mythological narratives of the origin of all the four varnas or classes or social categories of the people-the Aryans and the types of specific roles or functions assigned to each of them. "All the four varnas had to perform four distinct functions and were assigned specific ranks or statuses-higher and lower or superior and inferior, and any violation of these was subjected to punishment specifically in the form of ex-communication".[39] According to Ambedkar[40], "caste means an artificial chopping off of the population into fixed and definite units, each one prevented from fusing into another through the custom of endogamy". He further illustrates about the genesis of caste as an outcome of the super-imposition of endogamy over exogamy (as a form of marriage) which he considered as one of the mechanisms for the genesis as well as growth of caste. Again, commensality or commensal relations-taking food together cooked in the same kitchen, drinking water from the same pot and smoking frame the same smoking stem which has remained confined to the members of a caste. Over and above, the national ritual or religious purity of mind and body of members of a caste, especially higher in the caste-hierarchy, has made it separate from members of another caste.[41] Thus, exclusion means throwing away or boycotting, either permanently or temporarily member (s) of a caste. Such strategy has remained in operation since the early period, and operates even today, especially among the lower castes in rural society, though it is applied generally on temporary and not permanent basis.[42] The denial of opportunity resulting into deprivation, discriminatory behaviour, exploitation, etc., may be same of the manifestations of exclusion or social exclusion of a person or group in the contemporary Indian society. It is true that such a strategy or mechanism of the exclusion of the Dalits or Scheduled Castes is deeply rooted in the Hindu social structure as well as its social system where caste as an institution plays a crucial role. Anyway, not going into further details of exclusion and inclusion in the caste system as such, we shall examine briefly the views of our respondents on social exclusion of the Dalits in the state, particularly our studied locales-the village and the town from the various spheres of life and the specific reasons thereof.

Table 4.8: Caste-wise views of the Respondents on Social Exclusion of Dalits

Caste	Degree of Social Exclusion							
	Most	Less	Least	No	Most	Less	Least	No
	Bara Govind Village				Chakia Town			
Chamar	33(26.4)	7(5.6)	2(1.6)	-	7(5.6)	11(8.8)	3(.4)	21(16.8)
Dhobi	-	-	-	-	7(5.6)	4(3.2)	7(5.6)	29(23.2)
Dusadh	27(21.6)	5(4)	6(4.8)	-	5(4)	5(4)	8(6.4)	18(14.4)
Musahar	43(34.4)	2(1.6)	-	-	-	-	-	-
Total	**103(82.4)**	**14(11.2)**	**8(6.4)**	-	**19(15.2)**	**20(16)**	**18(14.4)**	**68(54.4)**

The respondent, Bhikhari Ram, whose parents pursued the caste-based traditional occupation[43] in the village of Bara Govind, has pointed out that people of the upper castes, and some middle level castes in the village have been maintaining distance and practicing untouchability widely against people of the lower castes or the Dalits. Due to the heinous practice of untouchability against the Dalits of the village, most of the respondents have given up their caste-based traditional occupations, but discrimination or social boycott and untouchability could not be stopped against them by people of the upper caste. Thus, the change of the traditional caste occupations has not eliminated the discriminatory attitudes of people of the upper and middle level castes towards the Dalits of the village. People of the upper as well as middle level castes do not let Dalits even to sit on the same cot and make distance from them in their day-to-day social relationship. Their discriminatory and unequal relationship exists with the Dalits including most of the respondents. Therefore, most of the Dalits of the village still experience social boycott or exclusion and discrimination because of the existing traditional caste hierarchy and their low rank or status of their caste and poverty. This has been supported by another respondent, Birendra Ram of the Chamar caste in the village. He has further stated that even unemployment has been contributing to social exclusion of most of the Dalits in the village. He has further stated that the people belonging to the upper castes and the middle level castes in the village are strong supporters of the caste system, and accordingly, they treat the Dalits as the lowest one and practice untouchability against them. According to him, there may be two causes of social exclusion of the Dalits (i) caste system is very well embedded in the socio-economic system or social systems, and (ii) there is wide economic disparity among the people of different castes-the upper and middle level castes on one hand and the Dalits castes on the other. The practice of untouchability and various forms of discriminatory behaviour by people of the upper and middle level castes towards people of all the Dalits castes remains a day-to-day phenomenon in villages, including the studied village, in the state.

Contrary to the village, people of all castes and communities in the town are somewhat conscious and aware of the repercussions of the untouchability and other forms of discriminatory behaviour towards people of the Scheduled Castes or the Dalits. They are also aware the negative consequences of the apparent form (s) of exclusion of social exclusion of the Dalits from the public spheres of life. Hence, the denials of rights and to access of Dalits by the non-Dalits to the public spheres in urban are somewhat subtle and hidden. As appears from Table 4.8 that a majority of the respondents –all castes, both literate and employed in the various types of jobs in the town have found less degree of discriminatory behaviour of people of the non-Dalit castes and communities. In fact, the change of educational level of occupational pursuit in income of the Dalits in the town has enhanced their social relationship with people of the upper and middle level castes and of other communities (see Tables 4.4 and 4.5 in Appendix-A). Such a change has created an inclusive atmosphere for them in the town, to have their access to and acquire better position in economic, educational, cultural and political domains of life than that in the villages. One may easily notice that people of the upper and middle level castes and non- caste communities been sympathetic and giving respect or prestige to a number of Dalits in the town due to their present socio-economic status. But most of the Dalits are still socially, economically, educationally, culturally and politically excluded from or deprived of their rights access to various awareness in the urban areas. They do not even freely interact with people of the different caste groups in the town.

Conclusion

The deprivations due to discriminations in various spheres of life, exploitation and exclusion of the Dalits have been found more in the village than in the town under the study. It has also focused, in this Chapter, how they have been getting excluded to the maximum degree from their access to social, economic, educational, political and cultural domains of life in the village due to powerful dominance of people of the upper and middle level castes in all the spheres. Not only that, but we have also noted views of the respondents expressing about the maximum extent of social and economic exploitation of the Dalits living in the village. So has been the case of social discriminations practiced, in the various forms, against them. Contrary to that, the respondents from the town, being relatively better in their socio-economic and educational positions have found somewhat social relation and social interaction of Dalits with people of non-Dalits castes and communities. Most of the respondents from different Scheduled Castes do not experience any sort of discrimination or untouchability from the non-Dalits and have accepted that the non-Dalits behave with the Dalits on equal term due to their better socio-economic and educational status and social consciousness.

Notes

1. Louis, Prakash (2001). *Casteism is Horrendous than Racism: Durban and Dalit Discourse*, Indian Social Institute, New Delhi, pp. 5-6.
2. Ram, Nandu (2008). *Caste System and Untouchability in South India*, Manak Publications, New Delhi, pp. 18-19.
3. Townsend, P. (1993). "The International Analysis of Poverty" in Baily, Nick and Spratt, Jenny & others (2004). *Deprivation and Social Exclusion in Argyll and Bute*, Report to the community Planning Partnership, Scottish Centre for Research on Social Justice, Universities of Glasgow & Aberdeen, p. 3.
4. Oommen, T.K. (1984). Sources of Deprivation and Styles of Protests: The Case of the Dalits in India, *Contributions to Indians Sociology* (n.s.) 18, 1 Sage Publications, New Delhi, pp. 46-7.
5. Referred in Dahrendolf, Ralf (1959). *Class and Class Conflict in Industrial Society*, Berkeley.
6. Omvedt, Gail (1994). *Dalits and the Democratic Revolution: Dr. Ambedkar and the Dalit Movement in the Colonial India*, Sage Publications, New Delhi, p. 47.

7. De Haan, Arjan (2008). *Social exclusion: Two Essays*, Critical Quest, New Delhi.
8. Berreman, Gerald D. (1979). *Caste and Other Inequities: Essays on Inequality*, Folklore Institute, New Delhi, p. 76.
9. Singh, Ashok "The Story of a Dalit family from a Sleepy North Bihar Village" in Ahmad , Imtiaz & Upadhaya, S.B (2010 ed.). by *Dalit Assertion in Society, Literature and History,* Orient Black Swan, New Delhi, pp. 90-1.
10. Ram, Nandu (2008). *Caste System and Untouchability in South India*, Manak Publications, New Delhi, p. 85.
11. Mayer, A.C. (1960). *Caste and Kinship in Central India: A Village and its Region*, Routledge and Kegan Paul, London.
12. Sachchidananda (1977). *The Harijan Elite*, Thomson Press(India) Limited, p. 46.
13. Vidyarthi, L.P & N. Mishra (1977). *Harijan Today*, Classical Publications, New Delhi, p. 209.
14. Mishra, Narayan (2004). *Exploitation and Atrocities on Dalits in India*, Kalpaz Publications, New Delhi, pp. 85-6.
15 Berreman, Gerald, D. (1979). *Caste and Other Inequities: Essays on Inequality*, Folklore Institute, New Delhi.
16. Lal, A.K. (1997). *Dalits in Action: An Evaluation of Bihar Dalit Vikas Samiti*, Concept Publishing Company, New Delhi, p. 24.
17. Lal, A.K. (1997). *Dalits in Action: An Evaluation of Bihar Dalit Vikas Samiti*, Concept Publishing Company, New Delhi.
18. Ramashray, Roy (1970). "Caste and Political Recruitment in Bihar", in Rajni Kothari (ed.), *Caste in Indian Politics*, Orient Longman Ltd, New Delhi, p. 229.
19. Referred in T.B. Bottomore (1962). *Sociology: A Guide to Problems and Literature*, Blackie & Son (India) Ltd, p. 262.
20. Wankhede, G.G. (2003). "The Scheduled Castes and Higher Education in India: Retrospects and Prospects", *Think India* 6(3), July-Sept, p. 37.
21. Salam, Jeebanlata (2004). *Social Exclusion and Education*, Indian Social Institute, New Delhi, p. 1.
22. Abdulraheem, A. (2011). "Education, Equality and Social Exclusion: A View", *Social Action*, July-September, Vol. 61, No. 3, p. 217.
23. Weber, Max (1948). *From Max Weber: Essays in Sociology*, (ed.) by H.H. Gerth and C. W. Mills, London, Routledge and Kenan Paul, p. 180.
24. Beteille, Andre (1966). *Caste, Class and Power*, Oxford University Press, New Delhi, p. 4.
25. Milner, Murray JR. (1994). *Status and Sacredness: A general theory of Status Relations and an Analysis of Indian Culture*, Oxford University Press, New York, p. 27.

26. Morrison, Ken (1995). *Marx, Durkheim, Weber: Formations of Modern Social Thought*, Sage Publications, New Delhi, p. 283.
27. Srinivas, M.N. "The Dominant Caste in Rampura", in Dipankar Gupta (ed.1991). *Social Stratification*, Oxford University Press, New Delhi.
28. Kumar, Vivek (2002). *Dalit Leadership in India*, Kalpaz Publications, New Delhi, p. 236.
29. Bharti, Indu (1990). "Dalits Gain New Izzat", *Economic and Political Weekly*, May 5-12, pp. 980-981.
30. Kunnath, George J. (2012). *Rebels from the Mud Houses: Dalits and the Making of the Maoist Revolution in Bihar,* Social Science Press, New Delhi, p. 20.
31. Lal, A.K. (1997). "Bihar: Old and New", *Seminar*, 450, February, p. 20.
32. Sen, Amartya (2004). *Social Exclusion, Concept, Application, Security,* Critical Quest, New Delhi, p. 11.
33. Kumar, Rabindra (2002). *Impact of Rural Development on Scheduled Castes*, Anmol Publications, New Delhi, p. 47.
34. Ashwani Kumar (2007). "Exile between Home and Memory", *Seminar*, December, p. 16.
35. Kumar, Rabindra (2002). *Impact of Rural Development on Scheduled Castes*, Anmol Publications, New Delhi.
36. Sharma, Mukul "The Untouchable Present: Everyday Life of Musahars in North Bihar", in Jodhka, S.S (ed.) Village *India* (2012). Orient Black Swan, New Delhi, pp. 99-100.
37. Ram, Nandu(1995). *Beyond Ambedkar:Essays on Dalits in India*, Har-Anand Publications, New Delhi, p. 33.
38. Haan, Arjan De (2008). *Social Exclusion: Two Essays,* Critical Quest, New Delhi.
39. See, Ram, Nandu (2008): *Caste System and Untouchability in South India*, Manak Publications, New Delhi.
40. Ambedkar, B.R. (1979). "Castes in India: Their Mechanism, Genesis and Development"(first published in 1917), in *Dr. Babasaheb Ambedkar: Writings and Speeches,* Vol. 1, Government of Maharashtra, Bombay.
41. See in details, Dumont, Louis (1966). *Homo Hierarchicus: The Caste System and its Implications*, Oxford University Press, New Delhi. And, Bougle, C. (1971). *Essays on the Caste System,* Translated and with an Introduction by D.F. Pocock, Cambridge University Press.
42. *Ibid.,* Ram (2008). pp. 7-8.
43. Carrying dead animals.

Chapter - 5

Status Formation among the Dalits

Introduction

We know that the ascribed status is assigned to a person by the group or society as a whole on the basis of his/her caste, gender, age, etc., whereas an achieved status is earned or required by the individual through his/her personal attributes. But in a society like India, particularly in the Hindu social system, the ascribed status of person of a particular caste is determined solely on the basis of his/her birth in that caste and other criteria like gender, age, etc. play the secondary role in it. So also, since there is religious or ritual hierarchy in which all castes have been placed in the descending order, in the caste system, there is an inherent hierarchy of the ascribed (castes) statuses in the caste system. It is also evident that in the majority of cases, the ascribed status always determines the nature and extent of their achieved status. In other words, the achieved status of a person is facilitated by his/her ascribed status, if it is in high esteem in the hierarchy of the ascribed status or may be hindered, if the latter one is in the low esteem. In this context, the present chapter tries to analyze about how the ascribed status of the Dalits either contributes to or hinders in the formation of their achieved status inclusive of their interaction and social relations with the non-Dalits in the exiting social structure of both the village and the town. In addition, the chapter focuses on the role of social and religious reforms, sanskritisation and the Constitutional Provisions in the formation of achieved status of the Dalits in general and the studied areas or locales in particular.

But before doing that, it is necessary to briefly look at the term status as conceptualised in its sociological understanding.

Defining Status or Social Status

According to Wolf[1], "In the past, status was juristic term connoting the individual' rights and duties as relevant to his (or her) condition and status in life....the sharp changes in status fortunes that emerged from the erosion of privileges (since the 19th century onwards) could not be encompassed by the old legalistic definition of the term, yet it was sometime before it was broadened sufficiently to be useful as a tool of analysis". It was, however, Ralf Linton[2] who perhaps for the first time attempted to define sociologically the term status. For him, status is primarily a position in a social structure, involving rights, duties, and reciprocal expectations of behaviour, none of which depends on the personal characteristics of the status occupant.[3] Referring to Max Weber's idea of status,[4] Wolf further says that, "In saying that status is an 'effective claim to social esteem in terms of positive and negative privileges'. Weber has emphasized its relational base and that a status claimant must have an audience from which to receive or to demand deferential response". Thus, the term status is relational and inter-subjective where its meaning and acceptance vary from person to person or from group to group. It is also positional and highly structural in terms of various or spheres and inclusive of its own properties.

In other words, Weber (1961) deals with status in terms of a quality of social honour. He argues that the economically determined class situation leads to status situation which is atypical component of the life situation of men and women. "This, in turn, is determined by a specific positive or negative social estimation of honour. This honour may be connected with quality shared by a plurality and, of course, can be linked, in the most varied ways, with the status distinction".[5] Similarly, in the caste system, castes as status groups are defined essentially in terms of style of life. Property and occupation enter as important elements in the style of life of a status group, but they need not be decisive. Social honour in the caste system is very closely tied to ritual values. Styles of life, which are highly esteemed, are generally associated with a large number of ritual restrictions. Thus, there are restrictions among Brahmins on the eating of various kinds of food.

Together with this there are ritual prescriptions with regard to the number of dress, the caste mark so on.[6]

A point may be mentioned here that the term status has been conceptualised primarily in the context of relatively open society where individual has been free to avail of opportunities enabling him/her to easily occupy a position or social position in the society. But in a relatively closed society, particularly the Hindu social system in India, occupying a status or position according to one's personal attributes or qualities has remained absent or restricted only individual of certain caste. So also, sociologists and social anthropologists from both India and abroad have hardly made any attempt to define the term status in the context of Indian society. However, Dumont[7] has attempted to define the term status in the context of caste system and has situated it in the religious and ritual domains only. In his opinion, the term status is to be explained only in terms of pure and impure caste of its member. But Saberwal[8] has stated that, "For one thing, the unit of social appraisal in urban India is increasingly not the corporate group but the individual; and the determinants of this appraisal include education, economic resources, political influence, general knowledgeability, etc., besides religious status. This composite evaluation of one's social standing by others and one's awareness of this evaluation by them will here be designated status with a capital S". Unlike Weberian formulation of status of social class, the formation of status or of social status of an individual in India, in Saberwal's sense, is based on the secular characteristics or criteria, i.e., education, economic resources, employment, power or authority or political influence which are achievable by him or her in the society, although his or her corporate group (caste) status does influence it positively or negatively. Hence, an individual may go up or down but his/her caste remains, by and large, static or stagnant due to its ascribed status which its members inherit in the caste system, in spite of a microscopic minority intending to disown it.

Interestingly, in defining the term status, Dumont keeps economic and political power separately. In other words, both status and power for him are disjointed. This lives the scope of defining the term status, separate from the one being religious or ritual in nature, based on economic and political power as well as social interaction and relations extracted from that. Then, Dumont's definition of status is either incomplete or it is supplemented by the economic and political power, which in his understanding may or may not be considered as crucial element of defining status. In a way, this is more explicit in Srinivas's[9] formulation of 'dominant castes' requiring necessarily to undergoing the process of sanskritisation for achieving higher status in the society of Hindu social system. But according to Ram,[10] a status exclusively based on purity and pollution does not sustain unless it is separated by economic and political power. In his own words, "now, in the changed situation, the social system is more complex and, as a result of that, the status-evaluation of a person or of a group has become a little difficult. Other aspect, such as economic and political power, with their specific sets of hierarchies also plays a significant role in determination of status. This does not mean that the caste hierarchy is completely eliminated or has grown weak. Rather, it has loosened its hold over the people in the public domain but retained it in the private one." Referring to Merton's status-set, i.e., status or position acquires in various domains, Ram has summed-up such statuses and termed it social status which also includes status or caste status of a person inherited from his/her caste.

Not going into further details of the conceptual explanation of the term status or social status, we may briefly look at the status arrangement of various castes and communities in Bihar.

If we see the views presented by many sociologists and social anthropologists, as referred earlier, about the caste system in India, we find the same complexity of Hindu caste system in Bihar. In the Hindu caste system, an individual is born, lives and dies within the limits of his caste, as stated earlier. Thus, a caste in contemporary rural Bihar is an endogamous group with a set of ritual practices which separate it from other castes. The caste of a person is determined by his/her birth. In the Hindu caste system, people belonging to a particular caste claim that the origin of their caste, is not only different but also superior from each other castes. This claim is legitimised on the basis of their various myths of origin of their caste, which constitute an important element of caste beliefs. People belonging to different castes create their internal hierarchies, according to their myths and beliefs about the origin of their caste.[11] The simplest and universally acceptable categorisation of all the Hindu castes in Bihar is three-fold: Forward, Backward and Scheduled Castes, as stated earlier. The Forward Castes (upper castes) are Brahmin, Bhumihar, Rajput and Kayastha and these have been historically dominant and continue to be so in both urban and rural areas. The Backward Castes (lower and upper) are a heterogeneous category in between the upper castes and the Scheduled Castes. The Scheduled Castes are at the lowest level of the caste hierarchy. In addition to these, three categories, there are also Muslims and a fifth category is Scheduled Tribes in Bihar[12], as mentioned in Chapter 3. If we see the caste composition among the people, especially Hindus, in Bihar, we find that they are divided into many caste groups, (see, Chapter 3). It mainly shows the rank or social status of a particular caste group in the caste hierarchy and accordingly it maintains its caste status in the society.

Therefore, in the present Chapter, the enquiry is made to find out as to why Dalits are socially excluded and whether their ascribed status contributes, in one way or the other, to improving or downgrading their social status in the Indian society as a whole. It would also find out the changes in their caste status on the basis of their interaction with non-Scheduled Castes. Finally, we shall enquire into status formation among the Dalits, including our respondents, in the studied locales.

Changes in Social Status in the Caste System

Castes operate not only in rural but also in urban areas, as is evident from a number of studies. It also influences, in one way or other, the other institutions such as education, economy, polity, etc. Therefore, a person's caste status in the caste system is taken into account while measuring his social status. There are two schools of thought regarding determination of a person's status in the caste system. According to one school[13], caste is an institution with a systemic form and a person's status is based on his birth in a particular caste (*Jati*), which has a definite rank in the caste hierarchy. This is his 'ascribed status' with which he is born and dies. It is also viewed in terms of his corporate group which is similar to his caste rank. Srinivas[14] has rightly stated that caste does not only simply place the people into higher or lower position, but it also determines their way of life, their customs, manners, occupations, social relations and status in the society. Caste also imposes certain restrictions on its members to avoid intermixing, maintaining purity and performing of certain vital tasks in the society. "The institution of caste, thus, cuts across diversity of groups and gives them all a common social idiom". The concept of 'ascribed status', taken from Linton,[15] deals with a person's status in a society wherein it is assigned to the person by the society, without regard for his/her unique talent or characteristics. It also deals with one's occupational pursuit and general social standing, which is determined at birth, but that may change over a period of time.

According to the second school[16], caste system is a dynamic one, and one is subjected to a variety of changes, especially in urban areas. A person's status (also his caste rank) is determined on the basis of a number of attributes acquired by him and the interaction between him and others. Such interaction is also guided by a person's socio-economic status and power position. There are also other criteria for status determination of a person and these are ritual purity and pollution, caste calling, etc., which themselves is subjected to change. Thus, on the basis of change in the pattern of interaction and social relation of a person with others, his status in the caste system is 'achieved' and remains changeable. In this sense, a person's status is his position which is accorded to or 'achieved' by him in the caste system, while rank of his caste is an order assigned to his caste in the caste hierarchy. In other words, the status is attributed to an individual, while rank is assigned to a caste as a corporate group. Status is changeable, while rank is almost fixed.[17]

It may then be said that caste still plays the key role in Indian society where a person's birth in a particular caste sums up his other position or status known as 'status summation'.[18] From this perspective, a person who has a low status in the caste hierarchy also has low status in other hierarchies such as economic or political hierarchies in the society.[19] In addition, caste also influences the mode of behaviour and pattern of life of the people.

Further, another respondent- Birendra Ram has stated that even those who are socially and economically a little well off are also treated inferior due to the caste feeling, which is still very much alive. He has further mentioned that it is the Brahmanical mindset or hegemony of the upper and even middle level castes, which has created layers of inequality among people of various castes by giving them a fixed rank or status. Thus, social interaction takes place among the people in accordance with their caste status. As a matter of fact, people of the upper and middle level castes do not pay respect to the people of the Dalit castes due to their low caste background. The Hindu *Dharma Shashtra* put people of the upper castes at the top and of the Dalit castes at the bottom in the caste hierarchy. Then, the notion of pure (upper castes) and that of impure (untouchables) emerges in the Indian society, especially the Hindu system.[20]

Having the lowest ascribed status in the caste hierarchy, the respondents achieve the lower status in the class or socio-economic status hierarchy. They also do not receive the amount of honour or respect from people of the upper and middle level castes in the village, as mentioned above. Therefore, the respondents having lowest ascribed status in the caste hierarchy are considered by people of the upper and middle level castes to be the lowest even after achieving higher position in other sectors or domains. We may take the case of Dr. K.R. Narayanan, the former President of India. After getting the highest position in the country, he was projected as the first Dalit President of India, in spite of his unique talent and qualifications. Another is the case of Mr. K.G. Balakrishnan, the Chief Justice of India. When he occupied the highest position in the office of the Judiciary, he was projected as the first Dalit Chief Justice of India. There are countless cases which reveal that due to the ascriptive criteria, Dalits are lowly evaluated by ignoring their personal qualifications and achievement. Even today, they do not receive the proportionate amount of honour or prestige from people of the higher castes.

In this context, it is interesting to note that the relationship of the respondents with the people of Bhumihar, Brahman and Yadav castes do not yield the required prestige or honour or respect, and they get the lower recognition in the village society. They are still attached with their low caste identity and there is no change in their caste status so far. If a Dalit with the lower ascribed status achieves the higher or highest status even then he is considered to be the lowest, by people of the upper and middle level castes, as mentioned earlier. But in the context of social relations with the Dalits even in the village, some change has taken place with the Dalits. That is why, people of the upper and middle level castes have started interacting with them by conferring certain amount of dignity and respect to them. However, it happens at the individual level but the group or caste, to such individual belongs, still remains socially degraded. In other words, an individual of the lower caste is included in the system through his/her positive social interaction with members of the upper and middle level castes, while his/her group or caste remains excluded from their social system. Here, it is pertinent to know whether ascribed status of a Dalit also gets changed and how his/her achieved status influences change, if any, in his/her ascribed status in the caste system. During the field study, what has been found is that the ascribed status of the Dalits in the village has not changed at all. Even the achieved status of a few Dalits has not contributed to any change in their ascribed status. People of the upper and middle level castes still believe in the caste hierarchy and even the achieved status of such Dalits is judged by them accordingly. Like other Dalits, they remain isolated and excluded group from their social rights and social respect as well as dignity in the village society. But it is also true that the minor change has taken place among the Dalits. Yet, people of the upper and middle level castes have somewhat better social interaction with them, but their achieved status has failed to influence their ascribed caste status at the village level.

On the other hand, the respondents of Dusadh caste have opined that the change of the caste-based occupation of the Dusadhs has not enhanced their social status in the eyes of the upper caste people. They continue to be humiliated, discriminated and isolated on the basis of their low ascribed caste status and remain socially excluded group from the socio-economic and political system of the village. Therefore, like other Dalits, the social status of the Dusadhs is low esteemed by people of the upper caste people. The respondent Awadh Paswan has highlighted that there is no way out of enhancement of the ascribed caste status in the Hindu caste system. It is given by the Hindu Society to the Dalits on the basis of the *Karma theory,* which is completely unscientific. In this context, location of caste status of the Dalits in the social hierarchy copes up with the lowest rank, compared to that of the other caste categories such as Brahmin, Bhumihar and Yadav. Hence, the ascribed status of Dusadhs does not get equal evaluation or esteem as compared to that of the upper and middle level castes in the village. Further, according to another respondents Ayodhya Paswan, Dalits are getting, now-a-days, a little bit improvement in their secular position due to government or private jobs, but somehow their achieved position or status does not carry the amount of honour or respect for them in the traditional, through being dynamic in some way, social structure in rural areas in general and the studied village in particular. On the ground of secular criteria, the upper and middle level castes have begun interacting with Dalits in the village for fulfilling their motives by using the latter. But even in this respect, it has been seen that the achieved status of the Dalits is still judged by the upper castes in relation to their ascribed status in the caste system practiced in the village. This simply means that caste still plays the vital role in deciding the social position of people in the Bara Govind village where Brahmans, Bhumihars and Yadavs enjoy the highest social status compared to the people of the remaining castes. Therefore, formation of social status of the Dalits in the village is very slow due to the upper castes' hegemony in all the available domains. For instance, in the domains of economic, educational and political authority, they lag behind other castes and these are the main obstacle of Dalits in the formation of social status in the positive distinction in the village. There is only slight improvement in the caste status of the Dalits through their social interaction and inter-dinning relationship. Such a change has taken place only with the educated respondents of the village, but a large majority of them are still deprived of such a change in their caste status.

Now, it is pertinent to analyze views of the respondents about formation of their status or social status as well as of Dalits in general in the caste system in the studied locales. The caste hierarchy in the Bara Govind village clearly appears in terms of '*Uchcha*' (upper) and '*Neecha*' (lower) *log* (people) or caste where the upper castes and middle level castes (Brahmins, Bhumihars and Yadav) are at the top and enjoy the highest social status and the Dalits (Chamar, Dusadh and Musahar) are placed at the bottom and are treated as low. The people of the upper and middle level castes of the village are known as twice-born. In the village, caste plays the vital role in deciding the social relations and interaction with people of the different caste groups. Most of the respondents have accepted that the purity and pollution is observed by people of the upper and even middle level castes against the Dalits of the village because of low caste status or rank assigned to them and their caste in the traditional caste system. On the basis of their low caste status, they are even physically segregation and untouchability is practiced against them by people of the *uchcha jatis*. Parvathamma[21] also has viewed that the ritual purity and pollution, the barrier which separates the untouchable groups from others in India, meant that these people could not be incorporated into the mainstream in Hinduism. This has not changed even after Ambedkar's neo-Buddhist movement. There is hardly a movement, with secular agenda, which attempts to influence minds of the people with secular agenda. She has further argued that the "religious ideologies act as opiate to masses. The constitutional benefits have covered only a fraction of the scheduled castes population since most of the deserving ones are hardly aware of their rights".

We have also found that the Dalits in the studied village are socially discriminated, physically isolated and economically deprived because of their low caste identity and status. Today, the social distance is very much observed between pure and impure or the upper and lower castes of the village. As far as the caste system is concerned, it is still a rigid form of stratification in the village where the social relations among members of the different caste exist on the basis of caste status. Most of the respondents from the village are economically handicapped and are totally dependent upon their labour which, in turn, influences their social status in the caste system practiced therein. Table 5.1 given below explains, in certain way, the social status of our respondents in terms of their sitting on a cot along with number of the upper and middle level castes, having commensal relations or taking food, water, smoking, etc. with them, and participating in the ritual or religious ceremonies performed by members of each castes in the village. The table also clearly shows that 18.4 percent of the total respondents of the Chamar, Dusadh and Musahar castes sit with people of the upper and middle level castes on the same cot. Similarly, 14.4 percent of the respondents are invited by people of the upper and middle level castes in their social functions. Apart from that, no respondent is invited by them on the ceremonial occasions celebrated by people of the upper and middle level castes in the village. Even those respondents who have established their social relationship with some people of the upper castes in the village, they do not get the considerable amount of honour or prestige from the latter due to their low caste status. Therefore, it can be said that despite a somewhat better economic status of a few respondents', caste plays the decisive role in determining the social status of even these of respondents in the Bara Govind village.

Table 5.1: Caste-wise views of the Respondents on changes in Caste Status of Dalits

Sl. No.	Changes in features of Caste	Caste of the Respondents					
		Bara Govind Village			Chakia Town		
		Chamar	Dusadh	Musahar	Chamar	Dhobi	Dusadh
1.	Sitting along with upper castes	11(8.8)	9(7.2)	3(2.4)	18(14.4)	22(17.6)	13(10.4)
2.	Commensal relation with upper castes	9(7.2)	7(5.6)	2(1.6)	11(8.8)	10(8)	9(7.2)
3.	On ceremonial occasions in upper castes house	5(4)	4(3.2)	1(0.8)	7(5.6)	9(7.2)	8(6.4)
4.	Upper castes on ceremonial occasions at own house	-	-	-	1(0.8)	3(2.4)	1(0.8)
5.	None	17(13.6)	18(14.4)	39	5(4)	3(2.4)	5(4)
	Total	**42**	**38**	**45**	**42**	**47**	**36**

Further, most of the respondents do not have privilege of sitting on the same cot with members of the upper and middle level castes due to their low caste background, and even those having such relations with them also face some sort of discriminations and untouchability in their day-to-day social life. This is equally true in the case of other Dalits or Dalit castes living in the village. It can, then, be said that the social status of the respondents as well as people of the Dalit castes as a whole is not elevated in the existing caste system because of their low caste rank or status. That is why, Dalits in the village face systematic exclusion from their participation in the various spheres of life, as already discussed in Chapter 4.

Unlike in the village, caste system in the town does not exist in the rigid form in day-to-day life of the people. In spite of Chakia town being a multi-castes people belonging to the Dalit castes do not experience the notion of purity and pollution. Presently, a majority of them have achieved better social status compared to those in the villages, even in the caste system after improving their socio-economic and educational status, though the status or rank of their castes remains the same in the caste-hierarchy existing in the town. Although the majority of them are spatially segregated from the localities of people of the non-Dalit castes, they do not come across the traditional hierarchical caste system where most of the respondents have experienced some change in their caste status through their secular roles, as well as their interaction and social relations with people of the non-Dalit castes and communities. Now-a-days, they do not experience the rigid form of caste discrimination, but are attributed to be having the low profile status in other domains. Therefore, it may be said that, presently, they have achieved some changes in their caste statuses after acquiring socio-economic and educational status, as mentioned earlier. On the basis of their achieved status, they have established somewhat better social interactions and relations with people of the different castes groups and enjoyed the considerable amount of respect there. Ram[22] also has mentioned about the changes occurred in statuses of the Scheduled Castes in urban areas. He has argued that congruence between both the achieved status in class structure and the ascribed status in the caste system in urban rural areas. According to him, "those Dalits who had achieved their status in class structure also found some meaningful changes in their caste status where, unlike their less achieving caste people, they were not subjected to any crude practice of untouchability and caste discrimination. They interacted "freely" with people of other castes and communities more in urban areas and enjoyed a considerable degree of respect from them". Keeping the above arguments in mind, we can look at the social status of the respondents, as given Table 5.1, as well as their views on status of Dalits, keeping their caste-based status intact, in the town.

The Table 5.1 shows the social relationships of the respondents, with members of the different caste groups, in terms of their sitting along with them on the chair or the same cot, their interacting freely with them and having commensality or taking food together and participating in their ceremonies in their houses one organised by people of the upper and middle level castes in the town. It is also evident from the table that less than fifty percent of the total respondents share the sitting arrangement (42.4%) and have commensal relationship with (24%) and are invited (19.2%) by people of the upper and middle level castes in the latter's celebration of the festivals or social functions. Interestingly, only (4 %) of the respondents are invited by them in their celebration of ceremonial occasions in their houses. It is, thus, very obvious that a majority of the respondents do not experience the rigid form of caste discrimination, as compared to the respondents from the studied village. In the urban areas, technological advancement and industrial and educational development of people in general, in that of the Dalits has loosened the traditional rigidity of the Hindus caste system. By and large, change is marked in the behaviour patterns of only such Harijans (Dalits) who are residing in the town or are the top achievers.[23] In the case of the Chakia town, it has been found that most of the respondents have accepted that they have cordial social relations with people of the upper and middle level castes and they do not face any severe form of caste discrimination because of change in their status in the caste system. They have enhanced their social status, despite of having a very low ascribed status in the hierarchy of caste system. This is equally true in many cases among the Dalits, access their caste, living in the town.

In the village, most of the respondents continue to be prohibited from taking water from the village wells, entering the village's Hindu temples and exercising their voting rights. The segregation of seating of the statutorily elected Dalit member in the village panchayat continues even today. In the Indian society, the 'lower' castes (that is, the Scheduled Castes) have traditionally been ranked 'low' in the caste hierarchy; and often this ranking has rarely been challenged till recently from any quarter.[24] Due to the "low rank of their castes, the Dalits have suffered from the cumulative inequalities in the economic, political and ritual systems".[25] In the Bara Govind village, we have found the social status of Dalits in general and of our respondents in particular similar to that as mentioned above by many social scientists where people's caste plays the main role in determining their social position or status. As we know, each caste in the caste system is traditionally assigned an occupation and the occupation is also ranked pure or impure in accordance with the rank of the caste in the caste hierarchy. As far as the Scheduled Castes or Dalits in the village are concerned, they have traditionally been assigned fixed occupations and rank as mentioned in the traditional Hindu caste system. However, most of the respondents have now given up their traditional occupations, but their social status has not changed due to status or rank of their caste in the traditional caste hierarchy existing there.

Further, the people belonging to a particular caste follow their caste's rituals and hold status accordingly, whereas the impact of their social interaction with different caste groups is very limited. Berreman[26] also has stated the same thing in his study by explaining that the village comprises of those "people whose statuses are largely a function of their membership in the corporate groups (families, sibs, castes). They tend to remain in their "home territory"-the familiar setting of the village and its local region. Religious diversity is often absent and where this is not the case, it is handled in traditional fashion, very often on the model of caste differences. Villagers interact in terms of their total identities on a personal basis with others who know them well. Status summation is the rule; well-to-do people are powerful people of high ritual and social status; poor people are relatively powerless and of low status". Similarly, Ghurye [27] argues that, "The status of a person (in a society) is depended not on his wealth as in the classes of modern Europe, but on the traditional importance of the caste in which he had the luck of being born".

The respondent Tutu Manjhi, a Musahar by caste, has stated that he and his caste members are not allowed to enter the houses of the upper and middle level castes with slippers and shoes. They have to put these off it outside and then inter in their *baranda*. The people of the upper castes consider them culturally slaves. "In an increasing conscious multi-cultural India, cultural casteism based upon heterophilia acquires legitimacy by representing caste discrimination as cultural differentiation and status distinction as cultural difference".[28] Thus, due to their low caste status, people belonging to the Dalits castes face social discrimination and social segregation in the village even now. In this context, most of the respondents from the village have stated that there is not any change in their caste-based status. In fact, the indicators like socio-economic, educational status and social power or authority, selected by us for measuring their status or knowing any enhancement in their status, are completely redundant, to know any enhancement in their status, due to domination of the upper and middle level castes in the village, as stated earlier. Even psycho-social changes among the respondents and the Dalits in general, i.e., their own perception of changes in the caste status and the pattern of their interaction and social relations, with non-Dalits are absent at the village level.

Parvathamma[29] has rightly described that, "social discrimination is loaded with differential values, often supported and sanctioned by religious beliefs and practices. Provisions to eliminate discrimination and to establish social equality have to be supported from other possible sources. Social inequality and discrimination are inherent and therefore ascriptive. It is hardly possible to alter ascriptive values by legislation". In this context, the view of a respondent, Sakal Manjhi is worth mentioned here. He tells his story to the present researcher about the existing social hurdle faced by him in the village. He states, "there is a Temple in the upper caste locality. During the ceremony, people of the upper castes only are allowed to worship in the temple. Whenever a Dalit male or female goes for worship in the temple, the priest of the temple does not permit him or her to go inside due to his/her low social status, prescribed or ascribed in the caste system. The Dalits of the village are allowed only to see or worship the idol from outside the gate. They are strictly prohibited to enter inside the temple. On the occasion of *Somari Puja* celebration or any other celebrations, the Dalits pour water at the gate of the temple because the gate is already closed for them". It may, then, be said that due to low caste status of Dalits in the local caste hierarchy, their social status is negatively observed by people of the upper and middle level castes. It is, thus, very obvious from the above that most of the respondents and the Dalits in general suffer from the incongruence between their caste status and their overall social status, compared to that of the higher castes. Their status or social status formation within the village is almost absent or non-starter due to their low ascribed (caste) status.

Social Status in Class (Socio-economic status) Structure

The notion of class has been analyzed by many Sociologists and Social Anthropologists in the western as well as in Indian societies. Generally speaking, the concept of class is associated with the economic status and accordingly life style of the people. In most cases, the term class is identified exclusively with the economic position vis-à-vis status of individuals without taking into account the social and political or power aspects. But such understanding of class is invariably located in a given mode of production or production relations, as analyzed extensively by Karl Marx. Opposed to that, Weber[30] has defined class in the given market situation and social relations therein. But such conceptualisation is based on the empirical social reality found in the open society or social structure. Marx[31] uses class in terms of owners and non-owners of the means of production in a pure economic sense. Apart from that, Bottomore[32] gives contradictory view on classes and status group by saying that "the difference, broadly, is between a hierarchy of a small number of organised or partly organised economic groups whose relations to each other are antagonistic, and a hierarchy of numerous groups, more correctly described as aggregates of individuals of equal social prestige based on similarities which are not exclusively economic, and whose relations to each other are not primarily antagonistic but are partially competitive and partially emulative". Weber[33] talks of classes only in a market economy: "… always this is the genetic connotation of the concept of class: that the kind of chance in the market is decisive moment which presents a common condition for the individual's fate. 'Class situation' is, in this sense, ultimately market situation" (*ibid*). As Ogburn and Nimkoff[34] wrote, "class societies may be represented as extending from those like the caste which are relatively rigid or closed to those which are flexible". Contrary to that, in a relatively closed society like that in India, the traditional institutions such as caste and religion besides the economic means of production, play a dominant role in deciding the economic position or status of an individual and group. For instance, the status of a poor Brahman and a poor Dalit is equally made by religion and caste in the formation of 'class' but also unequally made in the structural location in the social structure.[35]

Within the above mentioned analytical framework of class hierarchy, we find that most of the Dalits, including our respondents, are landless agricultural labourers and are dependent on land source of others for their livelihood in the Bara Givind village. Kumar[36] rightly mentions about the economic relation in rural Bihar being fundamentally represented in terms of '*Malik'* (upper castes land owners) and '*Praja*' (lower castes landless). Even urban areas are largely owned by the Malik-upper and middle level castes and the lower castes or Dalits are mostly skilled and unskilled labourers. This is true elsewhere also. For example, Andre Beteille [37] explains the relationship among the owners (the Brahmin), the tenants (the non-Brahmin), and the agricultural labourers (the Adi-Dravid) the untouchable castes in a village in Tamil Nadu. He shows that the caste system overlaps, to a larger extent, the class structure status or socio-economic status in the agrarian setting, although certain aspects of life as land ownership, occupation, etc. are not dependent upon caste as before.

Thus, in formation of class in rural areas, land plays the crucial role in determining the social status inclusive of economic, educational and the political status of people. Therefore, due to their deprivation or non-possession of the land, Dalits of the studied village are socio-economically most vulnerable and may be termed as lower class in the class hierarchy if we situate it in the village. In the case of land ownership in Bihar, Singh[38] has stated that "Since in a feudal or semi-feudal society the main source of wealth is land, it naturally belonged (since early time) to higher castes. It is difficult to imagine the lower castes owning the important means of wealth. Hence, to a great extent, the caste system was congruent with the class system. Those who owned the instruments of production were the higher castes (class) and those who laboured under them to produce were of the lower castes (class)". The Table 5.2 shows views of the respondents on the social status and class or the socio-economic status of the Dalits respondents in the village. There are (69.6%) of the respondents of all the three Dalits castes who have found the class or socio-economic status of the Dalits as low, followed by (25 or 20%) of the respondents whose views on class or socio-economic status of the Dalits is of middle level. And there are only 13 (10.4%) the respondents who have viewed the Dalits acquiring high' class or socio-economic status in the village. The table also shows that most of the respondents, who have viewed the Dalits of the village with low class or socio-economic, are illiterate, mostly landless agricultural labourers and who earn their wages mainly in kind, but their monthly income is less than Rs 100, and are totally dependent on their labour force. On the other hand, the respondents who have the middle level of socio-economic status are literate, agricultural labourers with some auxiliary source of income of more than Rs 100 p.m., compared to those who are educated upto matriculation and employed, with more than Rs 3000 p.m., both the public and private sectors organisations in the nearby town, have placed a few Dalits in high class or socio-economic status. It may not be out of context to mention the views of the respondent, Huseni Ram, who has stated that the social position of Dalits, compared to non-Dalits, is very low and the degraded one. They do not receive the amount of respect, prestige or honour from people of the upper and middle level castes because of their low caste status. Even those Dalits, who are socio-economically, educationally and politically a little better-off, also do not get the amount of respect or honour as the other non-Dalits of the similar position receive in the village. This amounts to status incongruence or incongruence between their both ascribed and achieved statues, about which we have discussed in details in the next Chapter. Thus, the ascribed status somehow influences their day-today social life in the village. It may, however, be clarified that the views of the respondents on the Dalits' class or socio-economic status being low, middle and high in class or socio-economic statuses are inter se, i.e., within the Dalits themselves and, by extension, the reflections of the respondents' own class or socio-economic status in the village, and in no way, are comparable with that of the non-Dalit castes in the village as well as both the Dalits and non-Dalits in the town. Secondly, since the frames of reference of class or socio-economic status are different in both the village and the town, the values of low, middle and high also differ. In other words, the 'high' class or socio-economic status in the village may perhaps be equal to low or slightly higher to that in the town (see Tables 5.1. in Appendix-A).

Table 5.2: Caste-wise views of the Respondents about the Class or Socio-economic status of the Dalits in the village and the town

Caste of Respondents	Class or Socio-Economic Status of the Dalits					
	Bara Govind Village			Chakia Town		
	Low	Middle	High	Low	Middle	High
Chamar	25(20)	10(8)	7(5.6)	9(7.2)	11(8.8)	22(17.6)
Dhobi	-	-	-	6(4.8)	13(10.4)	28(22.4)
Dusadh	23(18.4)	9(7.2)	6(4.8)	7(5.6)	13(10.4)	16(12.8)
Musahar	39(31.2)	6(4.8)	-	-	-	-
Total	**87(69.6)**	**25(20)**	**13(10.4)**	**22(17.6)**	**37(29.6)**	**66(52.8)**

As already stated, people in the towns or cities, compared to the village, are in better position due to availability of education and job opportunities with better wages or paid emoluments, as is evident from that of the respondents themselves. In fact, it is town or city where social structure of class or social class is distinctively visible, although it does not replace the caste system completely. Taking into account the ascribed status of the Dalit respondents in the erstwhile traditional social structure as well as the changing contemporary social set-up in the town, we have found that the social position consisting of social, economic, educational and political positions of the respondents is better than, say, ten years back. As far as the Dalits's social status, compared to that of the upper caste people in the town is concerned, according to the respondents, it is improving gradually because of improvement in their socio-economic status. They also do not face the extreme form of caste discrimination by people of the upper and middle level castes as the Dalits in general and the respondents in particular of village do. In the whole process, their ascribed (caste) status is certainly low in the traditional social structure of the Hindu caste system and because of that their social status is also rated low in the esteem of prestige by people of the upper and middle level castes in the society. Apart from that, the respondent Neeraj Ram, a Primary teacher, has narrated his own experiences about change in his caste status after his getting job in the government school. Earlier, people of the upper and middle level castes did not give respect to him, but now, they address him with regard and respect. By achieving somewhat better socio-economic status, most of the respondents feel elevated in extending their social relation with members of the different caste groups in the locality where they live in. At present, change of their caste-based occupations in the town has earned them social recognition from members of the other castes. Interestingly, it is these respondents who view about improvement in socio-economic status of the Dalits in the town. Taking cognizance of such change among the Dalits, Sachchidananda[39] has stated the same thing by saying that the barrier of the traditional society is breaking down because of social interaction of the Dalits with people of the higher castes in the state. For such type of change, many factors are playing the positive roles. For instance, the contemporary social development has changed the social climate and become favourable even for the Dalits, especially after Independence. Urbanisation also has improved their social, economic, and political conditions, whereas the government policy of protective discrimination has been considered as an effective force for bringing about the change in their style of life and has decreased the excessive influence of the caste Hindus. Harold Isaacs[40] also has articulated about such change by mentioning that the lower level (caste-based) occupations of ex-untouchables have gone considerable change due to their migration from village to city where they are associated with new kinds of jobs in both private as well as government organisations.

Hence, the Dalits living in the town are relatively in a more comfortable position. In other words, they are, at present, socially, economically and educationally better off than they were earlier. In the case of their social status, their educational level and thereby their employment position have played the primary role not only in the formation of their social status, but also in bringing about some changes in it in the recent decades. Therefore, education is an important means of achieving as well as enhancing social status of the Dalits in the class hierarchy. However, Teltumbde[41] argues that education, as a part of superstructure, is moulded by the needs of the economic system and the classes who control it. In general, the Indian Constitution has overlaid certain preferential provisions in favour of Dalits (and Tribals), which have proved to be instrumental in their educational progress. For instance, Article 46 deals with promotion of educational interests of the SCs, STs and other weaker sections of Indian society, and it has also been helping Dalits in achieving education up to certain level and the bureaucratic as well as non-bureaucratic job. The Dalits, including our respondents in Chakia town, have improved their socio-economic status after getting education and employment in jobs.

As stated earlier, the respondents have viewed that the social status of the Dalits from the town as improved their educational level and performing of secular roles, especially in the public and private sectors organisations and in petty-business. Due to their changing achieved socio-economic status, there is change in their caste-based status also, although the rank or status of their castes remains the same in the caste-hierarchy existing in the town. More specifically, there are a little more than half (52.8%) of the respondents who have accepted that the Dalits in the town have achieved 'high' social status not only in the class or socio-economic status structure, but also in their caste status. This has followed by less than one-third (29.6%) of the respondents who viewed the Dalits achieving middle level socio-economic vis-à-vis social status and around one fifth (17.6 %) of the respondents have viewed them with low status in the class or socio-economic status structure. Thus, we may say that the considerable number of respondents belonging to all three Dalit castes in the town have viewed the improved the social status of the Dalits in both caste system and class or socio-economic status structure in the urban areas. Such relationships with different caste groups in the town have also improved their social relations in terms of sitting together on the chair or same cot or any platform, having commensality or commensal relations and participation in ceremonial occasions. Nowadays, they feel more comfortable in their social relationship or interaction with people of the upper and middle level castes groups than that in earlier times.

Factors responsible for status formation among Dalits

We have analyzed above views of the respondents on achieving statuses both in caste and class or socio-economic status hierarchies by the Dalits in the studied village and town. Keeping aside the multiple-hierarchy or status hierarchy which simply means hierarchy of statuses or positions found in every spheres or domains of life, we shall examine here briefly the respondents' views on the process of formation of status or social status among the Dalits both in caste and class or socio-economic status hierarchies in the village and the town or in the rural and urban areas. In other words, we shall analyze their views on various factors contributing to formation of social status among Dalits, although these factors themselves might be acting as process in the status formation. Some of the factors may be consciousness or awareness resulting into assertion or otherwise, sanskritisation and reference group/individual behaviour, constitutional provisions, etc. We shall analyze below our respondents' views on impact of these factors on the formation of status of the Dalits in both caste and class or socio-economic status hierarchies in rural and urban areas, particularly in the studied locales of the village and the town.

Social consciousness and Status formation

It is true that certain types and levels of social consciousness and awareness have arisen among the Dalits in India in the modern time, particularly after Independence. In their growing consciousness and awareness, a number of social movements led by both the Dalit and non-Dalit leaders, before and after independence, have contributed a lot. Rajni Kothari[42] opines that "Dalit consciousness in no way is limited to the Scheduled Castes. It has begun to symbolise a much broader spectre of the oppressed and hitherto excluded from the social strata". Dalits have been excluded from the main residential settlement of the village and are also kept outside the social and cultural hierarchies, with people of the upper castes at the top due to their social and cultural settings or rankings in the caste hierarchy.[43] Even after achieving mobility through secular channels with their hard work, they are not accepted by people of castes ranked higher in the caste hierarchy. Due to the extreme form of social exclusion, Dalits could not accumulate 'social capital' which could generate or create potential to develop their socially assertive consciousness.[44]

In the case of Bara Govind village, the caste-based status of the Dalits has not changed because of their socio-cultural moorings at the lower level in the social hierarchy. In the opinion of most of the respondents, a large majority of the Dalits have accepted their low evaluation by people of the upper and middle level castes who have ever developed subordinate attitudes and behaviour towards them due to low status or rank of their caste in the caste hierarchy practiced in the village. A point may be mentioned here that Dalits, across their castes and degree of their socio-economic status, have remained helpless to accept their subordinated status or social status in the village, even if they have accumulated certain types of social and cultural capital which has ever been undermined by people of the upper and middle level castes in the studied village. More specifically, majority of the Dalits are conscious of well-being of their family members, their exploitation of various sorts, their discrimination and social exclusion, low ranking of their caste in the caste hierarchy, etc. According to many respondents from the village, Dalits have been conscious of their rights of equality or equal status, dignity or respect as well as respectful treatment towards them by people of the upper and middle level castes. But due to lack of independent source of their livelihood, negation of their social and cultural capital and lack of unity among them, they are unable to develop a positive consciousness and awareness among them to ascertain equality of their status or social status, whatsoever they have achieved, with that of people of other castes, irrespective of incongruity of both in caste status or rank and the one achieved by them.

Contrary to this, Dalits living in the studied town have acquired a considerable degree of social consciousness and awareness due to their access to the various avenues such as education, employment, political participation, etc., as discussed earlier. According to many respondents, a large number of Dalits living in the town, believe in the notion of liberty, equality and fraternity which was extracted from Buddhism and extended by Dr. Ambedkar to the socially excluded people in India in general and to the oppressed sections of the society in particular. Therefore, most of the respondents from the town have stated that a sizeable number of Dalits locate even the status or rank of their caste equal to the people of other castes in the Hindu caste system. This amounts, in a way, their insistence for a casteless society among the Hindus. On the other hand, people of the upper and middle level castes do not want to give equal status or rank to the Dalits due to their social hegemony as well as their insisting on the traditional notion of superiority of their castes over that of Dalits. The transition has taken place from the ascribed caste status to the achieved one among the Dalits due to their performing secular roles and occupying positions accordingly. Caste-wise views of the respondents on the degree of levels of consciousness or awareness of the Dalits contributing to status formation among the Dalits both the village and town can be seen from Table 5.3 below. As is clear from the table, the respondents' views explained that the Dalits within the town are more aware of their status or social status in both caste and class structure, of number of constitutional provisions, etc., they have been able to improve their social status-in several cases equal to or better than of non-Dalits both in village and town- in class or socio-economic status and caste hierarchy existing there. Similar are the views of those respondents who are educated upto certain level and employed in government as well as private sectors jobs on status formation of Dalits living in the village and the town (see Tables 5.2 and 5.3 in Appendix-A).

Table 5.3: Caste-wise views of the Respondents on Social Consciousness of Dalits

Caste of Respondents	Bara Govind Village				Chakia Town			
	Types of Social Consciousness							
	About their rights, i.e., Reservation, free education	Government schemes for them	Assertive against social discrimination	No	About their rights, i.e., Reservation, free education	Government schemes for them	Assertive against social discrimination	No
Chamar	7(5.6)	3(2.4)	2(1.6)	30	15(12)	12(9.6)	10(8)	5(3.2)
Dhobi	-	-	-	-	17(13.6)	13(10.4)	14(11.2)	3(2.3)
Dusadh	5(3.2)	3(2.4)	2(1.6)	28	9(7.2)	11(8.8)	11(8.8)	5(3.2)
Musahar	2(1.6)	-	-	43	-	-	-	-
Total	**14**	**6(4.8)**	**4(3.2)**	**101**	**41(32.8)**	**36(28.8)**	**35(28)**	**13(10.4)**

Emulation and Social Status

We have explained, at the out said, the concept of status or social status which remains a static conceptual category and becomes part of hierarchy of several such statuses placed in ascending and descending order. The status placed below obviously tries to reach to the level of the one placed above it and sometimes to supersede it not only through material achievement but also emulating its behaviour pattern and life style. Such process has been termed as sanskritisation in the Hindu caste system in India and reference group/individual behaviour in the class-based society in the West. More specifically on the basis of empirical data from the particular studied locale-a village, M.N. Srinivas[45] has termed this process as sanskritisation in which the lower caste and the tribals emulate the sanskritise life style and behaviour pattern of the upper castes, particularly Brahmins. According to him, Sanskritisation means, "a process by which low Hindu caste or tribal or other group change its customs, rituals, ideology and way of life in the direction of a high and frequently "twice -born" caste. Generally, such changes are followed by a claim to a higher position in the caste hierarchy than that traditionally concerned to be the claimant caste by the local community…it is generally accompanied by and often results in upward mobility for the caste in question; but mobility may also occur without Sanskritisation; resulting only in positional changes in the system and does not lead to any structural change". This means that position or status of people of the sanskritised castes changes, not leading to any change in the structural arrangement of the system or Hindu caste system itself.

It may not be out of context to be mentioned about a few studies conducted on sanskritisation and its impact among the lower caste in Bihar. For instance, Prasad[46] has explained that the high castes like Brahmins and Rajputs have positive urge to westernise their style of life for distinguishing themselves from others, whereas the lower castes try to sanskritise their style of life for building up the traditional status held by the high castes. On other hand, Sahay[47] deals with the limits of Sanskritisation in the selected villages of his field study in Bihar where he finds that the Dalits do not need this process, but only some lower castes, to improve their life style. Dalits are actually economically and politically powerless and are not at all ashamed of their caste identity. But on the contrary, they feel proud of them. This is substantiated by the fact that some of the so-called lower castes in the village have achieved so much economic and political (voting) power that, if they wished, they could sanskritise themselves. However, they do not feel inferior and, therefore, do not feel the need to sanskritise. He has given some examples of backward castes like Yadavs, Koeris and Dalits of Buxar district of Bihar.

Similarly, the process has been termed as reference group behaviour by R.K. Merton[48] on the basis of empirical data extracted from the American society. In the process of reference group/individual behaviour, members of inferior or lower class emulate the style of life of their superior class through the related process of anticipatory socialisation, with the hope of their getting accepted by the reference class. According to Merton, "In the language of reference group theory, therefore, attitudes (and behaviour also) of conformity to the official more can be described as positive orientation to the forms of a non-membership group that is taken as frame of reference. Such conformity to norms of an out-group is thus equivalent to what is ordinarily called non-conformity, that is, non-conformity to the norms of social recognition". In the case of Indian society, particularly in the caste system, Marriott[49] deals with the "multiple reference levels" in the process of status mobility. He has called these levels as 'zones of reference' by arguing that a "local caste group may perceive itself as living and striving in at least three successively larger zones and each of which has its different ordering of categories". According to him, these three zones are (1) "the zone of the village community and its directly connected part of the country, i.e., '*caste ranks*', (2) the zone of recognised cultural or linguistic region in terms of '*whole endogamous castes*', and (3) the zone of the whole civilisation where '*varna categories*' plays the key role". At the theoretico-analytical level, Damle[50] also has argued that the caste system is peculiarly characterised and the inclusion into a caste (jati) other than some one's own (without birth in it) is normally not possible. Citing the process of reference group behaviour, he further states that it sets forth the prerequisites for positive orientation in an open system, "where ultimate inclusion in the non-membership group is possible and often anticipated. If the ultimate inclusion of a person in another caste (jati) is normally not possible by the very nature of the caste system, would then the positive orientation of the person to a caste be dysfunctional for his or her?" He further states, "the paradox of caste lies in the fact that, although lower-caste persons cannot expect to be included in a higher caste (jati), and also because higher caste persons need not fear their inclusion, positive orientation for reference and imitation is permitted and even encouraged. Anticipatory socialisation can thus occur and it has the effect of reducing distance and repulsion between castes even if it does not ensure ultimate absorption or inclusion".[51]

Referring to the varna model of reference group behaviour in the case of Jatavas (Scheduled Caste) of Agra City in the early decades of 20th century, Lynch has found that the Jatavas could not succeed in getting their claim of being Kshatriya accepted by caste Hindus, but "Through the influence of the Arya Samaj they have gained in education, social status and self-respect".[52] However, a point may mention here that in the case of both sanskitisationa and reference group behaviour, the types and amount of resistance of the sanskitiser or referred group/individual as well as the success or failure of emulator or the referring group/individual in reaching to the superior status has not been enquired into.

Without going into further explanations of the concept of process of sanskritisation or reference group/ individual behaviour, it may be pertinent to mention that sanskritisation, being a process of emulation of sanskritic values and life styles of twice-born castes by the lower castes, may substantially be explained in terms of taking vegetarian meals, performing Hindu rituals and ceremonies, worshiping Hindu gods and goddess, believing in Hindu religious sects and reciting Hindu religious texts or books. Since these had supposedly been practiced by people of twice-born castes in the traditional caste system, these were ranked in the high esteem and people of the lower castes are said to be emulating that to reach to the level of high caste and thereby achieving upward social mobility in the traditional caste system. Anyway, since both the processes of sanskritisation and reference group/individual behaviour have been found present, in some forms, in our studied locales, we shall briefly analyze the views of our respondents on their adaptation by and its success or failure among the Dalits in contributing to status formation among them in the village and the town.

We have, thus, found that a sizeable number of respondents of all the three Dalit castes in the village have been practicing Hindu rituals and ceremonies, worshipping Hindu god and goddess and believing in Hindu religious sects. More or less, the same number of respondents from the town has also been doing so. So also have been their views about Dalits in general both in the village and the town. It may, however, be mentioned that Dalits in the village and the town have been practicing this as a general way of life due to their being Hindus, and no case they have accepted these as exclusive ways of life of the upper castes and intended to emulate that in both the studied locales. Secondly, their intention has not been so even if we take into account the different levels of their education, occupational pursuit and income position (see Tables 5.4, 5.5 and 5.6 in Appendix-A). Thirdly, emulating sanskritic lifestyle of the upper caste needs the adequate resources, including knowledge, financial capacity, etc., besides the persistent intention and purpose for the same. More than that, such emulation needs to be approved by caste of those whose sanskritic life style is being emulated. On this count also, we have found majority of the Dalits in the village being unable and also not permitted by the upper castes for doing so. For example, the respondent Bhagirath Ram, a Chamar by caste, has narrated his own case by saying that he has been the priest in the Hindu temple, with a small idol of Hanuman, since 2003. The villagers had decided to install the idol of Hanuman in the Temple, but people of the upper castes opposed it and said that during the period of the Chamar priest (pujari), the *Pranpratishtha* (installation) of Hanuman Idol was not be done. They opposed it by saying that *Chchoti jati ke logo ko ye adhikar nahi hai kee vay puja path karayen* (persons of the lower castes do not have right to perform the puja). In other words, they were of the view that a Chamar, having the lowest status in the caste system, does not have right to perform such a *Shubh* (ominous) act. He is the priest of that temple even now. But on the weekly or monthly or annual celebration of the idol, the upper caste people do not accept *Prasad* from him. Anyway, after this incidence, they called a Brahmin priest and the installation of Hanuman Idol was performed by him. According to the same respondent, people of the upper caste constructed another Temple where a Brahmin is appointed as a priest, and now only people of the twice-born castes are allowed to worship it. It is, however, interesting to mention that the emulation of the so-called sanskritic style of life by a few Dalits enhances their social status among people of their own castes and not is taken note of by the non-Dalits. In fact, people of upper and middle level castes go on ridiculing such lifestyle of the Dalits on one occasion or the other. This means that emulation of sanskritic lifestyle by people of the lower castes needs necessarily to be supported by their better socio-economic position or status for the purpose of its wider acceptance.

Table 5.4: Caste-wise views of the Respondents on Emulation of Way of Life

Types of Emulation	Bara Govind Village			Chakia Town		
	Caste of Respondents					
	Chamar	**Dusadh**	**Musahar**	**Chamar**	**Dhobi**	**Dusadh**
Taking vegetarian meal	5	4	-	7	9	7
Performing Hindu Rituals and ceremonies	7	7	8	5	6	5
Worshipping Hindu god and goddess	5	5	9	4	5	5
Believing in Hindu Religious sects	7	6	6	5	6	4
Reciting Hindu religious books	1	-	-	-	-	-
None	17	16	22	21	21	17
Total	**42**	**38**	**45**	**42**	**47**	**38**

But such situation does not exist in the town where the Dalits largely do not intend to undergo the process of sanskritisation by making people of the upper castes as their reference model. In fact, they perform Hindu rituals and ceremonies, worship Hindu god and goddess, believe in Hindu religious sects and recite Hindu religious texts or books for their own satisfaction and mental peace instead of accepting that as an instrument of they are getting sanskritised. Over and above, it has been said repeatedly by our respondents of the town that practicing of sanskritic life style is their right as a Hindu, and the question of attaching such life style with upper castes and emulating or copying the same does not arise.

We have also mentioned above, in this section, that emulating reference group behaviour also contributes to formation or enhancement of social status of Dalits in both caste and class or socio-economic status hierarchies. In this regard, we shall briefly look at the views of the respondents on the same among the Dalits in both studied locales. At the theoretical level, the reference group behaviour simply implies copying behaviour patterns-life style, patterns of interaction and relations, etc. and attitudes (towards that of members of other class or classes as well as society as whole) of members of upper or superior class by those of inferior of the lower class. Incidentally, the theory of reference group has been formulated on the basis of empirical data from the western society where such process has worked smoothly. But in a society like India, the process may very often get hindered by members of referred group itself. Secondly, even if the emulator particularly of a lower caste background succeeds in socialising himself/herself in anticipation of getting accepted by the superior group or class not of the same but of higher caste, there is every livelihood that such reference group behviour would not only be discouraged, but also lead to confrontation and negation. Incidentally, we have found such situation almost being absent among the Dalits in our studied village, except in the case of our respondent Shankar Manjhi, a Musahar by caste, who has narrated that a man of the Bhumihar caste came to him to call for some work. The child of Manjhi did not stand from his chair. At that time, Manjhi was humiliated and abused by the Bhumihar who complained about his child by saying- *tum log apne larko ko nahi sikhate ho ki kaise byawhar karna chahiye, ab tum log hum logo ki barabri karne lage ho*.....(You do not teach your children how to behave with people of the upper caste; now, you people want to be equal to us). It may not be out of mention here that sitting on the chair or cot, living in hygienic condition, putting on clean cloths and, in a word, living a comfortable life is everybody right, provided one is able to afford either in a village or a town. Hence, the question of the emulating behaviour and attitude of any reference group does not rise, as has been expressed by majority of our respondents from both the studied village and the town.

Socio-Religious Movements and Status Formation

The religious reforms movement in India has also occurred, during various period, among some Scheduled Castes in different parts of India. Referring to these reform movements, Stephen Fuchs[53] discussed the role played by some enlightened individuals in particular areas like Guru Ghasi Das in Chhattisgarh (M.P. but now in a separate State), Yogi Virabrahma in Andhra Pradesh, Narayan Guru in Kerala and the movements led by Swami Achhutanand and Shiv Narayan in U.P., and Mangoo Ram in Punjab. More precisely, Ghasi Das led the movement among the Chamars towards the Satnam (the true name), Narayan Guru initiated the movement of Shri Narayan Dharam Paripalan among the Pulayas` and other lower castes in Kerala, and Shiv Narayan led the movement among the Chamars of eastern U.P. and Achhutanand led the movement for among the Chamars for their being Adi Hindu in Central and western UP. Besides, two movements of Kabir Panth and Raidas Panth have also been quite active among the Chamars of earntern UP and Bihar. Similarly, Mangoo Ram led the Adi Dharam Movement among the Chamars of Punjab. Anyway, these movements ultimately helped the Dalits and other low castes in imitating some and rebelling more against most of norms of higher castes, and also encouraged them to rebel against the disabilities they had suffered at the hands of the caste Hindus. More recently, the Dalits, especially living in urban areas in Bihar have inclined largely towards Dalit movement as well as the conversion to Buddhism led by Ambedkar. It is necessary to mention here that these movements certainly contributed to not only negating the social disabilities and degraded status of the Dalits, but also enhancing their social status, in some ways, and making them conscious and aware of that, besides negating their social disabilities and inferior social status in the traditional caste system at the local levels.

It is appropriate to mention here some of the recent movements organised and being carried out even in the contemporary period in different parts, especially in urban areas, in Bihar. The Dalits living in urban areas like Patna, Bodh Gaya, Bettiah, Motihari, Chakia, etc.

are followers of Buddhism, Ambedkar movement, Kabir Panth, Ravi Das Panth, Jai Gurudeo Panth, etc. Anirudh Prasad[54], in his study of Musahars in the Bodh Gaya region of Bihar has mentioned about the changing ways of life and thinking of the Musahars in the state. Due to active participation of two voluntary organisations, i.e., the Chhatra Yuva Sanghrash Vahini and the Samanwaya Ashram, Musahars of the region have recorded considerable change in their life style in the material culture and thinking through the liberation of mind. In other words, change has been taking place in their living habits, dress pattern and traditional values. Our respondents have also informed about the Dalits, across the castes, both in the village and the town believing in and practicing the teachings/preaching of Buddhism, Kabir panth and Jai Gurudeo Sect. This can be seen in the Table 5.5 given below.

Table 5.5: Caste-wise views of the Respondents on Dalits' believing in different Religious Sects or Panths

Caste of Respondents	Bara Govind Village				Chakia Town			
	Believing in Religious Sects or Panths							
	Hindu believes	Buddhism	Kabir Panth	Jai Gurudeo Sect	Hindu believes	Buddhism	Kabir Panth	Jai Gurudeo Sect
Chamar	28	5	5	4	5	15	10	12
Dhobi	-	-	-	-	7	17	9	14
Dusadh	25	5	5	3	9	7	11	9
Musahar	42	1	1	1	-	-	-	-
Total	**95**	**11**	**11**	**8**	**21**	**39**	**30**	**35**

Without going into details of views expressed by respondents from both the village and the town about some of these sects and panths and their impact on social life and the status of Dalits in recent year, it may be interesting to note the views of our respondents from the village and the Chakia town. Awadesh Ram, follower of the Jai Gurudeo sect, has stated that "he does not believe in any Hindu gods and goddesses. He does not perform even Hindu rituals. Those who follow this sect attend the weekly meeting where they put their opinion about their communities. In this sect, most of the people belong to lower strata who have been the victim of age-old problem of the Hindu social order. Through participating in these meetings, they demand equal rights and respect from people of the upper and middle level castes". On the other hand, Neeraj Ram (a Kabirpanthi), who is a teacher in the government primary school, has said that those belonging to this panth do not find any caste-based discrimination practiced by any other castes. According to him, people of the upper caste give respect to him and treat him equally in social interaction in the locality. Even then, the followers of the Kabirpanth conduct meetings where they condemn the rigid form of caste system and the heinous practice of untouchability. Most of the respondents, especially educated ones have stated that this Panth has really enhanced their social status in the social-hierarchy (see Table 5.7 in Appendix-A). In the town, most of the respondents employed in both the public and private sectors jobs and engaged in petty-business with somewhat better socio-economic position or status, as stated earlier, have found the Dalits in the town with their enhanced acceptance and respectability of their caste position among the people in the respective localities due to their believes in and practices of some of the stated sects and panths.

Even a few Dalits who have embraced the *Buddhism*, *Kabir Panth* or *Jai Gurudeo sect* in the town, claim their equal status to other caste people. They do not believe in the Hindu caste system which has provided the fixed occupations to each caste and accordingly the ascribed status of individuals of the different caste groups. In the hierarchy of the Hindu caste system, the caste status of the respondents is fixed at the bottom, but they do not believe in such a rank given to the Dalit communities. Most of the respondents have described that the evaluation of the caste status of Dalits in the locality is being made by people of the upper castes on the basis of their present achieved social position. Thus, the constellation of diverse statuses like social, economic, educational, power or authority play major role in formation of status of Dalits in the locality. These achieved statuses also provide them equal status in the hierarchy of commensality and social interaction with people of the different caste groups. As far as change in the caste status of the Dalit respondents is concerned, it is occurring on the basis of their individual attributes rather than the group attributes; wherein individual is included in the system, while their group still remains excluded by people of the upper and middle level castes.

Moreover, the psychic change has taken place among the respondents after getting higher level jobs and drawing inspirations from the Dalits icons like *Ambedkar*, *Phule*, *Periyar*, etc. Yet, they do not hesitate to demonstrate their identity as a Dalit. Nowadays, people of the upper and middle level castes do not disregard people of Dalit castes in their social relationship, as stated earlier, and they equally exchange respect to each other caste group. In the entire process, what we have found that the roles of the type of employment, level of education and the form and amount of political power or authority have definitely improved the social status of the respondents, especially in the town. At present, children of the Dusadhs do not face any sort of caste discrimination in availing of education and they are allowed to study in both government and private schools. Even the Dalits children get financial assistance like stipend or free books, as stated earlier, which motivate them for their study in the schools.

Similarly, some of the respondents from the Dhobi caste, believing in the *Kabir Panth* and *Jai Gurudeo* sect and also being *Ambedkarite,* do not believe in the traditional hierarchical social structure created by the Hindu belief system for the benefit and social hegemony of the upper castes. In their opinion, they consider themselves equal to people of all castes and communities and give due respect to each caste group by negating the notion of the upper and middle level castes.

Thus, various social reform movements, including both old and new ones, have contributed for making the Dalits conscious and aware of their low social status as well as a number of social and religious disabilities imposed on them in the traditional Hindi system. Interestingly, the people believe in Hindu religious and social system vis-à-vis they practice the caste system continued even today in the society and the present democratic political system has failed to eliminate that. Anyway, the Dalits believe in participation in the number of socio-religious movements have enabled them to bring about change both qualitative and quantitative changes in their thinking and activities in their day-to-day life. This, in turn, has also brought about some change in their traditional status and thereby formation of social status in present time.

Constitutional Provisions and Status Formation

Finally, we shall analyze views of the respondents on impact of the various constitutional provisions and measures on the change in status formation among the Dalits in general and of the studied locales in particular. But it is necessary to mention briefly about the specific provisions and measures adopted and implemented for the protection, welfare and development of the Dalits in the country. The Constitution of India is one of the most important instruments that guarantee equality of opportunity, social and economic justice, liberty of thought and expression, etc., within the framework of a sovereign state. It clearly declares building of a new society by putting aside the differences of caste, race, religion and sex. Thus, the Constitution of India provides special provisions for the Scheduled Castes or Dalits for bringing them at par with others. The protective Constitutional measures are to the removal of untouchability and the prevention of physical as well as socio-psychological atrocities or violence inflicted on them. Similarly, welfare and developmental provisions vis-à-vis measures are related to relaxation in admission and provision of freeship and stipend or scholarship in the educational sphere, employment in the public sector organisations and political representation at the State and the Centre levels. In fact, the genesis of these special provisions for the Dalits or Scheduled Castes (and also for the Scheduled Tribes) can be traced back to the Poona Pact of September 24, 1932, signed by Dr. Ambedkar and the representatives of Mahatma Gandhi. This Pact had insured the then 147 seats in the provincial legislatures (now State Assemblies) and 18 percent of the general electorate seats in the Central legislature (presently Lok Sabha) were to be reserved for the Scheduled Castes due to Dr. Ambedkar's efforts.

However, the number of seats for the Scheduled Castes (and also for the Scheduled Tribes) in both the Lok Sabha and the State Assemblies are reserved in participation in proportion to their population in the country and in the state. It was also with Dr. Ambedkar's efforts that the Indian Constitution today contains several provisions and measures to protect the weaker sections, especially for the Dalits or the Scheduled Castes (and Scheduled Tribes) from exploitation and discrimination, on one hand, and provides them special privileges for their speedy development to equality with the rest of the population, on the other hand. For instance, Article 46, contained in Parts IV entitled Directive Principles of State Policy provides educational facilities to the weaker sections, and Articles 14 and 15 provide them equality, with others, before law. Article 17 and the added Untouchability Offences Act of 1955 call for abolition of the practice of untouchability. More precisely, Article 17 of the Constitution states that untouchability is abolished and its practice in any form is forbidden. Similarly, Articles 330, 332, 334 and 335 contain special provisions for the Scheduled Castes' reservation in public sectors jobs and their reservation in both the Centre and State Legislatures, besides making the provision of a special officer to ensure the proper implementation of these provisions. A number of constitutional provisions and adopted measures relating to the protection, welfare and uplift or development of the Scheduled Castes, deal with-

1. The removal of any form of their disability and liability, restrictions or conditions with regard to access to shops, public restaurants, hotels and places of public entertainment, the use of well, tanks, bathing ghats, roads and places of public resort maintained wholly or partially out of the state funds or dedicated to the use of the general public.
2. The throwing open of Hindu religious institutions of a public character to all classes and sections of the Hindus.
3. The forbidding of any denial of admission to educational institutions maintained by the state or receiving aid out of state funds.
4. The setting up of advisory councils and separate departments in the States and the appointing of a Special Official at the Centre to review about their administration of various measures Schemes for welfare and safeguard of their interest.
5. Special representation of the Scheduled Castes in Parliament and the State legislatures, and
6. The obligation of the State to consider their claim or reservation in making of appointments to public services.

But due to their improper and inadequate level of implementation, these provisions and related measures have not yet produced the desired results in favour of the Scheduled Castes. Parvathamma,[55] for instance, gives some account of frustration prevalent among the Scheduled Castes in the post-independent India. She believes that the ban on untouchability remains, more or less, a legal fiction. She also points out a big gulf between the Scheduled Castes politicians, the educated ones and the common men. According to her, most of the educated Dalits get Government jobs and are alienated from their own people. Thus, economic betterment has brought about class consciousness among them, but has not helped to remove the stigma of untouchability at all. On the other hand, Duskin and Galanter[56] also have analyzed the role of state action in bringing about positive social change among the Scheduled Castes. In the opinion of Glanter, sources of the government policy of protective discrimination, especially in education, are producing a growing number of educated Scheduled Castes who are not economically dependent and who have greater political skill, consciousness and aspirations. They may, sooner or later, provide leadership to remedy the present miserable condition of the Dalits or Scheduled Castes. Thus, the role of socially and politically conscious Dalits in both rural and rural communities, religious reforms, government efforts to abolish untouchability, and social and psychological responses of the people in general may bring about change of status of the Scheduled Castes.[57]

In the light of the above context, it is, then, pertinent to analyze views of the respondents on impact of the constitutional provisions and measures on change in status of Dalits in the traditional social structure and thereby formation of new type of status or social status among them in both rural and urban areas. In this regards, we have found of our respondents from some changes occurred through the implementation of the Constitutional Provisions, especially in the town where Dalits are socially conscious and economically better off than the respondents of the village about their rights. These provisions have played positive role in enhancing social status of the Dalits not only in caste system but also in class structures. Changes in the village are very slow as is evident from the fact that the village respondents are still not allowed to fetch water from the well commonly used by the caste Hindus. They have remained deprived of social, economic and political benefits of the various constitutional provisions and measurements and schemes for decades, while the respondents from the town are by far better off. It has been observed that such provisions have also contributed positive role in enhancing awareness of the respondents about their social rights more in the town than that in the village. The respondents who are socially, economically and educationally better off have got affirmative response from people of the other castes about their social status and even they have improved social relationship with them.

Without going into further details, it is pertinent to analyze here views of our respondents on impact of constitutional provisions in terms of protection, welfare and development on change in traditional status as well as formation of social status among the Dalits in the studied locales. In the case of formation of status or social status among the Dalits, most of the respondents from the village have expressed their views that the Dalits in general have not been benefited from the welfare and development provisions and measures adopted and implemented by the government in the forms of relaxation in admission, freeship and stipend in the educational institutions and employment in private and public sectors organisations. This is due to mismanagement of the allocated funds as well as jealousy and prejudices of people of the upper and middle level castes, who are mostly associated with implementing the provisions and measures meant for welfare and development of the Dalits or Scheduled Castes. See Table 5.6 given below.

Table 5.6 Caste-wise views of the Respondents on impact of Constitutional Provisions on Status formation among Dalits

Caste of Respon-dents	Bara Govind Village				Chakia Town			
	Impact of Constitutional Provisions related to							
	Welfare & Development	Freedom of Expression	Atrocity Act	No impact	Welfare & Development	Freedom of Expression	Atrocity Act	No impact
Chamar	7	3	2	30	15	12	10	5
Dhobi	-	-	-	-	17	13	14	3
Dusadh	5	3	2	28	9	9	11	7
Musahar	4	-	-	41	-	-	-	-
Total	**16**	**6**	**4**	**99**	**41**	**34**	**35**	**15**

Similarly, most of the respondents have also expressed their anger against the various forms of atrocities and untouchability practiced against the Dalits in the rural areas. They have opined that due to their socio-economic vulnerability, the Dalits do not dare to resist or even express their views against inflictor(s) of untouchability and atrocities against them. The constitutional provisions adopted and implemented by the government for the welfare and enhancement of status or social status or protection of social rights of the Dalits, have not reached in the studied village. Thus, it may be said that only a few Dalits living in rural areas and the studied village in particular have got benefited from some and not all provisions and measures given in the Constitution.

It is expected that the Constitutional provisions and measures adopted and implemented in the favour of the Dalits or Scheduled Castes have produced more positive results in urban areas. In the case of the town under study, most of the respondents from the town who are educated and employed in public and private sectors organisations as well as in petty-business have stated that the constitutional provisions and measures, especially related to welfare and development, have played the exclusive role in improving the socio-economic status and thereby enhancing status formation of a sizeable number of the Dalits living there (see Table 5.7 given below). More specifically, this has happened due to their achieving education and getting employment in both public and private sectors organisations, compared to those living in the village. Similar are the views of the respondents employed in public and private sectors organisations and petty-business with their improved economic position in the town, on the impact of the constitutional provisions and measures on status formation among the

Table 5.7: Education-wise views of the Respondents on impact of Constitutional Provisions on Status formation among Dalits

Education of Respondents	Bara Govind Village				Chakia Town			
	Constitutional Provisions of							
	Welfare and Development	Freedom of Expression	Atrocity Act	None	Welfare and Development	Freedom of Expression	Atrocity Act	None
Illiterate	9	7	7	45	-	-	-	-
Primary School	4	3	-	12	-	-	-	-
Middle School	4	2	-	7	2	2	2	5
High School	3	4	-	11	7	11	7	13
Intermediate	1	1	2	1	3	9	12	7
Graduation	-	1	1	-	11	14	13	-
Post-Graduation	-	-	-		3	2	2	-
Total	**21**	**18**	**10**	**74**	**26**	**38**	**36**	**25**

Dalits (see Tables 5.8, 5.9 and 5.10 in Appendix-A). Here, the Dalit children get stipend, freeship and free books in the government schools without any social hindrance. As far as the social discrimination, untouchability or atrocity are concerned, some of the respondents from the town have stated that people belonging to all the three Dalit castes do not hesitate to protest against those people who practice such a social evil against the lower castes. This simply means that Dalits from the town are socially conscious and aware about their social rights due to their present status or socio-economic status and education. Thus, it may be said that the constitutional provisions and related measures have played a positive role in the formation of status or social status of the Dalits, especially in the town.

Conclusion

In sum, it may be said that there are some visible changes in the traditional social status of the Dalits or Scheduled Castes as well as in their social relations and interactions with people of the upper and middle level castes in both urban and rural areas due to adoptation and implementation of the constitutional provisions and measures in Bihar. Vidyarthi and Mishra[58] also have stated that the relationships of Dalits with people of the higher castes in Bihar are on the verge of change. In their opinion, the enforcement of the Indian Constitution and Untouchability Offences Act, along with the SC and ST (Prevention of Atrocities) Acts, are being responsible for such change. Nowadays, a person belonging to a higher caste may be seen eating in the house of a Chamar, or Rajwar or Dusadh or Musahar. Earlier, the Dalits were not allowed to use utensils and also eat in the house of a higher caste. But now, they use the same utensils in which a higher caste person eats. Children of the higher castes sit together with children of the Scheduled Castes in the same classroom. Thus, due to impact of the constitutional provisions and measures, industrialisation, and modern means of communication, etc., some changes have taken place in the Hindu caste system also. People of the upper castes are not as allergic today to the Scheduled Castes as they had been in the past, though there exist the antagonistic relations, of one type or the other, between them. People of the upper castes are slowly but gradually shielding their irrational and traditional prejudices and inhibitions towards the Scheduled Castes or the Dalits both in villages and towns.

Notes

1. Wolf, C. (1985). "Status" in Kuper, Adam and Jessica Kuper (eds), *The Social Science Encyclopedia,* Routledge and Kegan Paul, London, pp. 825-27.
2. Linton, Ralf (1936). *The Study of Man: An Introduction*, New York, Appleton-Century-Crofts.
3. Wolf, C. (1985). "Status" in Kuper, Adam and Jessica Kuper (eds.), *The Social Science Encyclopaedia,* Routledge and Kegan Paul, London, pp. 825-27.
4. *Ibid.,* 825.
5. Bendix, R. and Lipset, S.M. (eds.1966). *Class, Status and Power*, London Rout ledge and Kegan Paul, p. 24.
6. See, Beteille, Andre (1966). *Caste, Class and Power*, Oxford University Press, New Delhi, pp. 188-9.
7. Dumont, Louis (1988). *Homo Hierarchicus: The Caste System and its Implications*, Oxford University Press, Delhi, p. 66.
8. Saberwal, Satish (ed.1972). *Beyond the Village: Sociological Explorations*, Indian Institute of Advanced Study, Shimla, p. 114.
9. Srinivas, M.N. (1982). *Social Change in Modern India*, Orient Longman, New Delhi.
10. Ram, Nandu (1988). *The Mobile Scheduled Castes: Rise of a New Middle Class*, Hindustan Publishing Corporation, Delhi, p. 70.
11. Sahay, Gaurang Ranjan (1998). "Caste System in Contemporary Bihar: A Case Study of Selected villages", *Sociological Bulletin*, 47(2), September, p. 207.
12. Gupta, Shaibal (1994). "Caste, Class and Landholding in the Analysis of Technology and Agricultural Production in Bihar", in K.L. Sharma (ed.). *Caste and Class in India*, Rawat Publications, Jaipur and New Delhi, p. 84.
13 Dumont, Louis (1966). *Homo Hierarchicus: The Caste System and its Implications*, Oxford University Press, New Delhi. Dumont may be regarded as representative of this school.
14. Srinivas, M.N. (1980). *India: Social Structure*, Hindustan Publishing Corporation, New Delhi.
15. Linton, Ralf (1936). *The Study of Man: An Introduction*, New York, Appleton-Century-Crofts.
16. Representatives of this school are Marriott, MacKim (1959, 1968). "Multiple References in Indian Caste System", in James Silverberge (ed.). *Social Mobility in the Caste System in India*, Mouton, The Hague. Mandelbaum, David G. (1972). *Society in India: Continuity and Change*, Popular Bombay, and Barreman, Gerald D. (1971, 1979). *Caste and Other Inequities: Essays on Inequality*, Folklore Institute, New Delhi.

See, these statements cited in Nandu Ram (1988). *The Mobile Scheduled Castes: Rise of a New Middle Class*, Hindustan Publishing Corporation, Delhi, Pp. 78-79.

17. Marriott, MacKim (1959, 1968). "Multiple References in Indian Caste System", in Jemes Silverberge (ed.). *Social Mobility in the Caste System in India*, Mouton, The Hague.
18. See for details, Saberwal, Satish (ed.). (1972). *Beyond the Village: Sociological Explorations*, Indian Institute of Advanced Study, Shimla., Bhatt, Anil (1975). *Caste, Class and Politics*, Manohar Book Service, Ram, Nandu (1988). *The Mobile Scheduled Castes: Rise of a New Middle Class*, Hindustan Publishing Corporation, Delhi.
19. *Ibid.*, 22-23.
20. See in details, Dumont, Louis (1966). *Homo Hierarchicus: The Caste System and its Implications*, Oxford University Press, New Delhi. and Ram, Nandu (2008). *Caste System and Untouchability in South India*, Manak Publications, New Delhi.
21. Parvathamma, C. (2012). "The Weaker Sections of Society: The Scheduled Castes in India", in Abhijit Dasgupta (ed.) *On the Margins, Tribe, Caste and Other Social Categories*, Sage Publications, Vol. 4, New Delhi, p. 5.
22. Ram, Nandu (1995). *Beyond Ambedkar: Essays on Dalits in India*, Har-Anand Publications, New Delhi, pp. 206-207.
23. See in details, Vidyarthy, L.P. & N. Mishra (1977:73). *Harijan Today*, Classical Publications, New Delhi. Sachchidananda (1977:127). *The Harijan Elite*, Thomson Press Limited, India.
24. Saberwal, Satish (1976). *Mobile Men: Limits to Social Change in Urban Punjab,* Indian Institute of Advanced Study, Shimla, Manohar Publications, New Delhi, p. 29.
25. Beteille, Andre (1969). *Castes: Old and New*, Asia Publishing House, New York, p. 93.
26. Berreman, G.D. (1979). *Caste and Other Inequalities: Essays on Inequality,* Folklore Institute, Meerut, p. 148.
27. Ghurye, G.S. (1961). *Caste, Class and Occupation*, Popular Book, Bombay, pp. 1-5.
28. Natarajan, Balmurli. "From Jati to Samaj", in Caste Matters: A Symposium on inequality, identities and disintegrating hierarchies in India, *Seminar* 633, May 2012, p. 56.
29. Parvathamma, C. (2012). "The Weaker Sections of Society: The Scheduled Castes in India", in Abhijit Dasgupta (ed.) *On the Margins, Tribe, Caste and Other Social Categories*, Sage Publications, Vol. 4, New Delhi, p. 7.
30. Weber, Max (1961). *From Max Weber: Essays in Sociology*, Routlegde and Kegan Paul, London. (translated by H.B. Gerth and C.W. Mills).

31. Referred in Dahrendolf, Ralf (1959). *Class and Class Conflict in Industrial Society*, Berkeley.
32. See, Statements cited in Andre Beteille (1996). *Caste, Class and Power*, Oxford University Press, New Delhi, p. 189.
33. *Ibid.,* p. 7.
34. Cited in Bhatt, Anil (1975). *Caste, Class and Politics*, Manohar Book Service, New Delhi, p. 21.
35. Kumar, Vivek (2010). "Teaching Caste and the Hindu Social Order: Dalits in Indian Sociology", in *Sociology in India: Intellectual and Institutional Practices* (ed.) by Maitrayee Chaudhuri, Rawat Publications, New Delhi.
36. Kumar, Rabindra (2002). *Impact of Rural Development on Scheduled Castes*, Anmol Publications, New Delhi.
37. Beteille, Andre (1966). *Caste, Class and Power*, Oxford University Press, New Delhi.
38. Singh, Shrawan Kumar. "Social Scenario of Scheduled Castes in Bihar", *Third World Concept*, April-June, 2011, p. 24.
39. *Ibid.,* p. 127.
40. Isaacs, Horald R. (1998). "The Ex-Untouchables", in *The Untouchables in Contemporary India* (ed.) by J. Michael Mahar, Rawat Publications, New Delhi, p. 378.
41. Teltumbde, Anand (2003). "Globalisation and Education for the Dalits: A Perspective for the Future", in *Globalisation and Social Movements: Struggle for a Humane Society*, (eds.) Jogdand. P.G. & S.M. Michael, Rawat Publications, New Delhi, p. 153.
42. Kothari, Rajni (1994). "Rise of the Dalits and the Renewed Debate on Caste", *Economic and Political Weekly*, Vol.XXIX, Issue 26, p. 1589.
43. Kumar, Vivek (2008). "Changing Trajectory of Dalits Assertion in Uttar Pradesh", in Nandu Ram (ed.) *Dalits in Contemporary India*, Vol. 1, Manak Publication, New Delhi.
44. *Ibid.,* 274.
45 Srinivas, M.N. (1980). *India: Social Structure*, Hindustan Publishing Corporation, New Delhi.
46. Prasad, N. (1970). *Change Strategy in a Development Society*, Meenakshi Prakashan, Meerut, p. 135.
47. Gaurang R. Sahay (2004). "Hierarchy, difference and the Caste System: A Study of Rural Bihar", *Contributions to Indian Sociology*, Vol. 38, p. 121.
48. Merton, R.K. (1968). *Social Theory and Social Structure*, American Publishers.
49. Marriott, McKim (1968). "Multiple Reference In Indian Caste System", in James Silverberg (ed.) *Social Mobility in the Caste System in India*, Mouton, the Hague, Paris, pp. 108-9.

50. Damle, Y.B. (1968). "Reference Group Theory, With regard to Mobility in Caste " in James Silverberg (ed.) *Social Mobility in the Caste System in India*, Mouton, The Hague, Paris, p. 98.

51. *Ibid.,* 98.

52. Lynch, Owen M. (1974). *The Politics of Untouchability*, National Publishing House, New Delhi.

53. Fuchs, Stephen (1965). *Rebellious Prophets*, Asian Publishing House, Bombay.

54. Prasad, Anirudh (1988). "Changing Life ways and Thought ways of Musahars in Bodh Gaya", in *Tradition and Development*, (eds.) by Sachchidananda, B.B. Mandal, K.K. Verma & R.P. Sinha, Concept Publishing Company, p. 134.

55. Parvathamma, C. (1968). The Case for Untouchables, *United Asia* 20, pp. 279-86.

56. Cited in Sachchidananda (1977). *The Harijan Elite*, Thomson Press (Limited) India, pp. 9-10.

57. Mahar, Mihael, J.M. (ed.1972). *The Untouchables in Contemporary India*, The University of Arizona Press, Tucson.

58. Vidyarthi, L.P. & N. Mishra (1977). *The Harijan Today*, Classical Publications, New Delhi, pp. 209-210.

Chapter - 6

Social Exclusion and Status Formation

Introduction

We have already discussed, in the previous Chapter, about the ascribed and achieved statuses among the Dalits in general and our respondents in particular in both rural and urban areas. We have also examined their relationship in terms of whether it is congruent or incongruent, and if incongruent, then how and what to extent their low ascribed (caste) status has facilitated or hindered their achieved status. We have, finally, enquired into the reverse process wherein the way and to the extent their achieved status has contributed to any enhancement in the lowest level of attributes vis-à-vis prestige in the society, especially in the caste system. In the same vein, we shall try to examine, in the present Chapter, the way in which the perennial exclusion of the Dalits, resulting into their low ascribed status in the traditional form of caste system is contributed or has attributed to their low status or position in the class or socio-economic status system or hierarchy. Finally, we shall analyze views of the respondents on how the perennial social exclusion of the Dalits from their deserving statuses or positions has affected positively, or otherwise, the formation of social status among them.

Social Exclusion and the Dalits

We have already discussed, in Chapters 1, and 4, about the conceptual explanations of social exclusion. However, before looking into the impact of social exclusion of Dalits in details, it is imperative to discuss briefly about the nature and forms vis-à-vis spheres or domains of the term social exclusion. In social science literature, there is general agreement on the core features of social exclusion and its principal indicators, which are related to poverty and inequality. De Haan[1], for instance, has explained social exclusion in terms of denial of equal opportunities by certain groups of people to others in a society, as already stated in Chapters 1 and 4. This leads to their inability to participate in the basic social, civil, political, economic and cultural functioning of the society in which they live. For Amartya Sen[2], social exclusion is a relational root of deprivation. He further distinguishes the constitutive relevance of exclusion (exclusion or deprivation is of intrinsic importance in its own rights) from its instrumental importance (exclusion itself is not impoverishing, but it can lead to the impoverishment of human life). He also differentiates between unfavourable exclusion and unfavourable inclusion, and active and passive exclusion, as mentioned in Chapter 1. On the other hand, Silver[3] focuses on three paradigms, i.e., solidarity, specialisation and monopoly of social exclusion where each paradigm has a different notion of social integration, explaining social exclusion to a different cause and is based on different form of monopoly.

In India, exclusion is embedded in the societal inter-relations and institutions or institutional arrangements that exclude, discriminate, isolate and deprive some groups of people on the basis of the groups' identities such as caste and ethnicity. The nature of exclusion or social exclusion, revolving around the caste system, needs to be understood and conceptualised. The caste system deals with fundamental characteristics of fixed civil or social, cultural and economic rights for each caste, with restrictions for one caste from undertaking the occupations of other castes.[4] The exclusion and discrimination in civil, cultural, political and economic- such as occupation and labour employment- spheres is, therefore, internal to the system and a necessary outcome of its governing principles. "In the market economy framework, the occupational immobility would operate through restrictions in various markets such as land, labour, credit, other inputs and services necessary for any economic activity. Labour being an integral part of the production process of any economic activity would obviously become a part of market discrimination".[5]

Thus, exclusion or social exclusion in India "…. is partly rooted in economic disability, the religiously-sanctioned segregation and ordering of occupations, with the lowest castes associated with the most stigmatised occupations. In addition, caste embodies various forms of symbolic devaluation which serve to define the lowest caste as despised category or having no caste at all and to legitimise various forms of injustice, including physical harm towards them".[6] Not only that, but contact of any kind through touching, having sexual relations, dining, drinking water from the same well or utensil and so on between institutionally-distanced castes would result in the higher of the two castes being polluted. Along with spatial segregation of residence with untouchable confined to the margins of village through which other villagers will not have to pass through, fears of pollution also regulate any form of physical interaction between the castes[7].

It is, then, pertinent to have a brief at the impact of exclusion or social exclusion on status formation among the Dalits in the village and the town. The people belonging to the Dalit castes in villages face not only multiple deprivations, but also remain the victim of cumulative domination. However, there are two crucial aspects of accomplishing the task of bringing about change among the Dalits. The first task is to recognize a hierarchy in the structure of deprivations, as perceived by Dalits. Second is the signal importance of the Dalits' participation in bringing about change or development among them.[8] But as far as the town is concerned, people of the Dalit castes do not face the similar form of physical segregation where they live in. They reside in the same street or locality where other caste people live in. Yet, they suffer from exclusion in many spheres to the other spheres of life, which we would like to examine below.

Caste-based Ascribed Status and Social Exclusion

We shall analyze briefly here the respondents' views on how the social exclusion is embedded in the caste-based low ascribed status of the Dalits in both the rural and urban areas. In other words, whether they are of the views that as the Dalits have ever been remained excluded from their access to social relations and interaction, and civil cultural or religious, economic and political spheres of life, they have been assigned or ascribed to low caste status or other way round?

Or, whether their low caste-based ascribed status and their exclusion from their access to various avenues of life go hand in hand? But before going into details of that, it is necessary to look at what Ambedkar[9] stated about caste. According to him, "caste in India means an artificial Chopping off of the population in fixed and definite units, each one prevented from fusing into another through the customs and endogamy", as stated in chapter 4. Caste as the system of ascriptive status also prescribes "a variety of distance creating gestures and expressions which is invested with socially derived meanings and values for the participation".[10] Further, "the system of caste happens to be a system of graded inequality (Ambedkar, 1979) wherein each caste is ranked higher or lower with unequal ranked status and with cumulative social and ritual inequality with the other. The inclusion mechanism was operative in the vertical and not horizontal fashion".[11] Further, Meillassoux[12] describes that caste in such a hierarchical arrangement "was (still) one weapon in the repressive ideological arsenal used in one direction only, arbitrary and opportunistically as a means of discrimination, oppression, and exploitation".

On the other hand, Dumont[13] has accepted the term status in religious sense, as stated in the previous Chapter. For him, status is the caste rank in the caste hierarchy where superiority of the pure to the impure underlies separation because the pure and the impure must be kept separate, and underlies where the division of labour because pure and impure occupations must likewise be kept separate. However, in view of the variety of changes occurred in the notion of pure and impure and in the occupational division of labour, that endogamy is the only characteristic that is peculiar to caste. In India, the caste system entirely constitutes a status-hierarchy, with Brahmin at the top and the Scheduled Castes or Dalits at the bottom. For Dumont, the basis of caste system in India is the principle of ritual purity and pollution. On account of their low ritual status and inferior occupations, often involving manual work and resulting in the low socio-economic status, the Scheduled Castes were ever deprived of or excluded from all social interaction and relations with people of the upper castes, as mentioned earlier.[14]

Keeping the above mentioned perspective or framework in mind, we would look at the views of our respondents on impact of exclusion or social exclusion on status formation of the Dalits in both the village and the town, with the caste-based ascribed status and the class or socio-economic status based achieved status existing side by side. As stated in the previous Chapters, caste system plays a very crucial role in determining social status as well as social relationships among people of different sections both in rural and urban areas. We have also mentioned that most of the respondents from the village reside in the respective *tolas* or *bastis,* which are socially and spatially segregated from the main village. In the tolas or bastis known by their caste names, caste factor plays the unique role in determining the socio-economic as well as cultural life of the people living there. It also decides the socio-personal relationship of the people on the basis of their caste and class or socio-economic status-position in the community or society or locality where they live in. Caste in the Bara Govind village is known in terms of *Uchcha Jati* (high caste) or *Neech Jati* (low caste), according to its status or rank in the hierarchy of castes mentioned in the Hindu religious texts, and each caste group is separated and maintains social segregation from other caste groups on the grounds of purity and pollution, commensality, marital relations, occupation, wealth and social power. The physical isolation exists between people of the upper castes and lower castes and also in the context of their settlement- people of the upper castes residing in the centre of the village, whereas the Dalits being located at the periphery or outside the village. Berreman[15] rightly states that, "caste system is abstract: a caste system occurs where a society is made-up of birth-ascribed groups which are hierarchically ordered and culturally distinct. The hierarchy entails differentially evaluation, rewards and association". In this context, the traditional caste system is one of the most underlying institutions of social exclusion of Dalits with ascribtive characteristics. It determines their social, economic, political and cultural or religious-ritual statuses as well. In the studied village, caste is the main basis of social exclusion of the Dalits and on the basis of their caste status their social interaction occurs with member of the different caste groups in the locality. The views of the respondents on the degree of exclusion or social exclusion of the Dalits and the degree or level of status formation among them in both the village and the town are presented in Table 6.1 given below.

Table 6.1: Caste-wise views of the Respondents on Exclusion and Status Formation among Dalits in Caste System

Caste of Respon-dents	Bara Govind Village						Chakia Town					
	Degree of Exclusion and Status Formation											
	Exclusion			Status Formation			Exclusion			Status Formation		
	Mst	Les	Lst	Hgh	Mddle	Lw	Mst	Les	Lst	Hgh	Mddle	Lw
Chamar	33	7	2	2	7	33	7	11	24	24	11	7
Dhobi	-	-	-	-	-	-	7	4	36	36	4	7
Dusadh	27	5	6	6	5	27	5	5	26	26	5	5
Musahar	43	2	-	-	2	43	-	-	-	-	-	-
Total	**103**	**14**	**8**	**8**	**14**	**103**	**19**	**20**	**86**	**86**	**20**	**19**

We have already mentioned, in Chapter 5, that the high, middle and low social status of the Dalits is non-comparable with that of people of the upper and middle level castes in the village and the town. It is also non-comparable of the Dalits of the town due to the obvious reasons. As is, however, clear from the above table, the respondents have viewed about the different degrees of social exclusion as well as different degrees or levels of status formation among Dalits in the village and the town. They have also opined that all the castes, i.e., *Chamar*, *Dhobi*, *Dusadh* and *Musahar* from the village and the town are, in one way or the other, socially excluded from their social rights, and their status formation is also slow in the caste-hierarchy found there. In fact, Musahars are the most excluded group and the pace of their status formation is also very low, whereas the Chamars and Dusadhs are less or least excluded and their status formation is comparatively faster in terms of discrimination, untouchability, social relations, commensality and interaction with others in the village. Most of the respondents have expressed their views that because of their low ascribed identity or caste status, the Dalits are socio-economically, culturally and politically deprived and discriminated by people of the upper and middle level castes in the village. In this sense, the caste-based exclusion of and discrimination practiced against the Dalits continues to be one of the main reasons for low as well as slow status formation among the Dalits even after achieving some changes within it. In fact, majority of the respondents, being socially excluded to the maximum level or degree and having the low social status with the slowest pace of its formation have expressed their views about the maximum level of social exclusion of the Dalits from their participation in all the existing spheres of life and the low level of formation of their social status in the village society.

In this context, it has already been observed that the Dalits in the village are socially and economically deprived of their rights and due to their low caste background or identity; they are facing different forms of discrimination. Their relationship with the upper castes has not only been discriminatory, but also humiliating. It is in this sense that the people belonging to the upper and middle level castes do not accept cooked food and water from the hands of the Dalits. They also do not have commensality or inter-relationship with them, as already mentioned in Chapter 4. This certainly reflects the degree of their social exclusion as well as formation, with slow pace, of their social status with the caste system practiced in the village.

On the other hand, the nature and degree of social exclusion as well as status formation among the Dalits in the town is somewhat different. But before going into details of that, it is pertinent to have a brief look at caste system and change taken place within it in the town. The respondents are of the view that the Dalits living in the town do not face more rigid form of caste discrimination than those in the village. Most of them have also improved their social relations with people of the different caste groups, after improving their socio-economic status. Now, a sizeable number of Dalits get a considerable amount of honour or respect from people of the upper castes. At present, they have perceived certain changes in their caste status in terms of commensality or inter-dining, and social interaction and social relations with the different castes people in their locality. For instance, their present socio-economic, educational and political status, which forms their social status, has brought about substantial positive change in their social status. In views of many respondents', a sizable number of Dalits in the town have achieved such status or social status through the benefit of protective discrimination policy as well as changes in the attitudes and behaviour of people of the upper castes. This can be seen from the above Table.

More specially, the respondents are of the views that the degree or level of status formation among the Dalits in the town as well as degree of their exclusion from its somewhat relaxed caste system are analogous to their being more socially conscious and aware about their rights than those in the village. Yet, according to them, the Chamars are most socially excluded in the town and degree of their status formation is also 'low', compared to those of the Dusadhs and the Dhobis. On the other hand, Dhobis are relatively better off than the other Dalit castes not only in terms of their exclusion, but also in the degree or level of their status formation. But despite all the social hurdles, a majority of the Dalits, according to the respondents, has improved their social status in the caste-system through the improvement in their socio-economic status.

Sharma and Pimpley[16] have mentioned about three strategies for improvement of social status of the Scheduled Castes. First, improvement of their status through the legal abolition of the stigma of Untouchability; the second strategy for improvement of their status is through job reservation, and the third is the spread of education among them. In the case of our study also, most of the respondents have stated that with the improvement in the socio-economic status of the Dalits due to benefits of protective discrimination policy, their social relationship with people of the upper and middle level castes has also improved in terms of their sitting together, commensality or inter-dining, etc., as stated earlier. Now, they do not experience the worst form of social segregation, discrimination, humiliation or any form of disregard in the town on the basis of their low caste background or identity as the Dalits in the village face. In fact, the relationship between people of the upper and middle level castes and the Dalits in the town has changed to the extent of eating cooked food together, inviting each other in social gatherings and ceremonies, etc. But all goes along the educational level, employment and income positions of the Dalits in the town and the village (see Tables 6.1, 6.2 and 6.3 in Appendix-A).

Class (Socio-economic status) Status and Exclusion

We shall discuss here the views of the respondents about the social exclusion of and status formation among the Dalits in the class-based status system or hierarchy found in both the studied village and town. As already mentioned in Chapter 2, both Marx and Weber have explained the term class differently. For instance, Marx[17] has viewed class in the economic sense, whereas Weber[18] has explained it in terms of human behaviour and attitudes, beliefs, values, etc. For the purpose of present analysis, we have put both the views together. In rural areas, land is the main source of livelihood of the people. Agriculture is the basic economic activity where people from the upper and middle level castes hold almost entire land and majority of the Dalits are landless agricultural labourers and are totally dependent on their labour for their survival as well as of their family members, as already mentioned in Chapter 4. Subrahmanyam[19] has rightly said that, "landownership is clearly the single most important determinant of power in the jajmani system". Anyway, the landless and other social occupational groups forcefully depend on the traditional landowning communities for their livelihood. Barik[20] also states that the zamindars, under the laws of permanent settlement, succeeded in utilising the caste system for exploiting the tenants of the lower-castes. Kunnath[21] has analyzed the Dalits' subordination in the colonial and post-colonial Bihar by stating that in the *Zamindari System* of land rights, the upper castes landlords established an enduring dominance which led to the main factor of the Dalit exploitation and marginalisation in Bihar. Even today, a few landowing zamindars of the upper castes control the destiny of the Dalits or Scheduled Castes agricultural labourers in the village. The Dalits are socially and geographically segregated from others, and their roles and statuses in the village society are decided for them by others. In most of the villages, the life of a Dalit is reduced to total dependent on the landlords, as stated above. Also, in many cases, the semi-bonded agricultural labourer is the only source of livelihood of the Dalits, So also, their political life is often reduced to the status of being vote-banks for those who control their life.[22]

Anyway, without going into details of the sorry state of affairs about Dalits in rural Bihar or elsewhere in the country, it is necessary to analyze here the views of our respondents on the social exclusion of and status formation among the Dalits in the class or socio-economic status-based hierarchy found in both the village and the town under the study.

Table 6.2: Caste-wise views of the Respondents on Social Exclusion and Status Formation among Dalits in Class (Socio-Economic Status) Structure

Caste of Respondents	Bara Govind Village						Chakia Town					
	Degree of Exclusion and Status Formation											
	Exclusion			Status Formation			Exclusion			Status Formation		
	Mst	Les	Lst	Hgh	Mddle	Lw	Mst	Les	Lst	Hgh	Mddle	Lw
Chamar	25	10	7	7	10	25	9	11	22	22	11	9
Dhobi	-	-	-	-	-	-	6	13	28	28	13	6
Dusadh	23	9	6	6	9	23	7	13	16	16	13	7
Musahar	39	6	-	-	6	39	-	-	-	-	-	-
Total	87	25	13	13	25	87	22	37	66	66	37	22

Table 6.2 clearly shows views of the respondents on status formation among the Dalits in terms of its being low, middle and high as well as degree of their social exclusion being less, least and most in the class or socio-economic status hierarchy found separately in the village and the town. In the village, the Musahars are socially and economically most excluded and the formation of their social status in the socio-economic status hierarchy is low, compared to that of the Chamars and Dusadhs, as stated earlier. This is so in spite of the fact that they do not follow any traditional occupation and most of them are landless agricultural labourers. On the other hand, the Chamars are relatively less excluded from their access to the economic opportunity and the formation of their social status is also high, whereas the Dusadhs are economically least excluded and the socio-economic status formation among them is high in the village. But a majority of the respondents are of the view that the overall socio-economic status formation among the Dalits in the class or socio-economic status hierarchy is low. This may be so as their economic relations with people of upper castes is of the '*Malik*' (upper caste landlord) and '*Praja*' or Naukar[23], as stated earlier. Thus, in the class or socio-economic status hierarchy in the village, the upper castes control the maximum land in the village, whereas the Dalits are landless agricultural labourers and are totally deprived of economic facilities since decades. Due to the landownership, people of the upper and a few middle level castes not only control the economic activities, but also dominate social, educational and political domains in the

village. Although untouchability has been abolished by law, the Dalits or Scheduled Castes still suffer from the inferiority complex and social disabilities imposed on them by the upper and middle level castes people in the village. The rigidity of caste system is glaring in the rural areas of Bihar, including the village under study, where practically no social change has taken place. The society is still basically feudal and exploitative, and the phenomena of bonded labour, atrocities on weaker communities, social segregation, and orthodox practices are still prevalent. With such scenario found in the studied village, a majority of the Dalits with low social status are remained excluded from their free participation in all domains in the village.

Contrary to this, the socio-economic status of the Dalits in the Chakia town, according to the respondents, is far better than the respondents who are living in the village. It is interesting to mention that quite a few Dalits, like our respondents, are educated and employed as primary school teachers, clerks and fourth-grade employees in Government and semi-Government offices, employees in private sector organisations, and are businessmen. Due to their jobs and thereby better and regular income position (see Tables 6.4 and 6.5 in Appendix-A), they have achieved somewhat better socio-economic status in the class or socio-economic status hierarchy in the town. Ram[24] has also stated that the socio-economic position of the Dalits is relatively better in urban areas, where they are free from the traditional bondage, though their majority is employed even there in the menial and semi-skilled jobs in the unorganised sector. In the case of the Chakia town, we also have found a somewhat similar situation where the Dalits, belonging to the different Dalit castes, are 'free' from the traditional prejudices and have improved their socio-economic status in both caste and class or socio-economic status hierarchies through their personal attributes, although having low degree or level of status in the caste structure. At present, they do not face any rigid form of traditional caste prejudices of people of the upper and middle level castes, according to the majority of the respondents. They are also free to interact with member (s) of any caste group where they find that the notion of superiority and inferiority between them has been minimized.

Table 6.3: Employment-wise views of the Respondents on Social Exclusion and Status Formation among Dalits in Class (Socio-Economic Status) Structure

Employment of Respondents	Bara Govind Village						Chakia Town					
	Degree of Exclusion and Status Formation											
	Exclusion			Status Formation			Exclusion			Status Formation		
	Mst	Les	Lst	Hgh	Mddle	Lw	Mst	Les	Lst	Hgh	Mddle	Lw
Traditional	6	-	-	-	-	6	-	-	-	-	-	-
Agri-Labourer	90	6	-	-	6	90	-	-	-	-	-	-
Non-agriculture labourer	5	2	-	-	2	5	4	-	-	-	4	5
Govt. Jobs	-	3	-	-	3	-	-	22	25	25	22	-
Private Jobs	-	4	-	-	4	-	5	9	10	10	9	5
Petty-Business	-	-	-	-	-	-	3	6	10	10	6	3
Other Occupations	9	-	-	-	-	9	15	8	8	8	8	15
Total	**110**	**15**	**-**		**15**	**110**	**27**	**45**	**53**	**53**	**45**	**27**

Regarding social exclusion of and status formation among the Dalits in the class or socially and economic status hierarchy in the town, we have found that the Chamars are socio-economically most excluded and their status formation is also low, compared to that of the Dusadhs and Dhobis, according to our respondents. In fact, the Dusadhs are less excluded from their access to the available socio-economic opportunities and the degree or level of their status formation is higher than that of the Chamars. On the other hand, the Dhobis are socially and economically in better position than the Chamars and Dusadhs, and, so also, their status formation is higher in the town as shown in the above Table. It is also clear, from the above table, that quite a few Dalits have improved their social status in both caste and class hierarchies after achieving socio-economic status, as opined by the respondents. Presently, a majority of them do not perceive any sort of discrimination in their day-to-day life, and their social relationship with members of the different castes groups is also improved after independence. Most of the respondents have stated that many people of the upper and middle level castes, visit the homes of their acquaintance, including their own, and take meals together on the certain occasions of ceremonies; they also invite them at their homes on occasions of celebration of a few festivals. Thus, with their improved socio-economic status, many Dalits have achieved change in their social status as well as in their relationship with people of the upper and middle level castes in the town, stated above. In this context, Mishra[25] also has stated that today the situation has change where Dalits are free to lead a respectable life. They are free to educate themselves, to make journey to sit with anyone in public, to eat with anyone in public hotels, to contest elections and to select occupations of their own choice. These developments have definitely brought changes in the status of Dalits in the town. It is true that those Dalits whose social, educational and economic status is similar to that of people of the upper and middle level castes do not perceive any caste discrimination as well as in their class or socio-economic relations in the town. But a large majority of those Dalits who have not achieved the expected level of change in their social status, they experience incongruity in their achieved and ascribed status, as discussed in the following section.

Relationship between Ascribed and Achieved Statuses: Congruity and Incongruity of Statuses

We have stated earlier in this Chapter as well as in the previous Chapter, about the relationship between the ascribed status (the status or rank of caste in the caste-hierarchy) and the achieved status (one a person achieves or acquires on the basis of personal attributes and making use of that). Here, we may briefly look at the views of the respondents on the relationship between ascribed and achieved statuses of the Dalits in terms of how their given status (caste status) influences or affects the achieved one (class status) and gets manifested in the local and wider contexts in Indian society. However, a point may be reiterated that an ascribed caste status plays a very substantial role in determining a person's social status and if he/she belongs to a low caste in the caste hierarchy, he/she not only carries his/her low caste status, but also does not receive due honour or respect in accordance with achieved position or status by him/her in the society, as stated earlier in the Chapter 5.

Before going into analyzing the status congruity and incongruity among the Dalits, it is necessary to have a brief look at the concepts of status congruity and incongruity and also to see how it is similar to or different from the concepts of status consistency and inconsistency. Referring to Homans' theory of status congruence[26], Ram[27] has stated that "if there are persons who have their status factors (variety of work, office responsibility, pay, seniority and work autonomy) in an organisation 'in line', they claim their status congruity and those whose status factors are 'out of line', do not. In Homans' terminology, in-lineness may be a condition of relative and distributive justice for such individuals, whereas 'out-lineness' may lead to status anxiety". Similarly, explaining the concepts of status consistency and inconsistency Lenski[28] has stated that "Persons with a low degree of status crystallisation are more likely to be subjected to disturbing experiences in the interaction process and have greater difficulty in establishing rewarding patterns of social interaction than others. In this sense, persons whose status is poorly crystallised constitute a social category peculiarly vulnerable to rebuffs, embarrassments and disappointments".

In view of the above, we shall analyze views of the respondents on status congruity and incongruity and by extension the status consistency and inconsistency among the Dalits in both the village and the town under study. According to our respondents, the ascribed status of the Dalits is not getting changed due to the fact that it is fixed in the caste system. With the lowest ascribed status in the caste hierarchy, the Dalits, according to the respondents, of the village have the lower and in many cases even the lowest status in the class or socio-economic status hierarchy in the village. So also, they are deprived of their rights of access to social, cultural, educational, economic and political opportunities. Most of the respondents from the Bara Govind village have stated that the Dalits are unequally behaved by people of the upper and middle level castes due to their low birth-ascribed status. Even then, a few Dalits in the village have been able to improve their socio-economic status and thereby forming their social status, which is not generally appreciated by people of the upper and middle level castes. Not only that but they have been facing multiple social hurdles like deprivation from opportunities, oppression and exploitation during the work, untouchability in social relations, social isolation and socio-economic disparity, less social interaction by people of the upper and middle level castes in the village. That is why there is a contradiction between ascribed and achieved statuses as Parvathamma[29] has also stated by describing that "the conflict between the achieved status and ascribed status or between class and caste cannot be easily resolved in the case of Scheduled castes. What the scheduled castes desire is an honourable social position to the entire lot, no matter what kind of intention contradictions persist among themselves. The social hierarchy and gradation have always figured in public relation in the Indian context. So mere abolition of untouchability practices and making the observance a cognizable offence, involving the legal practices has made the situation more and complicated". In many cases, there exist status congruity and incongruity between the ascribed and achieved statuses of the Dalits under the studied village.

Gerald Berreman has rightly stated that "Indian caste system has been customarily described as system of stratification-unusually rigid, birth-ascribed, and permitting of no individual mobility, but nevertheless examples of ranked aggregate of people".[30] He has mentioned further that membership in castes is determined by birth means that an individual is assigned his lifelong and unalterable status according to his parentage-a status which he shares with others of similar birth who are therefore assigned to the same group (caste). A common means of guaranteeing this status is by prescribing endogamous marriage in the caste, and assigning to the child the caste affiliation, of its parents. But this method is by no means universal even in India, for caste, like kin-groups affiliation can be assigned unilineally or according to other, more complex, rules based on birth.[31] Taking about upward social mobility of a person in the caste system, he has stated that "mobility striving in a caste system, while intrinsic, is constant threat to the *status quo*. As a consequence, it is suppressed whenever possible, but the process of suppression is difficult and never completely effective. Caste systems are always in disequilibrium, like pots of water on fire, always threatening to boil over. They are characterised not by consensus but by conformity. They are maintained not by agreement but sanctions. When change occurs it is quickly rationalised in order to maintain the system and the myth of its stability. That social order prevails most of the time does not mean that those comprise the system willingly accept their position within it any more than it means that it is static".[32]

Regarding relationship between ascribed and achieved statuses of the Dalits in the town, we have found that caste still plays an important role in terms of social interaction and social relations, commensality or inter-dinning, etc. with people of the different caste but it is not in as rigid form as it found to be in the village. Most of the respondents have accepted that they as well as other Dalits do not face any form of caste discrimination, untouchability, etc. by people of the other castes on the basis of their ascribed caste status. Instead, they have improved, at present, their social relations with people of the upper and middle level castes due to their improved socio-economic and educational status, as stated earlier. Although, the ascribed status or rank of their castes remains static or stagnant but some changes have occurred in their social status in the dynamic form of each system found in the town. Here, people of the other castes and community accept cooked food and water in the houses of Dalits and the latter are also invited by them on the ceremonial occasions and festivals, as already stated in and this previous Chapters. Now, they sit together, take tea at the same stall or eat with anybody in the public hotel, make journey with anybody and educate their children in both public and private schools. They are also allowed to enter the Hindu temples and worship the deity. They are free to do their business transaction with people of other castes and communities without any social hurdle. Such change has occurred among the Dalits in the town due to their achieved status in the class or socio-economic status hierarchy as well as benefits of the protective discrimination policy provided in the Indian Constitution. We have also mentioned, in the previous Chapter, that a certain level of social consciousness and awareness, a number of socio-religious movements, etc. have contributed, in the positive ways, to enhancing their social status in the town.

Thus, it may be said that, in the comparison to Dalits from the village, the Dalits from the town have achieved changes in both their caste and class-based statuses. A point may, however, be mentioned here that we have accepted the term social status as the one achieved in the class or socio-economic status hierarchy. Thus, social status of quite a few numbers of Dalits in the caste-hierarchy is 'high', compared to their low status in the caste hierarchy due to their personal achievement. Thus, having low caste-status in the hierarchy, they have perceived upward mobility in their both types of statuses, i.e., ascribed and achieved ones. On the basis of their social status, they have received a considerable amount of respect from people of the upper castes. In this context, it may be mentioned that their caste as well as class statuses are playing the substantial roles in formation of their social status where ascribed status is constant while the achieved one is changeable and, in this way, their ascribed status influences their achieved status in their day-to-day life in the social hierarchy. Therefore, both the caste and class statuses contribute to in the formation of a new type of social status, i.e., active assertive status among the Dalits. This simply means that the people of lower castes or Dalits are continuously demanding equal social status and equal self-respect with people of the other castes in the hierarchy of the caste system. They are also demanding their equal participation in the socio-economic, educational, political and cultural spheres where people of the higher castes have held their grips for decades. Even they also want to change their given status, i.e., ascribed one through availing the benefits of the Constitutional Provisions related to social economic and educational progress and that of the power political power and authority. Yet, they are evaluated even now as one with low status by people of the upper and middle level castes in the society. In this context, a point may be mentioned here that the Dalits, with achieved status, have been termed by social anthropologists[33] have been termed as neo-Brahmans or Elite, or a new middle class. But their number is, of course, very small and the huge majority of the Dalits living in both the rural and urban remains with low social status in both the caste and class or socio-economic status hierarchy. In this regards, we may look into the issues of whether an achieved status of the Dalits in the class or socio-economic status hierarchy affects the status in the caste hierarchy or not. Whether there is congruence or incongruence between the two?

Then, looking at the views of the respondents we find that the majority of them have opined about the incongruent status of the large number of Dalits in the village due to the fact that both the ascribed and achieved statuses are low. Contrary to that, a sizeable number of the respondents have found the status incongruence of quite a few Dalits living in the town. This can be seen from the Table 6.4 given below. More specifically, majority (87.2%) of the respondents from the village are of the views that the Dalits suffer from the status of incongruity due to their caste status in the caste-hierarchy and consequently low status in the incongruity in the class or socio-economic status hierarchy as well. In this context, it may be said that the caste system is one of the key instruments which determine the incongruity of status of the Dalits, compared to that of the other castes in the caste hierarchy. This is, more or less, similar to what many sociologists and social anthropologist have found in their studies of different locales. In our study also, it has been observed that a majority of the respondents have opined that the Dalits, with even little change in their status, experience the status incongruity in terms of their social interaction, inter-dining and sitting together with people of the upper and middle level castes in the village. They also face segregation, discrimination and untouchability in their day-to-day life due to their caste background or low caste status or rank assigned to their caste in the caste hierarchy. It is in this sense; caste plays the decisive role in the inclusion as well as the exclusion of the individual in the caste hierarchy in Indian society.

Table 6.4: Caste-wise views of the Respondents on changing status of Dalits in the Hindu caste system

Caste of Respondents	Bara Govind Village			Chakia Town		
	Types of Status					
	No respect due to caste back-ground	Respect due to caste back-ground	Equal respect in caste hierarchy	No respect due to caste back-ground	Respect due to caste back-ground	Equal respect in caste hierarchy
Chamar	35(28)	7(5.6)	-	9(7.2)	21(16.8)	12(9.6)
Dhobi	-	-	-	8(6.4)	23(18.4)	16(12.8)
Dusadh	32(25.6)	6(4.8)	-	8(6.4)	15(12)	13(10.4)
Musahar	42(33.6)	3(2.4)	-	-	-	-
Total	**109(87.2)**	**16(12.8)**	-	**25(20)**	**59(47.2)**	**41(32.8)**

Contrary to this, it has been observed that most of the respondents from the town have opined that quite a few Dalits, including respondents themselves, have enhanced their status in both the caste and class (socio-economic status) and subsequently the caste hierarchies through improving their socio-economic status as well as the social interaction and relations with and acceptance from people of the upper and middle level castes. In other words, 80 percent of the respondents have found Dalits not experiencing incongruity in their statuses in the caste as well as class hierarchies, in spite of their caste status in the caste-hierarchy. Thus, their status congruity is seen in terms of amount of honour or prestige received from people of the upper and middle level castes. Apart from that, only few respondents have viewed the Dalits suffering from the status incongruity due to their low case status in the caste-hierarchy.

This simply means that most of the Dalits in the town are relatively better off in terms of their socio-economic status, educational level and employment position than those from village. They are also socially conscious about their rights where they seek equal social status not only in the class or (socio-economic status) but also in the caste hierarchy. Caste system in the town is not as rigid and discriminatory against the Dalits in the terms of commensality, social interaction, sitting together temple entry, etc. as compared to that in the village. So also, most of the Dalits in the town have improved their social relations with people of the upper and middle level castes by choosing modern or secular occupations based on their education and other achieved attributes. With such status, the Dalits have achieved status congruence in both the caste and class hierarchies, as stated above. This is also to be seen in the light of the fact in the recent time with the benefits of the Constitutional policy of protective discrimination and related measures, Dalits have succeeded in improving their educational, economic, political and cultural positions or statuses congruent with others in the hierarchical domains.

Consequences of Formation of Social Status

Even those who have achieved changes in their both ascribed as well as achieved statuses, they become separated from people of their own castes and try to mingle with members of the upper strata. But they neither go up nor down. For such situation, Issacs[34] has mentioned that "the educated ex-untouchables pull up and away from the sodden bleakness of their past estate, they do not quite get *nowhere*, but neither do they reach *somewhere*. They are people who want to become different from what they were and what their fathers were. They want to leave all that behind, to forget it, to blot it out, but they come into a situation where too little is changing too slowly; a society still govern by caste does not allow them to abandon their past, to forget it, to blot it all out, become in the state of "Semi-limbo". Needless to say that quite a few Dalits in urban areas in general and our studied town in particular are in the state of semi-limbo, though they get in a former way, the maximum possible honour and respect from the people of their own caste whenever they visit them.

Conclusion

We have analyzed, in this Chapter 6, the views of our respondents about the impact of social exclusion on status formation among the Dalits of both the village and the town under the study. In this regards, we have examined how caste system plays the substantial role in assigning the social status to the Dalits in the village. Due to their caste-based status or identity, most of the respondents have opined that the Dalits are evaluated low by people of the upper and middle level castes even after their achieving relatively high status or position in the class or socio-economic status hierarchy and, thus, their social exclusion on their low caste ascribed status. In this sense, their caste-based status is constant or stagnant in the Hindu caste system despite their having a little change in their commensality or social interaction with people of the other castes. Those Dalits who have achieved changes in their both caste and class-based statuses have improved their social status and with their relations people of the other castes because of their achieved attributes, especially in the town.

Notes

1. De Haan, Arjan (1997). Poverty and Social Exclusion: A Comparison Debate on Deprivation, Poverty Research Unit, Working Paper No. 2, University of Sussex, Brighton.
2 Sen, Amartya (2004). Social Exclusion: Concept, Application and Scrutiny, *Critical Quest*, New Delhi.
3. Silver, Hilary (1995). "Reconceptualizing Social Disadvantage: Three Paradigms of Social Exclusion" in *Social Exclusion: Rhetoric, Reality, Responses* (eds.) by Rodgers, Gerry, and et. al., International Institute of Labour Studies, United Nations Development Programme, Geneva.
4 Ambedkar, B.R (1989). *Away from the Hindu*, Writings and Speeches, Vol.5, Government of Maharashtra, Bombay.
5. Thorat, S. & Newman, S. Katherine (2007). "Caste and Economic Discrimination: Causes, Consequences and Remedies", *Economic and Political Weekly*, October 13, p. 4122.
6. Kabeer, Naila (2008). Social Exclusion, Poverty and Discrimination towards an Analytical Framework, *Critical Quest*, New Delhi, p. 23.

7. Kabeer, Naila (2008). "Social Exclusion, Poverty and Discrimination towards an Analytical Framework", *Critical Quest*, New Delhi.
8. Oommen, T.K. (1984). Sources of Deprivation and Styles of Protest: The Case of the Dalits in India, *Contributions to Indian Sociology* (n.s.) 18, 1, p. 59.
9. Cited in Rodrigues, Valerian (ed.) (2002). *The Essential Writings of B.R Ambedkar*, Oxford University Press, New Delhi, p. 245.
10. Statements cited in Sachchidananda(1977). *The Harijan Elite,* Thomson Press (India) Limited, p. 38.
11. Ram, Nandu (2008). *Caste System and Untouchability in South India*, Manak Publication, New Delhi, p. 10.
12. Meillassoux, C. (2001). "Are There Castes in India", referred in "Caste and Agrarian Class: A View from Bihar", by Anand Chakravarti, *Economic and Political Weekly*, Vol. 36, No. 17, April-May, p. 1451.
13. Dumont, Louis (1966). *Homo Hierarchicus: The Caste System and its Implications*, Oxford University Press, New Delhi, p. 43.
14. Pathak, Sumanlata (1985). "Self -images of Scheduled Castes, Girl students of Chandigarh" in *Struggle for Status* edited by Sharma, S.K & P.N. Pimpley B.R. Publishing Corporation, New Delhi, p. 218.
15. Berreman, Gerald. D. (1979). *Caste and Other Inequalities*, Folklore Institute, Meerut, p. 73.
16. Sharma, S.K. & P. N. Pimpley (1985). *Struggle for Status*, B.R. Publishing Corporation, New Delhi, pp. 2-3.
17. Darendolf, Ralf (1959). *Class and Class Conflict in Industrial Society*, Berkeley, p. 3.
18. Weber, Max (1969). "Class, Status and Party", in C.G. Helles (ed.) *Structural Social Inequality: Readers in Comparative Stratification*, New York, p. 25.
19. Subramanyam, V. (2010). "Context Social Exclusion and Inclusion of Weaker Sections", in Subramanyam, V. & K. Sekhar (eds.). *Social Exclusions, Integration and Inclusive Policy*, Rawat Publications, New Delhi, pp. 22-23.
20. Barik, R.K. (2006). *Land and Caste Politics in Bihar*, Shipra Publication, New Delhi, p. 16.
21. Kunnath, Geaorge J. (2012). *Rebels from the Mud Houses: Dalits and the Making of the Maoist Revolution in Bihar*, Social Science Press, p. 19.
22. Kananaikil, Jose (1983). "Marginalisation of Scheduled Castes: A Sociological Interpretation", in *Schedules Castes and the Struggle against Inequality* (ed.) by Kananaikil, Jose, Indian Social Institute, New Delhi, p. 62.

23. Kumar, Rabindra (2002). *Impact of Rural Development on Scheduled Castes*, Anmol Publications, New Delhi, p. 47.
24. Ram, Nandu (1995). *Beyond Ambedkar: Essays on Dalits in India*, Har-Anand Publications, New Delhi, p. 33.
25. Mishra, N. (2004). *Exploitation and Atrocities on the Dalits in India*, Kalpaz Publications, New Delhi, p. 350.
26. Homans, G.C. (1962). *Sentiments and Activities: Essays in Social Science*, Routledge and Kegan Paul, London.
27. Ram, Nandu (1988). *The Mobile Scheduled Castes: Rise of a New Middle Class,* Hindustan Publishing Corporation, New Delhi.
28. Lenski, Gerhard (1956). "Social Participation and Status Crystallisation", *American Sociological Review,* Vol. 21, No. 4, pp. 458-464.
29. Parvathamma, C. (2012). "The Weaker Sections of Society: The Scheduled Castes in India", in Abhijit Dasgupta (ed.) *On the Margins, Tribe, Caste and Other Social Categories*, Sage Publications, Vol. 4, New Delhi, p. 14.
30. Berreman, Gerald D. (1979). *Caste and Other Inequalities: Essays on Inequality*, Folklore Institute, Meerut, p. 72.
31. *Ibid.,* p. 74.
32. *Ibid.,* p. 89.
33. For instance, see, Saberwal, Satish (ed.), (1972). *Beyond the Village: Sociological Explorations*, Indian Institute of Advanced Study, Shimla. Ram, Nandu (1988). *The Mobile Scheduled Castes: Rise of a New Middle Class,* Hindustan Publishing Corporation, New Delhi, pp. 13-14. And, Barreman, Gerald D. (1971, 1979). *Caste and Other Inequities: Essays on Inequality*, Folklore Institute, New Delhi.
34. Issacs, Horald R. (1998). "The Ex-Untouchables", in *The Untouchables in Contemporary India,* (ed.) by Mahar, Michael. J., Rawat Publications, New Delhi, p. 396.

Chapter - 7

Summary and Conclusion

Historically, the Scheduled Castes or Dalits have been the most excluded caste or communities of the society in India. They have been the most discriminated, exploited, subordinated and physically segregated communities in India in general and Bihar in particular. So also, they have remained socio-economically, educationally, politically and culturally most backward, compared to the people of other castes and communities. They have also been the stigmatized people and suffering from numerous disabilities due to their low ascribed status, i.e., caste status which has remained regulated through the religious beliefs and practices. The majority of them also have low socio-economic status, lack of political power, low literacy and educational level and social mobility.

In this concluding chapter, an attempt has been made to give a brief summary of findings of the analysis of data made in the preceding chapters. The first chapter is introducing the theme or subject matter studied in the thesis has elaborately been stated. In brief, the statement of the problem, research questions, universe of the study, selection of study areas and sample size, sources and methods of collection and analysis of data have been included in the chapter. Finally, the review of literature related to theme of the study and chapterisation have been elucidated in this Chapter.

The second chapter, the conceptual and theoretical framework of social exclusion as well as status and its formation have been spelt out. We have discussed, in this Chapter, about the genesis of the term social exclusion in the mid-1970s and its adaptation in the academic discourses in many developed and developing countries. The concept of social exclusion, being a global phenomenon, affects adversely individuals, groups and communities. Being accepted as a multi-dimensional concept in social sciences, social exclusion basically explains the institutionalised attempt to keep a few segments of population away from their participation in the various aspects of life in a given society. Apart from that, we have also analyzed, in details the concept of status and its types, ascribed and achieved statuses. In Indian context, we have included the notion of hierarchy to look into how the Hindu social system is hierarchically arranged where one caste is put at the top, while another are is at the bottom due to their ritual status or rank of caste.

The third chapter three elucidates the research setting of the study in which the socio-political geography, socio-demographic profile, social structure, socio-political and administrative structure of Bihar have been discussed. Besides describing briefly about including the agrarian structure in Bihar and the profile of East Champaran district. The Chapter elaborately unfolds the socio-economic and political features of the studied locales- the Bara Govind village and the Chakia Town. This has followed the maping of the socio-personal background of the respondents drawn from both the studied locales. We have found that while the respondents from the village are socio-economically, educationally, politically and culturally the most backward and thereby excluded one, the respondents from the town are relatively better off in all the above mentioned spheres due to their being free from the traditional cleavages and getting employed in the non-traditional jobs in both public and private sectors, petty-business and other menial works.

We have discussed, in details, the discrimination vis-à-vis deprivation, exploitation and exclusion of Dalits in India in general and in the studied village and the town in particular in Chapter four. In this chapter, we have analyzed that how Dalits have historically been excluded in the Hindu caste system because of their low caste background or ascribed criteria. Not only that but we have also mentioned that the exclusion or social exclusion is an inherent part of the organisational or arrangement of the structures (caste and sub-castes) of the Hindu caste system in which numerous structures or castes are in the hierarchy and these are separated through endogamy, commensality, etc.[1]

It is true that such a policy or social organisational arrangement of exclusion of the Dalits or Scheduled Castes is deeply rooted in the Hindu social structure as well as its social system where caste as an institution plays a decisive role. On the basis of their caste background, the Dalits face even today many social hurdles like discrimination, exploitation, untouchability, etc., in the society. In the state of Bihar, nearly two dozen Scheduled Castes or Dalits castes are treated as *Neech jati* (lower castes) by those who considered themselves as *Uchcha jati* (upper castes) in the hierarchy of castes. People of the higher castes do not have regular social interaction or relationship with people of the *Neech jati* (low caste includes Chamars, Dusadhs, Musahars, etc). Caste as a status of a person in the village plays the key role in deciding his/her social interaction or relationship with another person of a lower or higher caste. We have found, in this Chapter, that the Dalits with their low caste status, are completely segregated, discriminated, exploited in the village. They are unequally treated by people of the upper and middle level castes in their day-to-day interaction. This simply means that they are socially, culturally, economically and politically excluded by the upper and middle castes people in the studied locales.

But in the case of the town, most of the Dalits are socially, economically, educationally in better position and because of their such position or status they do not experience any form of caste discrimination. Caste in the town does not play the rigid form of discrimination as it is in the village, and a majority of the respondents have viewed of the Dalits perceived positive changes in their social relations with people of the upper and middle level castes. They do not find any discriminatory and humiliating attitudes and behaviour of people of the upper and middle level castes their social interaction and relations in the locality. In the case of commensal relationship, people of the upper castes do not hesitate in taking food whether it is *kachcha* or *pucca* or (cooked) food in the house of a Dalit friend. Even the higher caste people invite Dalits in their socio-cultural or religious celebrations. They are served meals with people of the higher castes in the same *pandal* or eating place.

The status formation among the Dalits in general and the Dalits of the Bara *Govind* village and *Chakia* town in particular have been analyzed, in details, in Chapter 5. The chapter primarily incorporates, in it, the detailed analysis of data on the hierarchy of caste system and social status achieved in both the caste hierarchy and class or socio-economic status hierarchy. The status formation among the Dalits through the constitutional provisions and emulation of some reference models, etc. it is a fact that caste still dominates the social system in Indian society, especially among the Hindus, despite the roles of other secular institutions such as education, economy, polity, etc. Castes operate not only in rural but also in urban areas as is evident from a number of studies.

Therefore, a person's caste status in the caste system is taken into account while measuring his social status. There are two schools of thought regarding determination of a person's status in the caste system. According to one school, caste is an institution with a systemic form and a person's status is based on his birth in a particular caste (*Jati*) which has a definite rank in the caste hierarchy. This is his 'ascribed status' with which he is born and dies. According to the second school, caste system is a dynamic one, and while being member of a caste one is subjected to a variety of changes, especially in urban areas. A person's status (also his/her caste rank) is determined on the basis of a number of attributes acquired by him and the interaction between him and others. Such interaction is also guided by a person's socio-economic status and power position. There are also other criteria for status determination of a person and these are ritual purity and pollution, caste calling, etc., which themselves is subjected to change and have undergone variety of changes in modern time. Thus, on the basis of change in the patterns of social interaction and relations with others, a person's status in the caste system is also 'achieved' and remains changeable. In this sense, a person's status is his position which is accorded to or 'achieved' by him in the caste system, while rank of his caste is an order assigned to it in the caste hierarchy. In other words, the status is attributed to an individual, while rank is assigned to a caste as a corporate group. Status is changeable, while rank is almost fixed.

The caste hierarchy in the Bara Govind village clearly appears in terms of 'high' and 'low' where the upper (Brahmins and Bhumihars) and middle level caste, (Yadav), etc. at the top are enjoying the highest social status and the Dalits (Chamar, Dusadh and Musahar) placed at the bottom are treated as low. Most of the respondents have accepted that the purity and pollution is observed by people of the upper and even middle level castes against the Dalits in the village. In fact, Dalits in the village are socially isolated and economically deprived because of their low caste status. The physical isolation of the Dalits is very much observed by the upper and middle level castes in the village, besides the social distance perceived and practiced by them. Due to this, most of the Dalits in the village are socially and economically handicapped and are totally dependent on their labour for their survival. In this way, Dalits face systematic exclusion in the village due to their ascribed status.

On the other hand, a sizeable number of Dalits in the town are, at present, socially, economically and educationally better off. Most of the respondents from the town have expressed their views that such Dalits have experienced change in their class or socio-economic status through their secular roles. Now, they do not experience the rigid form of caste discrimination, although they have low status in the caste system existing in the town. Yet, they have achieved change in their both caste and class statuses. On the basis of their achieved status, they have positive or non-discriminatory social interaction and relations with people other caste groups and enjoy the considerable amount of respect from them. This has been possible due to impact on them of a number of movements such as Ambedkar movement, *Kabir Panth,* and *Jai Gurudeo,* the process of *Sanskritisation* and of the *Constitutional provisions* of the protective discrimination policy, and prohibition of Untouchability Act, etc. These have played the positive role in elevating their social status in the caste as well as class hierarchies in the town. Thus, the Constitution of India is one of the most important instruments that guarantee equality of opportunity, social and economic justice, liberty of thought and expression within the framework of a sovereign and democratic republic. It clearly declares building of society by putting aside the differences of caste, race, religion and sex. In this way, the constitution of India provides special privileges to the Scheduled Castes or Dalits. Because of these provisions and measures, most of the respondents have achieved changes in their social status, especially in urban areas. Besides, a number of caste associations like Valmiki Ashram, Kabir Ashram, Dusadh Mahasabha, Ravidas Mahasabha, etc. formed by the Dalits have also played important role arousing their consciousness and thereby claiming higher social status in the town. Some of these have provided them the knowledge of Sanskritic symbols like vegetarian food, taboo on beef eating, refusal to take up such tasks as are ritually degrading, use of the sacred thread, etc.

In the sixth and the last chapter, we have enquired into the impact of social exclusion on status formation among the Dalits in both the village and town. In this chapter, we have tried to analyze how social exclusion is deeply embedded in the societal interrelations and institutions that exclude, discriminate, isolate and deprive some groups or caste on the basis of the group or identity. Thus, this Chapter has analyzed the nature of exclusion or social exclusion and status formation revolving around the caste status and class or socio-economic status. The caste system deals with fundamental characteristics of fixed civil, cultural and economic rights for each caste, with restrictions for other castes or from undertaking the occupations of other castes.[2] The exclusion from and discrimination in the civil, cultural, economic and political spheres is, therefore, internal to the caste system. Not only that, but it also influences the formation of status of the people even in the class or socio-economic status hierarchy.

Within such perspectives or framework, we have tried to examine, in this Chapter, the impact of social exclusion of the Dalits on their status formation in both the studied village and the town. The ascribed caste status of the Dalits is not getting changed due to it fixed status or rank in the existing caste system. Being the lowest ascribed status in the caste hierarchy, the Dalits of the village, as perceived by the respondents have lower status in the class or socio-economic status hierarchy also. With thier lowest status, they are socially, culturally, educationally, economically and politically deprived of their civil rights. Most of the respondents from the Bara Govind village have accepted that the Dalits are also unequally behaved with by people of the upper and middle level castes due to their low birth-ascribed status. Even majority among them do not have commensality or inter-dining relations with them. Therefore, the status formation of the Dalits in the village is 'low' and even slow in the both caste and class hierarchies.

Due to this, most of them face multiple social hurdles like deprivation from access to available opportunities, oppression and exploitation during the work, untouchability in social relations, social isolation and less social interaction with people of the upper and middle level castes in the village. Even they do not receive the minimum humanly honour or respect from them in their day-to-day social life.

Similarly, caste in the Chakia town in too plays an important role in terms of social relations, commensality or inter-dinning and social interaction, etc. with people of the different caste groups, but it is not in the rigid form as it happens to be in the village. Most of the respondents have accepted that they and other Dalits, similar social status or position do not face any form of caste discrimination, untouchability, etc. on the basis of their low caste ascribed status from people of the other castes and communities. They have presently improved their social relations with people of the upper and middle level castes due to their present better socio-economic and educational position or status, as stated earlier in this as well as earlier Chapters. Although their ascribed caste status does not change but some changes have been occurred in it in terms of commensality or inter-dinning, sitting together and social interaction and relations with people of castes. As stated earlier, people of the other castes do not accept cooked food and water in the houses of their Dalits friends. They sit together take tea at the same tea stall or eat with anybody in the public hotel and educate their children in both the public and private schools. They are allowed to freely enter the Hindu temple and worship. They are also free to do their business without any social hurdle, especially in the town. This simply means that with the improved in class or socio-economic status of the Dalits, there is considerable degree of improvement in their caste status, although the status or rank of their caste remains the same in the caste-hierarchy as it exists in the town. This also means that the impact of their social exclusion, due to low status or rank of their caste in the caste hierarchy, has loosened its grip over status formation among a sizable number of the Dalits in the town. Finally, we have tried, in the Chapter 6, to find out the nature and degree of status congruence and incongruence of the Dalits in the village and the town. Going by G.C. Homans theoretical framework or status congruence and incongruence, we have attempted to enquire into the status of the Dalits achieved in the class or socio-economic status hierarchy is in line or outline of their achieved status in the caste hierarchy. Thus, on the basis of our data we have found, in the caste of some Dalits, the status congruity and incongruity in many other cases, especially in the town. In the village, there is congruity between the ascribed low caste status and low class status, though a little improvement in class status of a few Dalits in the village is not taken into congruence by people of the upper and middle level castes.

In sum, both caste and class statuses of the Dalits do contribute in the formation of a new type of social status i.e., Active Assertive Status among the Dalits. By active assertive status is meant that the Dalits continuously demand for equal social status and equal self-respect in the hierarchy of the caste system. They also demand equal participation in the socio-economic, educational, political and cultural spheres where people of the higher and middle level castes have been holding their grips for decades. They want to even change their given ascribed status one through the benefits of the Constitutional Provisions and their own socio-political consciousness and awareness of them and others in the society.

N otes

1. Ambedkar, B.R. (1979). "Castes in India: Their Mechanism, Genesis and Development" (first published in 1917), in *Dr. Babasaheb Ambedkar: Writings and Speeches,* Vol. 1, Government of Maharashtra, Bombay. Ram, Nandu (2008). *Caste System and Untouchability in South India*, Manak Publications, New Delhi.
2. Ambedkar, B.R. (1989). *Away from the Hindu*, Writings and Speeches, Vol. 5, Government of Maharashtra, Bombay.

Bibliography

Books

Abrams, Dominic, M.A. Hogg, and J.M. Marques, (eds.) (2005). *The Social Psychology of Inclusion and Exclusion*, Psychological Press, New York.

Ambedkar, B.R. (1979). "Castes in India: Their Mechanism, Genesis and Development" (first published in 1917), in *Dr. Babasaheb Ambedkar: Writings and Speeches,* Vol. 1, Government of Maharashtra, Bombay.

Ambedkar, B.R. (1989). *Away from the Hindu, Writings and Speeches*, Vol.5, Government of Maharashtra, Bombay.

Bailey, F.G. (1958). *Caste and Economic Frontier,* Oxford University Press, Bombay.

Barik, R.K. (2006). *Land and Caste Politics in Bihar*, Shipra Publication, New Delhi.

Bendix, R. and S.M. Lipset (eds.) (1966). *Class, Status and Power*, Routledge and Kegan Paul, London.

Benjamin, Joseph (1989). *Scheduled Caste in Indian Politics and Society*, ESS ESS Publications, New Delhi.

Berreman, Gerald D. (1979). *Caste and Other Inequities: Essays on Inequality*, Folklore Institute, New Delhi.

Beteille, Andre (1966). *Caste, Class and Power*, Oxford University Press, New Delhi.

…………(1969). *Castes: Old and New*, Asia Publishing House, New York.

Bhatt, Anil (1975). *Caste, Class and Politics*, Manohar Book Service.

Bottomore, T.B. (1962). *Sociology: A Guide to Problems and Literature*, Blackie & Son, India.

Bougle, C. (1971). *Essays on the Caste System,* Translated and with an Introduction by D.F. Pocock, Cambridge University Press.

Byrne, David (2005). *Social Exclusion*, Rawat Publications, Jaipur and New Delhi.

Cohn, Bernard S. (1955). "The Changing Status of a Depressed Caste", in *Village India* (ed.) by McKim Marriott, Asia Publishing House, Bombay.

Dahrendolf, Ralf (1959). *Class and Class Conflict in Industrial Society*, Berkeley.

Damle, Y.B. "Reference Group Theory and the Mobility in the Caste System", in James, Silverberg (ed.1968). *Social Mobility in the Caste System in India*, Mouton, The Hague, Parish.

Das, Arvind, N. (1992). *The Republic of Bihar*, Penguin Books, New Delhi.

David, Kinsley (1949). *Human Society*, The Macmillan Company, New York.

De Haan, Arjan (1997). "Poverty and Social Exclusion: A Comparison of Debates on Deprivation", Working Paper No. 2, Poverty Unit, Sussex University, Brighton.

De Haan, Arjan (2008). *Social exclusion: Two Essays*, Critical Quest, New Delhi.

Diwakar, R.R. (1959). *Bihar Through the Ages,* Orient Longman, New Delhi.

Dumont, Louis (1988). *Homo Hierarchicus: The Caste System and its Implications*, Oxford University Press, New Delhi.

Evans, Martin, Serge Paugam, and Joseph S. Prelis, (1995). "Chunnel Vision: Poverty, Social exclusion and the Debate on Social Welfare in France and Britain", London School of Economics, Welfare State Programmme, Discussion Paper WSP 115.

Fuchs, Stephen (1965). *Rebellious Prophets*, Asian Publishing House, Bombay.

Ghurye, G.S. (1961). *Caste, Class and Occupation*, Popular Book, Bombay.

Gore, Charles, Jose B. Figueiredo, & Garry Rodgers, (1995). "Introduction: Market, Citizenship and Social Exclusion", in *Social Exclusion: Rhetoric, Reality, Responses*, (eds.) by Rodgers, G. C. Gore, and Jose B. Figueiredo, International Institute for Labour Studies, Geneva.

Gupta, Shaibal (1994). "Caste, Class and Landholding in the Analysis of Technology and Agricultural Production in Bihar", in K.L. Sharma (ed.), *Caste and Class in India*, Rawat Publications, Jaipur and New Delhi.

Harcourt, Max (1977). "Kisan Population and Revolution in Rural India", in D.V. Low, (ed.), *Congress and the Raj,* South Asia Books, Colombia.

Homans, G. C. (1961). *Social Behavior*, New York, Harcourt.

……………… (1962). *Sentiments and Activities: Essays in Social Science*, Routledge and Kegan Paul, London.

Horton, Paul B. and Chester Hunt (1964). *Sociology*, The McGraw-Hill Companies, New York.

Isaacs, Harold R. (1965). *India's Ex-Untouchables*, Asian Publishing House, Bombay.

……………….. (1998). "The Ex-Untouchables", in *The Untouchables in Contemporary India* (ed.) by J. Michael Mahar, Rawat Publications, New Delhi.

Jannuzi, Tomasson F. (1974). *Agrarian Crisis in India: The Case of Bihar*, University of Taxes Press, California.

Johnson, Harry M. (1960). *Sociology: A Systematic Introduction*, Allied Publisher, New Delhi.

Kabeer, Naila (2008). "Social Exclusion, Poverty and Discrimination towards an Analytical Framework", *Critical Quest*, New Delhi.

Kamble, N.D. (1982). *The Scheduled Castes*, Ashish Publishing House, New Delhi.

Kananaikil, Jose (1983). "Marginalisation of Scheduled Castes: A Sociological Interpretation", in *Schedules Castes and the Struggle against Inequality* (ed.). by Kananaikil, Jose, Indian Social Institute, New Delhi.

Kothari, Rajni (ed.) (1970). *Caste in Indian Politics*, Orient Longman, New Delhi.

Kumar, Rabindra (2002). *Impact of Rural Development on Scheduled Castes*, Anmol Publications, New Delhi.

Kumar, Raj (ed.) (2003). *History and Culture Series: Essays on Dalits*, Discovery Publishing House, New Delhi.

Kumar, Vivek (2002). *Dalit Leadership in India*, Kalpaz Publications, New Delhi.

.... (2008). "Changing Trajectory of Dalits Assertion in Uttar Pradesh", in Nandu Ram (ed.) *Dalits in Contemporary India*, Vol. 1, Manak Publication, New Delhi.

...................(2010). "Teaching Caste and the Hindu Social Order: Dalits in Indian Sociology", in *Sociology in India: Intellectual and Institutional Practices* (ed.). by Maitrayee Chaudhuri, Rawat Publications, New Delhi.

Kunnath, George J. (2012). *Rebels from the Mud Houses: Dalits and the Making of the Maoist Revolution in Bihar,* Social Science Press, New Delhi.

Lal, A.K. (1997). *Dalits in Action: An Evaluation of Bihar Dalit Vikas Samiti*, Concept Publishing Company, New Delhi.

.................(2008). "Dalits of Bihar" in "*Dalits in Contemporary India: Discrimination and Discontent*" (ed.) by Nandu Ram, Vol.1, Siddhant Publications, New Delhi.

Linton, Ralf (1936). *The Study of Man: An Introduction*, New York, Appleton-Century-Crofts.

Louis, Prakash (2001). *Casteism is Horrendous than Racism: Durban and Dalit Discourse*, Indian Social Institute, New Delhi.

.... (2002). "Social Exclusion of Dalits: Agony and Assertion of an Outcasted Community" in *Social Exclusion: Essays in Honour of Dr. Bindeshwar Pathak"* (ed.). by A.K. Lal, Concept Publishing Company, New Delhi.

.... (2008). "Social Exclusion: A Conceptual and Theoretical Framework", Working Paper, p. 4.

Lynch, Owen M. (1974). *The Politics of Untouchability*, National Publishing House, New Delhi.

Mahar, Mihael, J.M. (ed.) (1972). *The Untouchables in Contemporary India*, The University of Arizona Press, Tucson.

Mandelbaum, David G. (1972). *Society in India: Continuity and Change*, Popular Bombay. Barreman, Gerald D. (1971, 1979). *Caste and Other Inequities: Essays on Inequality*, Folklore Institute, New Delhi.

Marriott, Mckim (1968). "Multiple Reference in Indian Caste Systems", in James, Silverberg (ed.). *Social Mobility in the Caste system in India*, Mouton, The Hague, Parish.

Marshal, T.H. (1963). *Sociology at the Cross Roads*, London, Heinemannn.

Marshall, Gordon, and J. Scott (1995). *Oxford Dictionary of Sociology*, Oxford University Press.

Massey, James (1995). *Dalits in India*, Manohar Publishers and Distributers, New Delhi.

Mayer, A.C. (1960). *Caste and Kinship in Central India: A Village and its Region*, Routledge and Kegan Paul, London.

Merton, R.K. (1968). *Social Theory and Social Structure*, American Publishing Co. PVT.

Milner, Murray JR. (1994). *Status and Sacredness: A general theory of Status Relations and an Analysis of Indian Culture*, Oxford University Press, New York.

Mishra, B. B. (1961). *The Indian Middle Class: Their Growth in Modern Times*, Oxford University Press, London.

Mishra, Narayan (2004). *Exploitation and Atrocities on the Dalits in India,* Kalpaz, Publications, New Delhi.

Morrison, Ken (1995). *Marx, Durkheim, Weber: Formations of Modern Social Thought*, Sage Publications, New Delhi.

Muddiman, Dave (1999). "Theories of Social Exclusion and the Public Library', Working Paper, 1.

Ojha, K.P. (1959-60). *Bihar: Facts and Figure*, Directorate of Public Relations, Bihar.

Omvedt, Gail (1994). *Dalits and the Democratic Revolution: Dr. Ambedkar and the Dalit Movement in the Colonial India*, Sage Publications, New Delhi.

Parvathamma, C. (1968). The Case for Untouchables, *United Asia* 20.

.... (2012). "The Weaker Sections of Society: The Scheduled Castes in India", in Abhijit Dasgupta (ed.) *On the Margins, Tribe, Caste and Other Social Categories*, Sage Publications, Vol. 4, New Delhi.

Pathak, Sumanlata (1985). "Self -images of Scheduled Castes, Girl students of Chandigarh" in *Struggle for Status* edited by Sharma, S.K & Pimpley P. N. B.R. Publishing Corporation, New Delhi.

Patwarthan, S. (1973). *Change among India's Harijans: Maharashtra: A Case Study,* Orient Longman Ltd, New Delhi.

Prasad, Anirudh (1988). "Changing Life ways and Thought ways of Musahars in Bodh Gaya", in *Tradition and Development*, (eds.). by Sachchidananda and others Concept Publishing Company, New Delhi.

Prasad, Jagdish (2007). *Bihar: Dynamics of Development*, Mittal Publications, New Delhi.

Prasad, N. (1970). *Change Strategy in a Development Society*, Meenakshi Prakashan, Meerut.

Ram, Nandu (1988). *The Mobile Scheduled Castes: Rise of a New Middle Class*, Hindustan Publishing Corporation, Delhi.

……………….. (1995). *Beyond Ambedkar:Essays on Dalits in India*, Har-Anand Publications, New Delhi.

……………….. (2008). *Caste System and Untouchability in South India*, Manak Publications, New Delhi.

………………..(ed.) (2008). *Dalits in Contemporary India: Discrimination and Discontent*, Vol. 1, Siddhant Publications, New Delhi.

Ramashray, Roy (1970). "Caste and Political Recruitment in Bihar", in Rajni Kothari (ed.), *Caste in Indian Politics*, Orient Longman, Ltd, New Delhi.

Ramashray, Roy (1999). *Dalits, Development and Democracy*, Shipra Publication, New Delhi.

Rodrigues, Valerian (ed.) (2002). *The Essential Writings of B.R Ambedkar*, Oxford University Press, New Delhi.

Rowe, William. L. (1968). "The New Cauhans: A Caste Mobility Movement in North India", in *Social Mobility in the Caste System in India* (ed.) by James Silverberg, Houton, The Hague.

Roy Chaudhury, P.C. (1960). *Bihar District Gazatteers,* Saran Secretariat Press, Patna.

…………………… (1964). *Bihar District Gazetteers*, Darbhanga Secretariat Press, Patna.

Saberwal, Satish (1990). *Mobile Men: Limit to Social Change in Urban Punjab,* Indian Institute of Advanced to Study, Shimla in Association with Manohar Publication, New Delhi.

Saberwal, Satish (ed.), (1972). *Beyond the Village: Sociological Explorations*, Indian Institute of Advanced Study, Shimla.

Sachchidananda (1977). *The Harijan Elite*, Thomson Press (India) Limited.

Salam, Jeebanlata (2004). *Social Exclusion and Education*, Indian Social Institute, New Delhi.

Sen, Amartya (2004). *Social Exclusion: Concept, Application and Scrutiny*, Critical Quest, New Delhi.

Sharma, K. L. (1994). *Social Stratification and Mobility*, Rawat Publications, Jaipur &New Delhi.

Sharma, Mukul. "The Untouchable Present: Everyday Life of Musahars in North Bihar", in Jodhka, S.S. (ed.) (2012). Village *India*, Orient Black Swan, New Delhi.

Sharma, S.K. & P. N. Pimpley (1985). *Struggle for Status*, B.R. Publishing Corporation, New Delhi.

Shyamlal (2006). *Untouchable Castes in India*, Rawat Publications, Jaipur and New Delhi.

Sigh, Yogendra (1986). *Modernisation of Indian Tradition*, Rawat Publications, New Delhi.

Silver, Hilary (1995). "Reconceptualizing Social Disadvantage: Three Paradigms of Social Exclusion" in *Social Exclusion: Rhetoric, Reality, Responses* (eds.) by Rodgers, Gerry, et. al., International Institute of Labour Studies, United Nations Development Programme, Geneva.

Singh, Ashok (2010). "The Story of a Dalit family from a Sleepy North Bihar Village" in Ahmad, Imtiaz & Upadhaya, S.B. (ed.). by *Dalit Assertion in Society, Literature and History,* Orient Black Swan, New Delhi.

Singh, Shyama Nand (1990). *Reservation: Problems and Prospects*, Uppal Publishing House, New Delhi.

Srinivas, M.N. (1977, 1982). *Social Change in Modern India*, Orient Longman, New Delhi.

…………….. (1980). *India: Social Structure*, Hindustan Publishing Corporation, New Delhi.

……………..(1991). "The Dominant Caste in Rampura", in Dipankar Gupta (ed.). *Social Stratification*, Oxford University Press, New Delhi.

Subramanyam, V. (2010). "Context Social Exclusion and Inclusion of Weaker Sections", in Subramanyam, V. & K. Sekhar (eds.). *Social Exclusions, Integration and Inclusive Policy*, Rawat Publications, New Delhi.

Teltumbde, Anand (2003). "Globalisation and Education for the Dalits: A Perspective for the Future", in *Globalisation and Social Movements: Struggle for a Humane Society,* Jogdand. P.G & S.M. Michael (eds.). Rawat Publications, New Delhi.

Townsend, P. (1993). "The International Analysis of Poverty" in Baily, Nick and Spratt, Jenny & others (2004). *Deprivation and Social Exclusion in Argyll and Bute*, Report to the community Planning Partnership, Scottish Centre for Research on Social Justice, Universities of Glasgow & Aberdeen.

Vidyarthi, L. P. & N. Mishra (1977). *Harijan Today,* Classical Publications, New Delhi.

Weber, Max (1961). *From Max Weber: Essays in Sociology*, Routlegde and Kegan Paul, London. (translated by H.B. Gerth and C.W Mills) .

..................(1991). "Class, Status and Party" in *Social Stratification*, (ed.) by Dipankar Gupta, Oxford University Press, New Delhi, pp. 462-63.

.... "Class, Status and Party", in C.G. Helles, (ed.1969), *Structural Social Inequality: Readers in Comparative Stratification*, New York.

Wolf, C. (1985). "Status" in Kuper, Adam and Jessica Kuper (eds), *The Social Science Encyclopedia,* Routledge and Kegan Paul, London.

JOURNALS

Abdulraheem, A. (2011). "Education, Equality and Social Exclusion: A View", *Social Action*, July-September, Vol. 61, No. 3, p. 217.

Beteille, Andre (2000). "The Scheduled Castes: An Inter-Regional Perspective", *Journal of Indian School of Political Economy*, Vol. 12, July- December, p. 372.

Bharti, Indu (1990). "Dalits Gain New Izzat", *Economic and Political Weekly*, May 5-12, pp. 980-81.

Blair, Harry W. (1980). "Rising Kulaks and Backward Classes in Bihar", *Economic and Political Weekly*, Vol. 15(2) January, p. 67.

Dumont, Louis (1966). "A fundamental Problem in the Sociology of Caste", *Contributions to Indian Sociology*, No. 9.

Gaurang, R. Sahay (2004). "Hierarchy, difference and the Caste System: A Study of Rural Bihar", *Contributions to Indian Sociology*, Vol. 38, p. 121.

Imtiaz, Ahmad (1971). "Caste Mobility Movements in North India", *The Indian Economic and Social History Review*, Vol.VIII, No, December, p. 166.

Jha, Hetukar (2000). "Promises and Lapses: Understanding the Experiences of Scheduled Castes in Bihar in Historical Perspective", *Journal of Indian School of Political Economy*, July-December, Vol. 12, No. 342., p. 423.

Joshi, P.C. (1978). "Organising Rural Poor: Some Basic Issues", *Mainstream*, 12 August, New Delhi, p. 7.

Kothari, Rajni (1994). "Rise of the Dalits and the Renewed Debate on Caste", *Economic and Political Weekly*, Vol. XXIX, Issue 26, p. 1589.

Kumar, Ashwani (2007). "Exile between Home and Memory", *Seminar*, December, p. 16.

Lal, A.K. (1997). "Bihar: Old and New", *Seminar*, 450, February, p. 20.

Lenski, Gerhard (1956). "Social Participation and Status Crystallisation", *American Sociological Review,* Vol. 21, No. 4.

Meillassoux, C. "Are There Castes in India", referred in "Caste and Agrarian Class: A View from Bihar", (2001). by Anand Chakravarti, *Economic and Political Weekly*, Vol. 36, No. 17, April-May.

Natarajan, Balmurli " From Jati to Samaj", in Caste Matters: A Symposium on inequality, identities and disintegrating hierarchies in India, *Seminar* 633-May 2012, p. 56.

Oommen, T.K. (1984). Sources of Deprivation and Styles of Protests: The Case of the Dalits in India, *Contributions to Indians Sociology* (n.s.) 18, 1 Sage Publications, New Delhi.

Prasad, Pradhan H. (1975). "Agrarian Unrest and Economic Change in Rural Bihar: Three Case Studies", *Economic and Political Weekly*, June, 14, p. 1979.

Room, G. J. (1999). "Social Exclusion, Solidarity and the challenge of Globalisation", *International Journal of Social Welfare*.

Seminar 580- December, 2007, p. 29.

Sharma, Alakh N. (2005). "Agrarian Relation and Socio-Economic Change in Bihar", *Economic and Political Weekly*, Vol. 40, No.10, March 5-11, pp. 960-72.

Silver, Hilary (1995). "Social Exclusion and Social Solidarity: Three Paradigms", *International Labour Review,* Vol. 133, 1994/5-6.

Singh, J.P. (2001). "Caste and Morphology of Rural Settlement", *The Eastern Anthropology*, Vol. 54, No. 2, April-June, p. 159.

Singh, Shrawan Kumar (2011). "Social Scenario of Scheduled Castes in Bihar", *Third World Concept*, April-June, p. 24.

Sinha, Arun. "Caste and Factions in Bihar Politics", *Times of India* (July 9, 1986).

Sinha, Arvind and Indu Sinha (1996). "State, Class and 'Sena' Nexus", *Economic and Political Weekly,* No. 2.

Teltumbe, Anand (2012). "Identity politics and the Annihilation of Castes", in Caste Matters: A Symposium on inequality, identities and disintegrating hierarchies in India, *Seminar* 633-May, pp. 28-29.

Thorat, S. & Newman, Katherine. S. (2007). "Caste and Economic Discrimination: Causes, Consequences and Remedies", *Economic and Political Weekly*, October 13, p. 4122.

Thorat, Sukhdeo (2008). "Social Exclusion in the Indian Context: Theoretical Basis of Inclusive Policies", *Indian Journal of Human Development*, Vol. 2, No. 1.

Wankhede, G.G. (2003). "The Scheduled Castes and Higher Education in India: Retrospects and Prospects", *Think India* 6(3), July-Sept, p. 37.

GOVERNMENT REPORTS

Bihar District Gazetteers, Champaran, Secretariat Press, Patna, 1960.

Bihar District Gazetteers, Dharbhanga, Secretariat Press Patna, 1964.

Concurrent Evaluation of IRDP (September 92 to 93). Government of India, Ministry of Rural Development (Monitoring Division) March 1995.

Concurrent Evaluation of JRY (Jan-Dec 1992). A Report, Government of India, Ministry of Rural Development, July 1994.

Planning Commission, Government of India, 2006.

Rural Development (Monitory Division), March 1995.

The Nature of Determinations of Social Status, Year Book of Education, London, 1953.

Economic Survey 2008-09, Government of Bihar.

NEWSPAPER

Indian Nation 1975.

Times of India July 9, 1986.

Frontline, November 9, 2001.

UNPUBLISHED

Ram, Jitendra (2008). *Changing Status of Dalits in Post-Independent Bihar*, Unpublished M.Phil Dissertation, Jawaharlal Nehru University, New Delhi.

CENSUS REPORTS

Census of India, 1991, series Bihar Registrar, Pushpa Bhawan, New Delhi.

Census of India, 2001, series Bihar Registrar, Pushpa Bhawan, New Delhi.

INTERNET

www.mapsofindian.com

www.allaboutbihar.com

www.bihar.com

www.eastchamparan.com

Appendices

Appendix-A

Chapter 3

Table 3.1: Literacy Rates in India during 1961-2001

Decades	Gen			SC		
	Male	Female	Total	Male	Female	Total
1961	40.40	15.35	28.30	16.96	3.29	10.27
1971	45.96	21.91	34.45	22.36	6.44	14.67
1981	56.38	29.76	43.57	31.12	10.93	21.38
1991	64.13	39.29	52.21	49.91	23.76	37.41
2001	75.30	53.70	64.80	66.64	41.90	54.69

Source: *Education of Scheduled Castes and Scheduled Tribes 1997-98*, Department of Secondary and Higher Education, Ministry of Human Resource Development, Government of India, New Delhi.

Chapter 4

Table 4.1: Monthly Income-wise views of the Respondents on Social Discrimination against Dalits

Income (in Rs.) of Respondents	Degree of Social Discrimination							
	Most	Less	Least	No	Most	Less	Least	No
	Bara Govind Village				Chakia Town			
In Kind	49	2	-	-	-	-	-	-
Less than 1000	37	12	2	-	-	-	-	-
1001-2000	13	7	3	-	-	-	-	-
2001-3000	-	-	-	-	7	11	21	10
More than 3000	-	-	-	-	2	13	5	56
Total	**99**	**21**	**5**		**9**	**24**	**26**	**66**

Table 4.2: Educational-wise views of the Respondents on Social Discrimination against Dalits

Education of Respondents	Degree of Social Discrimination							
	Most	Less	Least	No	Most	Less	Least	No
	Bara Govind Village				Chakia Town			
Illiterate	65	3	-	-	-	-	-	-
Primary School	15	3	1	-	-	-	-	-
Middle School	9	3	1	-	5	3	3	-
High School	13	3	2	-	6	7	13	12
Intermediate	1	2	2	-	3	5	9	14
Graduation	-	1	1	-	-	6	13	19
Post-Graduation	-	-	-	-	-	-	1	6
Total	**103**	**15**	**7**		**14**	**21**	**39**	**51**

Table 4.3: Employment-wise views of the Respondents on Exploitation of Dalits

Employment of Respondents	Bara Govind Village				Chakia Town			
	Degree of Exploitation of Dalits							
	Most	Less	Least	No	Most	Less	Least	No
Traditional	6	-	-	-	-	-	-	-
Agricultural labourer	91	5	-	-	-	-	-	-
Non-agricultural labourer	4	2	1	-	4	-	-	-
Govt. Jobs	1	1	1	-	3	12	11	21
Private Jobs	2	1	1	-	4	2	5	13
Petty Business	-	-	-	-	2	3	3	11
Other Occupations	3	4	2	-	11	3	5	12
Total	**107**	**13**	**5**		**24**	**20**	**24**	**57**

Table 4.4: Education and caste-wise views of the Respondents on Social Exclusion of Dalits

Educational Level of Respondents	Caste of Respondents																							
	Chamar				Dusadh				Musahar				Chamar				Dhobi				Dusadh			
	Bara Govind Village												Chakia Town											
	Degree of Social Exclusion																							
	M	**L**	**L**	**N**	**M**	**L**	**L**	**N**	**M**	**L**	**L**	**N**	**M**	**L**	**L**	**N**	**M**	**L**	**L**	**N**	**M**	**L**	**L**	**N**
Illiterate	20	-	-	-	14	-	-	-	42	-	-	-	-	-	-	-	-	-	-	-	-	-	-	-
Primary School	5	1	-	-	4	1	1	-	2	-	-	-	-	-	-	-	-	-	-	-	-	-	-	-
Middle School	3	2	1	-	3	2	1	-	-	1	-	-	2	1	-	-	1	2	2	-	1	1	1	-
High School	3	2	2	-	5	2	2	-	-	-	-	-	6	4	-	3	5	4	2	2	2	3	2	3
Intermediate	1	1	-	-	1	1	-	-	-	-	-	-	-	-	2	9	-	1	1	11	-	1	1	9
Graduation	-	-	1	-	-	1	-	-	-	-	-	-	-	-	1	12	-	-	1	12	-	-	-	10
Post-Graduation	-	-	-	-	-	-	-	-	-	-	-	-	-	-	1	1	-	-	-	3	-	-	-	2
Total	**32**	**6**	**4**		**27**	**7**	**4**		**44**	**1**			**8**	**5**	**4**	**25**	**6**	**7**	**6**	**28**	**3**	**5**	**4**	**24**

Table 4.5: Caste and Income-wise views of the Respondents on Social Exclusion of Dalits

Income of Respondents	Caste of Respondents																							
	Chamar				Dusadh				Musahar				Chamar				Dhobi				Dusadh			
	Bara Govind Village												Chakia Town											
	Degree of Social Exclusion																							
	M	L	L	N	M	L	L	N	M	L	L	N	M	L	L	N	M	L	L	N	M	L	L	N
In Kind	15	3	2	-	11	3	2	-	32	1	-	-	-	-	-	-	-	-	-	-	-	-	-	-
Less than 1000	9	5	3	-	7	2	3	-	4	2	1	-	-	-	-	-	-	-	-	-	-	-	-	-
1000-2000	1	2	2	-	5	3	2	-	2	2	1	-	-	-	-	-	-	-	-	-	-	-	-	-
2001-3000	-	-	-	-	-	-	-	-	-	-	-	-	3	7	3	11	4	5	6	7	4	1	2	10
More than 3000	-	-	-	-	-	-	-	-	-	-	-	-	2	2	2	12	-	4	2	19	1	3	4	11
Total	**25**	**10**	**7**	**-**	**23**	**8**	**7**	**-**	**38**	**5**	**2**	**-**	**5**	**9**	**5**	**23**	**4**	**9**	**8**	**26**	**5**	**4**	**6**	**21**

Table 4.6: Age-wise views of the Respondents on Social Discrimination against Dalits

Age Group (in Years) of Respondents	Spheres of Social Discrimination									
	ISR	CR	RP	PP	N0	ISR	CR	RP	PP	N0
	Bara Govind Village					Chakia Town				
20-30	3(2.4)	5(4)	6(4.8)	5(4)	-	-	2(1.6)	4(3.3)	3(2.4)	19(15.2)
30-40	7(5.6)	9(7.2)	11(8.8)	9(7.2)	-	-	7(5.6)	5(4)	6(4.8)	15(12)
40-50	8(6.4)	11(8.8)	13(10.4)	8(6.4)	-	3(2.4)	6(4.8)	9(7.2)	5(4)	13(10.4)
50 Above	7(5.6)	9(7.2)	8(6.4)	6(4.8)	-	5(4)	4(3.2)	2(1.6)	6(4.8)	11(8.8)
Total	**25**	**34**	**38**	**28**	**-**	**8**	**19**	**20**	**20**	**58**

ISR-Interaction and Social Relations, CR-Commensal Relations, RP-Religious Participation, PP- Political Participation.

Table 4.7: Caste-wise views of the Respondents on Spheres of Social Discrimination against Dalits

Spheres of Social Discrimination	Bara Govind Village			Chakia Town		
	Caste of the Respondents					
	Chamar	Dusadh	Musahar	Chamar	Dhobi	Dusadh
Interaction and Social Relations	8(6.4)	6(4.8)	6(4.8)	2(1.6)	1(0.8)	2(1.6)
Commensal Relations	11(8.8)	10(8)	13(10.4)	3(2.4)	2(1.6)	1(0.8)
Religious Participation	15(12)	14(11.2)	17(13.6)	7(5.6)	6(4.8)	4(3.2)
Participation in Panchayat	8(6.4)	8(6.4)	9(7.2)	3(2.4)	3(2.4)	2(1.6)
No Discrimination	-	-	-	27(21.6)	35(28)	27(21.6)
Total	**42**	**38**	**45**	**42**	**47**	**36**

Table 4.8: Occupation-wise views of the Respondents on Social Discrimination against the Dalits

Occupation of Respondents	Degree of Social Discrimination							
	Most	Less	Least	No	Most	Less	Least	No
	Bara Govind Village				Chakia Town			
Traditional	6	-	-	-	-	-	-	-
Agricultural labourer	89	5	2	-	-	-	-	-
Non-agricultural labourer	3	3	1	-	2	2	-	-
Govt. Jobs	1	1	1	-	2	13	11	21
Private Jobs	2	1	1	-	1	3	7	13
Petty Business	-	-	-	-	2	3	3	11

Other Occupation	3	4	2	-	5	7	7	12
Total	**104**	**14**	**7**		**12**	**28**	**28**	**57**

Table 4.9: Caste-wise views of Respondents on Degree of Discrimination in (Ascending/Descending Order) against Dalits

Caste of Respondents	Bara Govind Village		Chakia Town	
	Degree of Discrimination (in Ascending/Descending Order)			
	Ascending Order	Descending Order	Ascending Order	Descending Order
Chamar Dhobi Dusadh Musahar	Dusadh> Chamar> Musahar	Musahar< Chamar <Dusadh	-	-
Chamar Dhobi Dusadh Musahar	Musahar> Chamar> Dusadh	Musahar< Chamar <Dusadh	Chamar> Dusadh> Dhobi	Chamar< Dusadh< Dhobi
Chamar Dhobi Dusadh Musahar	Musahar> Chamar> Dusadh	Musahar< Chamar >Dusadh	Chamar> Dusadh> Dhobi	Chamar< Dusadh< Dhobi

Note: >Ascending Order, < Descending Order

Table 4.10: Caste-wise views of the Respondents on Political Participation of Dalits

Caste of Respondents	Bara Govind Village		Chakia Town	
	Political Participation of Dalits in			
	Gram Panchayat	Political Party	Nagar Panchayat	Political Party
Chamar	33(26.4)	9(7.2)	28(22.4)	14(11.2)
Dhobi	-	-	30(24)	17(13.6)
Dusadh	28(22.4)	10(8)	18(14.4)	18(14.4)
Musahar	37(29.6)	8(6.4)	-	-
Total	**98(78.4)**	**27(21.6)**	**76(60.8)**	**49(39.2)**

Table 4.11: Education and caste-wise views of the Respondents on Exploitation of Dalits

Education of Respondents	Caste of Respondents																							
	Chamar				Dusadh				Musahar				Chamar				Dhobi				Dusadh			
	Bara Govind Village												Chakia Town											
	Degree of Exploitation in Education																							
	M	L	L	N	M	L	L	N	M	L	L	N	M	L	L	N	M	L	L	N	M	L	L	N
Illiterate	18	2	-	-	13	1	-	-	42	-	-	-	-	-	-	-	-	-	-	-	-	-	-	-
Primary School	5	1	-	-	4	1	1	-	2	-	-	-	-	-	-	-	-	-	-	-	-	-	-	-
Middle School	3	2	1	-	3	2	1	-	-	1	-	-	2	1	-	-	1	2	2	-	1	1	1	
High School	3	2	2	-	4	2	3	-	-	-	-	-	6	4	-	3	5	4	4	-	5	3	2	
Intermediate	1	1	-	-	1	1	-	-	-	-	-	-	-	1	2	8	-	1	1	11	-	1	1	9
Graduation	-	-	1	-	-	1	-	-	-	-	-	-	-	2	1	10	-	-	1	12	-	-	-	10
Post- Graduation	-	-	-	-	-	-	-	-	-	-	-	-	-	-	1	1	-	-	-	3	-	-	-	2
Total	**30**	**8**	**4**		**25**	**8**	**5**		**44**	**1**			**8**	**8**	**4**	**22**	**6**	**7**	**8**	**26**	**6**	**5**	**4**	**21**

Chapter 5

Table 5.1: Income-wise views of the Respondents about the Class or Socio-economic status of the Dalits

Income of Respondents	Bara Givind Village			Chakia Town		
	Class or Socio-Economic Status of the Dalits					
	Low	Middle	High	Low	Middle	High
In Kind	102		-	-	-	-
Less than1000	17	-	-	-	-	-
1001-2000	-	6	-	-	-	-
2001-3000	-	-	-	19	10	20
More than 3000	-	-	-	6	30	40
Total	**119**	**6**	**-**	**25**	**40**	**60**

Table 5.2: Education-wise views of the Respondents about the Class or Socio-economic status of the Dalits

Income of Respondents	Bara Givind Village			Chakia Town		
	Class or Socio-Economic Status of the Dalits					
	Low	Middle	High	Low	Middle	High
Illiterate	68	-	-	-	-	-
Primary School	19	-	-	-	-	-
Middle School	10	3	-	7	4	-
High School	10	8	-	15	6	17
Intermediate	2	3	-	2	9	20
Graduation	-	2	-	-	15	23
Post – Graduation	-	-	-	-	3	4
Total	**109**	**16**	**-**	**24**	**37**	**64**

Table 5.3: Employment-wise views of the Respondents about the Class or Socio- economic status of the Dalits

Employment of Respondents	Bara Govind Village			Chakia Town		
	Class or socio-economic Status of the Dalits					
	Low	Middle	High	Low	Middle	High
Traditional occupation	6	-	-			
Agri-labour	90	6	-			

Non-agri-labourer	5	2	-	4	-	-
Govt. Jobs	-	3	-	-	22	25
Private Jobs	-	4	-	5	9	10
Perry- Business	-	-	-	3	6	10
Unemployed	9	-	-	15	8	8
Total	**110**	**15**	-	**27**	**45**	**53**

Table 5.4: Education-wise views of the Respondents on Emulation of Hindu caste system

Education of Respon-dents	Bara Govind Village						Chakia Town					
	Types of Emulation											
	TVM	P H RC	W HGG	BH RS	RHRB	N	TVM	P H RC	W HGG	BH RS	RHRB	N
Illiterate	-	10	9	12	-	37	-	-	-	-	-	-
Primary School	1	3	5	2	-	8	-	-	-	-	-	-
Middle School	-	4	4	3	-	2	-	2	2	5	-	2
High School	-	4	3	2	-	9	4	4	5	5	2	18
Intermediate	-	2	2	1	-	-	3	4	5	6	2	11
Graduation	-	1	1	-	-	-	-	6	5	3	-	24
Post-Graduation	-	-	-	-	-	-	2	1	1	-	-	3
Total	**1**	**24**	**24**	**20**	-	**56**	**9**	**17**	**18**	**19**	**4**	**58**

Note: TVM: Taking vegetarian meal, **P H RC:** Performing Hindu Rituals and ceremonies, **W HGG:** Worshipping Hindu god and goddess, **BH RS:** Believing in Hindu Religious sects, **RHRB:** Reciting Hindu religious books.

Table 5.5: Employment wise-views of the Respondents on emulation of Hindu Caste system

Employment of Respondents	Bara Govind Village						Chakia Town					
	Types of Emulation											
	TVM	P H RC	W HGG	BH RS	RHRB	N	TVM	P H RC	W HGG	BH RS	RHRB	N
Traditional occupation	-	2	2	2	-	-	-	-	-	-	-	-
Agri-cultural labourer	1	7	9	9	-	70	-	-	-	-	-	-
Non-agri-cultural labourer	-	2	2	2	-	1	-	2	1	1	-	
Govt. Jobs	-	1	1	1	-	-	12	-	-	-	2	33
Private Jobs	-	2	1	1	-	-	3	2	1	1	2	15
Petty-Business	-	-	-	-	-	-	-	3	5	3	-	8
Unemployed	-	3	3	3	-	-	2	4	5	-	-	20
Total	1	17	18	18	-	71	17	11	12	5	4	76

Note: TVM: Taking vegetarian meal, **P H RC:** Performing Hindu Rituals and ceremonies, **W HGG :** Worshipping Hindu god and goddess, **BH RS** : Believing in Hindu Religious sects, **RHRB :** Reciting Hindu religious books

Table 5.6: Income-wise views of the Respondents on Emulation of the Hindu caste system

Income of Respondents	Bara Govind Village						Chakia Town					
	Types of Emulation											
	TVM	P H RC	W HGG	BH RS	RHRB	N	TVM	P H RC	W HGG	BH RS	RHRB	N
In Kind	-	5	9	7	-	30	-	-	-	-	-	-
Less than 1000	-	9	9	7	-	26	-	-	-	-	-	-
1001-2000	1	4	7	3	-	8	-	-	-	-	-	-
2001-3000	-	-	-	-	-	-	6	7	11	7	2	16
More than 3000	-	-	-	-	-	-	4	7	9	13	2	41
Total		**18**	**25**	**17**		**64**	**10**	**14**	**20**	**20**	**4**	**57**

Note: TVM: Taking vegetarian meal, **P H RC :** Performing Hindu Rituals and ceremonies, **W HGG :** Worshipping Hindu god and goddess, **BH RS** : Believing in Hindu Religious sects, **RHRB :** Reciting Hindu religious books

Table 5.7: Education-wise views of the Respondents on Dalits believing in different Religious Sects or Panths

Education of Respondents	Bara Govind Village				Chakia Town			
	Believing in Religious Sects or Panths							
	Hindu believes	Buddhism	Kabir Panth	Jai Gurudeo Sect	Hindu believes	Buddhism	Kabir Panth	Jai Gurudeo Sect
Illiterate	45	7	7	9	-	-	-	-
Primary School	12	3	3	1	-	-	-	-
Middle School	7	2	2	2	5	2	2	2
High School	9	4	3	2	13	13	7	5
Intermediate	1	1	2	1	3	9	12	7
Graduation	-	1	1	-	-	14	13	11
Post-Graduation	-	-	-	-	-	2	3	2
Total	**74**	**18**	**18**	**15**	**21**	**40**	**37**	**27**

Table 5.8: Education-wise views of the Respondents on impact of Constitutional Provisions on Status formation among Dalits

Education of Respondents	Bara Govind Village				Chakia Town			
	Constitutional Provisions of							
	Welfare and Development	Freedom of Expression	Atrocity Act	None	Welfare and Development	Freedom of Expression	Atrocity Act	None
Illiterate	9	7	7	45	-	-	-	-
Primary School	4	3	-	12	-	-	-	-
Middle School	4	2	-	7	2	2	2	5
High School	3	4	-	11	7	11	7	13
Intermediate	1	1	2	1	3	9	12	7
Graduation	-	1	1	-	11	14	13	-
Post-Graduation	-	-	-		3	2	2	-
Total	**21**	**18**	**10**	**74**	**26**	**38**	**36**	**25**

Table 5.9: Employment-wise views of the Respondents on impact of Constitutional Provisions on Status formation among Dalits

Employment of Respondents	Bara Govind Village				Chakia Town			
	Constitutional Provisions of							
	Welfare and Development	Freedom of Expression	Atrocity Act	None	Welfare and Development	Freedom of Expression	Atrocity Act	None
Traditional occupation	-	-	-	6	-	-	-	-
Agricultural labourer	12	7	7	70	-	-	-	-
Non-agricultural labourer	2	2	2	1	2	2	-	-
Govt. Jobs	1	1	1	-	9	17	18	3
Private Jobs	2	1	1	-	5	10	9	-
Petty-Business	-	-	-	-	4	5	5	5
Unemployed	3	3	3		7	7	12	5
Total	**20**	**14**	**14**	**77**	**27**	**41**	**44**	**13**

Table 5.10: Income-wise views of the Respondents on impact of Constitutional Provisions on Status formation among Dalits

Income of Respondents	Bara Govind Village				Chakia Town			
	Constitutional Provisions of							
	Welfare and Development	Freedom of Expression	Atrocity Act	None	Welfare and Development	Freedom of Expression	Atrocity Act	None
In Kind	10	4	4	33	-	-	-	-
Less than 1000	5	7	7	32	-	-	-	-
1001-2000	5	3	3	12	-	-	-	-
2001-3000	-	-	-	-	17	13	14	5
More than 3000	-	-	-		23	25	19	9
Total	**20**	**14**	**14**	**77**	**40**	**38**	**33**	**14**

Table 5.11: Education-wise views of the Respondents on changes in Caste Status

Education	Changes in features of caste									
	SUC	CRUC	OCOU C H	UCC OOH	None	SUC	CRUC	OCOU C H	UCC OOH	None
	Bara Govind Village					Chakia Town				
Illiterate	-	-	-	-	68	-	-	-	-	-
Primary School	-	-	-	-	19	-	-	-	-	-
Middle School	5	-	-	-	8	3	2	-	-	6
High School	7	1	-	-	10	14	10	7	-	7
Intermediate	2	2	1	-	-	11	6	7	-	7
Graduation	1	1	-	-	-	13	9	9	-	7
Post-Graduation	-	-	-	-	-	3	2	2	-	-
Total	**15**	**4**	**1**		**105**	**44**	**29**	**25**	**-**	**27**

SUC-Sitting along with upper castes, **CRUC**-Commensal relation with upper castes, **OCOUC H**-On ceremonial occasion in upper castes house, **UCCOOH-** Upper castes on ceremonial occasion at own house

Table 5.12: Income-wise views of the Respondents on changes in features of caste

Income	Changes in features of caste									
	SUC	CRUC	OCOU C H	UCC OOH	None	SUC	CRUC	OCOU C H	UCC OOH	None
	Bara Govind Village					Chakia Town				
In Kind	-	-	-	-	51	-	-	-	-	-
Less than1000	-	-	-	-	51	-	-	-	-	-
1001-2000	7	3	-	-	13	-	-	-	-	-
2001-3000	-	-	-	-	-	11	15	7	-	16
More than 3000	-	-	-	-	-	16	32	21	-	7
Total	**7**	**3**	**-**	**-**	**115**	**27**	**47**	**28**	**-**	**23**

Table 5.13: Employment-wise views of the Respondents on changes in features of caste

Employment	Changes in features of caste									
	SUC	CRUC	OCOU CH	UCC OOH	None	SUC	CRUC	OCOU CH	UCC OOH	None
	Bara Govind Village					Chakia Town				
Traditional Occupation	-	-	-	-	6	-	-	-	-	-
Agri-Labour	3	3			90	-	-	-	-	-
Non-Agri- Labourer	1	1	-	-	5	-	-	-	-	4
Govt. Job	1	1	1	-	-	11	13	18	-	5
Private	2	1	1	-	-	7	5	4	-	8
Petty-Business	-	-	-	-	-	5	7	3	-	4
Unemployed	1	1	-	-	7	9	11	5	-	6
Total	**8**	**7**	**2**	**-**	**108**	**32**	**36**	**30**	**-**	**27**

Table 5.14: Caste-wise views of the Respondents on Social Consciousness of Dalits

Caste of Respon- dents	Bara Govind Village				Chakia Town			
	Types of Social Consciousness							
	About their rights, i.e., Reservation, free education	Government schemes for them	Assertive against social discrimination	No	About their rights, i.e., Reservation, free education	Government schemes for them	Assertive against social discrimination	No
Chamar	7(5.6)	3(2.4)	2	30	15	12	10	5
Dhobi	-	-	-	-	17	13	14	3
Dusadh	5(3.2)	3()	2	28	9	9	11	7
Musahar	2(1.6)	-	-	43	-	-	-	-
Total	**14**	**6**	**4**	**101**	**41**	**34**	**35**	**15**

Table 5.15: Education-wise views of the Respondents on social consciousness of the Dalits

Education of Respondents	Bara Govind Village				Chakia Town			
	Types of Social Consciousness							
	About their rights, i.e., Reservation, free education	Government schemes for them	Assertive against social discrimination	No	About their rights, i.e., Reservation, free education	Government schemes for them	Assertive against social discrimination	No
Illiterate	-	-	-	68	-	-	-	-
Primary School	6	6	-	7	-	-	-	-
Middle School	2	4	-	7	-	-	-	11
High School	5	8	-	5	9	9	11	9
Intermediate	2	3	-	-	9	11	7	4
Graduation	1	1	-	-	14	11	13	-
Post-Graduation	-	-	-	-	2	2	3	-
Total	**16**	**22**	**-**	**87**	**34**	**33**	**34**	**24**

Table 5.16: Employment-wise views of the Respondents on social consciousness of the Dalits

Employment of Respondents	Bara Govind Village				Chakia Town			
	Types of Social Consciousness							
	About their rights, i.e., Reservation, free education	Government schemes for them	Assertive against social discrimination	No	About their rights, i.e., Reservation, free education	Government schemes for them	Assertive against social discrimination	No
Traditional occupation	-	-	-	6	-	-	-	-
Agricultural labourer	-	6	-	90	-	-	-	-
Non-agricultural labourer	2	3	-	2	-	-	-	4
Govt. Jobs	2	1	-	-	23	15	9	-

Private Jobs	2	2	-	-	9	10	5	-
Petty-Business	-	-	-	-	5	7	2	5
Unemployed	-	-	-	9	5	7	5	14
Total	**6**	**12**	**-**	**107**	**42**	**39**	**21**	**23**

Table 5.17: Caste-wise views of the Respondents on Emulation of Hindu Caste system

Types of Emulation	Bara Govind Village			Chakia Town		
	Caste of Respondents					
	Chamar	**Dusadh**	**Musahar**	**Chamar**	**Dhobi**	**Dusadh**
Taking vegetarian meal	5	4	-	11	13	7
Performing Hindu Rituals and ceremonies	15	9	20	7	6	10
Worshipping Hindu god and goddess	12	13	19	9	11	10
Believing in Hindu Religious sects	9	12	6	11	13	9
Reciting Hindu religious books	1	-	-	4	4	-
Total	**42**	**38**	**45**	**42**	**47**	**36**

Table 5.18: Employment-wise views of the Respondents on Dalits believing in different religious panths and sects

Employment of Respondents	Bara Govind Village				Chakia Town			
	Believing Religious Sects or Panths							
	Hindu believes	**Buddhism**	**Kabir Panth**	**Jai Gurudeo Sect**	**Hindu believes**	**Buddhism**	**Kabir Panth**	**Jai Gurudeo Sect**
Traditional occupation	6	-	-	-	-	-	-	-
Agricultural labourer	71	7	9	9	-	-	-	-
Non-agricultural labourer	4	1	1	1	4	-	-	-

Govt. Jobs	-	1	1	1	4	13	12	18
Private Jobs	-	1	2	1	5	7	6	6
Petty-Business	-	-	-	-	5	6	3	5
Unemployed	-	3	3	3	3	13	9	6
Total	**81**	**13**	**16**	**15**	**21**	**39**	**30**	**35**

Table 5.19: Income-wise views of the Respondents on Dalits believing in different religious Panths and Sects

Income of Respondents	Bara Govind Village				Chakia Town			
	Constitutional Provisions of							
	Hindu believes	Buddhism	Kabir Panth	Jai Gurudeo Sect	Hindu believes	Buddhism	KabirPanth	Jai Gurudeo Sect
In Kind	45	2	2	2	-	-	-	-
Less than 1000	43	3	3	2	-	-	-	-
1001-2000	7	6	6	4	-	-	-	-
2001-3000	-	-	-	-	9	10	18	11
More than 3000	-	-	-	-	12	29	13	32
Total	**95**	**11**	**11**	**8**	**21**	**39**	**31**	**34**

Chapter 6

Table 6.1: Education-wise views of the Respondents on Social Exclusion and Status Formation of Dalits in socio-economic status

Educational Level of Respondents	Bara Govind Village						Chakia Town					
	Degree of Exclusion and Status Formation											
	Exclusion			Status Formation			Exclusion			Status Formation		
	Mst	Les	Lst	Hgh	Mddle	Lw	Mst	Les	Lst	Hgh	Mddle	Lw
Illiterate	68	-	-	-	-	68	-	-	-	-	-	-
Primary school	19	-	-	-	-	19	-	-	-	-	-	-
Middle school	10	3	-	-	3	10	7	4	-	-	4	7
High school	10	8	-	-	8	10	15	6	17	17	6	15
Intermediate	2	3	-	-	3	2	2	9	20	20	9	2

Graduation	-	2		-	2	-	-	15	23	23	15	-
Post- graduation	-	-	-	-	-	-	-	3	4	4	3	-
Total	**109**	**16**	**-**	**-**	**16**	**109**	**24**	**37**	**64**	**64**	**37**	**24**

Table 6.2: Employment-wise views of the Respondents on Social Exclusion and Status Formation of Dalits in socio-economic status

Employment of Respondents	Bara Govind Village						Chakia Town					
	Degree of Exclusion and Status Formation											
	Exclusion			Status Formation			Exclusion			Status Formation		
	Mst	Les	Lst	Hgh	Mddle	Lw	Mst	Les	Lst	Hgh	Mddle	Lw
Traditional	6	-	-	-	-	6	-	-	-	-	-	-
Agri-Labourer	90	6	-	-	6	90	-	-	-	-	-	-
Non-agriculture labourer	5	2	-	-	2	5	4	-	-	-	4	5
Govt. Jobs	-	3	-	-	3	-	-	22	25	25	22	-
Private Jobs	-	4	-	-	4	-	5	9	10	10	9	5
Petty- Business	-	-	-	-	-	-	3	6	10	10	6	3
Other Occupations	9	-	-	-	-	9	15	8	8	8	8	15
Total	**110**	**15**	**-**		**15**	**110**	**27**	**45**	**53**	**53**	**45**	**27**

Table 6.3: Income-wise views of the Respondents on Social Exclusion and Status Formation of Dalits in socio-economic status

Income of Respondents	Bara Govind Village						Chakia Town					
	Degree of Exclusion and Status Formation											
	Exclusion			Status Formation			Exclusion			Status Formation		
	Mst	Les	Lst	Hgh	Mddle	Lw	Mst	Les	Lst	Hgh	Mddle	Lw
In Kind	102	-	-	-	-	-	-	-	-	-	-	-
Less than1000	17	-	-	-	-	-	-	-	-	-	-	-
1001-2000	-	6	-	-	-	-	-	-	-	-	-	-
2001-3000	-	-	-	-	-	-	19	10	20	20	10	19
More than 3000	-	-	-	-	-	-	6	30	40	40	30	6
Total	**119**	**6**	**-**	**-**	**-**	**-**	**25**	**40**	**60**	**60**	**40**	**25**

Table 6.4: Education-wise views of the Respondents on Social Exclusion and Status Formation of Dalits in socio-economic status

Educational Level of Respondents	Bara Govind Village						Chakia Town					
	Degree of Exclusion and Status Formation											
	Exclusion			Status Formation			Exclusion			Status Formation		
	Mst	Les	Lst	Hgh	Mddle	Lw	Mst	Les	Lst	Hgh	Mddle	Lw
Illiterate	68	-	-	-	-	68	-	-	-	-	-	-
Primary school	19	-	-	-	-	19	-	-	-	-	-	-
Middle school	10	3	-	-	3	10	7	4	-	-	4	7
High school	10	8	-	-	8	10	15	6	17	17	6	15
Intermediate	2	3	-	-	3	2	2	9	20	20	9	2
Graduation	-	2	-	2	-	-	15	23	23	15	-	25
Post-graduation	-	-	-	-	-	-	-	3	4	4	3	-
Total	**109**	**16**	**-**	**-**	**16**	**109**	**24**	**37**	**64**	**64**	**37**	**24**

Table 6.5: Income-wise views of the Respondents on Social Exclusion and Status Formation of Dalits in socio-economic status

Income of Respondents	Bara Govind Village						Chakia Town					
	Degree of Exclusion and Status Formation											
	Exclusion			Status Formation			Exclusion			Status Formation		
	Mst	Les	Lst	Hgh	Mddle	Lw	Mst	Les	Lst	Hgh	Mddle	Lw
In Kind	102	-	-	-	-	-	-	-	-	-	-	-
Less than 1000	17	-	-	-	-	-	-	-	-	-	-	-
1001-2000	-	6	-	-	-	-	-	-	-	-	-	-
2001-3000	-	-	-	-	-	-	19	10	20	20	10	19
More than 3000	-	-	-	-	-	-	6	30	40	40	30	6
Total	**119**	**6**	**-**	**-**	**-**	**-**	**25**	**40**	**60**	**60**	**40**	**25**

Table 6.6: Education-wise views of the Respondents on changing status of Dalits in the Hindu caste system

Education of Respondents	Bara Govind Village			Chakia Town		
	Types of Status					
	No respect due to caste background	Respect due to caste background	Equal respect in caste hierarchy	No respect due to caste background	Respect due to caste background	Equal respect in caste hierarchy
Illiterate	68	-	-	-	-	-
Primary School	19	-	-	-	-	-
Middle School	5	8	-	7	4	-
High School	7	11	-	8	13	17
Intermediate	-	5	-	2	9	20
Graduation	-	2	-	-	15	23
Post-graduation	-	-	-	-	3	4
Total	**99**	**26**	-	**17**	**44**	**64**

Table 6.7: Employment-wise views of the Respondents on changing status of Dalits in the Hindu caste system

Employment of Respondents	Bara Govind Village			Chakia Town		
	Types of Status					
	No respect due to caste background	Respect due to caste background	Equal respect in caste hierarchy	No respect due to caste background	Respect due to caste background	Equal respect in caste hierarchy
Traditional occupation	6	-	-			
Agri-labourer	90	6	-			
Non-agri-labourer	5	2	-	4	-	-
Govt. Job	-	3	-	-	22	25
Private Job	-	4	-	5	9	10
Perry-Business	-	-	-	3	6	10
Unemployed	5	4	-	15	8	8
Total	**106**	**19**	-	**27**	**45**	**53**

Table 6.8: Income-wise views of the Respondents on changing status of Dalits in the Hindu caste system

Income of Respondents	Bara Govind Village			Chakia Town		
	Types of Status					
	No respect due to caste background	Respect due to caste background	Equal respect in caste hierarchy	No respect due to caste background	Respect due to caste background	Equal respect in caste hierarchy
In Kind	102	-	-	-	-	
Less than 1000	9	7	-	-	-	-
1001-2000	-	6	-	-	-	-
2001-3000	-	-	-	19	10	20
More than 3000	-	-	-	6	30	40
Total	**111**	**13**	**-**	**25**	**40**	**60**

Appendix-B

INTERVIEW SCHEDULE

I. Socio-Personal Background

1. Name (Head of the household)--
2. Age:----------------- Sex:------------------- Education:---------------------------
3. Spouse Name:------------------Age-------Sex---------Education-----------------
4. Caste/Sub-caste:-------------------------------Religion---------------------------
5. No. of dependents: Wife/ Husband/Children No.-----Grandchildren No.---- parent(s)----------Grandparent(s)----------------
6. Present occupations? Main----------subsidiary ------
7. Income from all sources? Rs.---------
8. Per month expenditure (in Rs.-------) on------food;------children's education-----; medical treatment------; clothing---------; any other (please explain)----------
9. How long are you residing in this village/town? Since birth/ for----------- years
10. In case not since birth, you have migrated from which village ----------- or town/city and areas/ region/ ---------------------------------
11. What has been your caste based traditional occupation? (carrying dead animals, making shoes/chappals, toddy tapper, washing cloth, others) please specify---------?

11.(a) In case you or your family members have not discontinued the caste-based occupation, do you or your family members still practice it? Yes/ No please give reason(s)-----------

12. Would you like to continue or leave caste-based occupation? Yes/No
    Please explain------------------------
13. Have you ever experienced any discrimination because of such occupation? Yes/No

    If yes, please describe--------------------

II. (A) Social Exclusion: Social Interaction and Relations

14. Do the Dalits in your village/town still practice traditional occupation imposed on them in village/town? Yes /No

    If yes, give reason(s)--------------------

15. Being an SC or Dalit, how do you identify yourself in relation to other caste people in your village, mohalla or locality or neighbourhood in the town?

    Please explain--------------------

15(a). Do you have social interaction with different caste groups in your village /town? Yes/No if yes, whether it is a short term/long term b) spontaneous/ purposive--------------- please explain------------

16. With whom social interaction takes place? Whether it takes place with an individual or a group in village /town? Please Explain -------------

17. How do you address the upper caste people in your village/ town?--------

18. How do the upper caste people address you or your caste members in the village/ town?----------

19. Are you called by your caste name by the upper and middle level castes people in your village/ town? Yes/No

    Please explain--------------------

20. Have they ever discriminated you publically in their social relationship or social interaction with you in the village/town? Yes/No

    If yes, please describe---------------------

21. Have you ever been humiliated or abused by them in public?

    Yes/No If yes, give reason -----------------

22. How do the other caste people treat you in general? Equally or unequally in village/town? Please describe----------------------

23. Are the upper and middle level castes people's discriminatory and humiliating attitudes and behaviour towards the Dalits in your village/ town based on the latter's practice of traditional occupation? Yes/No

    Please explain-------------

(B) Commensal Relations

24. Do the upper caste people accept *kachcha, pukka* food cooked by you or any other member of your caste in your village/town? Yes/No

    Please describe----------------------

25. Have you ever been invited by the people of upper and middle level castes in your village/town for taking meals together? Yes/No

    Please explain-----------

26. Are you served meals along with the people of upper and middle level castes in your Village/Town? Yes/ No

If yes, do they serve you meal refreshment along with people of other castes?

Please give reason-------------

(C) Socio-Cultural Domain: Ceremonies and Festivals, Temple Entry, etc.

27. Which festival(s) or whose birth anniversary (ies) do you or your caste members celebrate in your village/town? Please describe------------
28. Do the other caste people invite you in their celebrations of some solemn occasions? Yes/ No

    (a) If yes, please specify the type of celebrations-------------------------

    (b) If no, give reason(s)--------------------------
29. Do they practice an overall discrimination against you during the celebrations? Yes/No

    Please elaborate----------------------
30. If no, do they serve you meal separately during these celebrations? Yes/No

    Please give reason(s)-----------------
31. Are you allowed to enter the caste Hindu temples in your village/ locality in town? Yes/No

    Please explain-------------
32. Are you invited by the people of upper and other backward castes to participate in their marriage ceremony and/ or other social functions or any other in your village/town? Yes/ No.
33. If yes, whether they treat you equally or unequally. If yes, Please elaborate -------------------------
34. Do the upper and middle castes people participate in marriage ceremony solemnised equally in your and or other Dalit's house? Yes/No.
35. If yes, do they eat food cooked in at your/other Dalit's house? Yes/No

    Please elaborate--------------
36. Are you allowed to celebrate *Chhat Puja* along with the people of upper and/or other middle level castes in your village/town? Yes/No

36(a) If yes, are you allowed to celebrate it at the Ghat or separate Ghat? Same/ other? Yes/No

If no, please explain----------------------

(D) Discrimination and Untouchability

37. Is there a community hall or Panchayat Ghar common to people of all castes and communities in your village/town? Yes/ No

    If yes, are you allowed to use it in need? Yes/No------------------

    If no, why----------------------?

38. Do you face social isolation due to your caste background and the practice of certain specific rituals in your village/town? Yes/No

    Please give reason-----------------

39. Do the upper and middle level castes treat you inferior due to your caste background in your village/town? Yes/No

    If yes, where do you locate yourself in the caste hierarchy?------------------

    If no, please give reason(s)---------------------------

40. Do your female members work as maid servant in the houses of Hindu caste people? Yes/No if yes, Do they face discrimination or untouchability in their household? Yes/ No

    If yes, give reason(s) ------------------------

41. Do the upper and middle level castes people exclude the Dalits as whole from their participation the social, economic, political and cultural life in your village/town? Yes/No Please explain-----------------

42. Do the upper and middle level castes people claim to be inherently superior to the Dalits in your village/town? Yes/No Please explain-----------------

43. Do the upper and middle level castes people practice untouchability against you and in your other Dalits in the village or town? Yes/No

    Please give reason------------------

44. In case of no, do you still face any form of caste-based discrimination, oppression, exploitation and isolation in your village/town? Please describe--------------------

III. Status or Social status

45. What is your or your any other caste member's social position or status as compared to the upper caste people in your village/town?

    Please explain---------------------

46. Does your ascribed status get equal evaluation or esteem as the upper castes do in your village or town? Yes/No

    If yes, please explain--------------------

    If no, please explain-----------------------

47. Is your or your any other caste member's achieved status enhanced your or your caste member's social position in your village/town? Yes/No

    If yes, please explain--------------------

    If no, please explain-----------------------

IV. Social Status Formation

48. Is there any change in your caste-based status at present in the village/town? Yes/No please explain--------------?

49. How do you locate the status or rank of your caste in the Hindu caste system? Please Describe----------------

50. Where do the people of upper and middle level castes locate your caste in the hierarchy of the caste system?----------

51. Being a Dalit, do you think that your caste status gets respect in the Hindu caste systems practiced in your village/town? Yes/No please explain-------------

51(a) If no, do you think that you are discriminated by other caste people due to your low caste status? Yes/No please explain-------------

V. Economic Status

52. Have you or any member of your family's/relatives's ever applied for a job in the government or private sector? Yes/No. (a) if yes, whether selected? Yes/No (b) if no, was it due to your low caste background Yes/No.

    Please explain---------------------

    (c) If selected, in what type of job?--------------------

    (d) If employed, have you/ any member of your family/ relatives faced/ face any discrimination because of your caste background? Yes/No. Please explain---------------

53. If no, has the government/private sector job enhanced your family member's/relatives social position in the village/town? Yes/No

    If yes, in what way?----------------

    If yes, how much?-------------

54. Have you/ any Dalits in your village/town benefited from the land reform and various other state sponsored economic measures like NREP, IRDP, JRY, MNREGA, etc. introduced in state? Yes/No

    Please explain----------------

VI. Educational Status

Is there any government/ private school located in your or nearly village/town? Yes/no

55. Where is the school located? In the mixed castes locality? Please explain---------

56. If yes, are your/other Dalits children allowed to go to that school? Yes/No------------------

57. Have you or your children faced been facing any discrimination in availing of education in village/town? Yes/No

    Please explain--------------------

58. Have you or your children faced been facing any discrimination in availing of stipend, freeship, free books, or any other economic facility in the school? Yes/No?

    Please explain------------------------

59. Whether the mid-day meals are served to the children in the School? Yes/no

59(a) if yes, whether it is served separately or with the group of upper and middle castes children in the school? Yes/No, please describe----------------

60. Do the educated Dalits face the similar social discrimination as non-educated in your village/town? Yes/No

    Please explain------------

VII. Status of Power and Authority

61. Is there any Gram/Nagar Panchayat in your village/town? Yes/No

62. Does Gram /Nagar Panchayat function properly in your village/town? Yes/No? Please describe---------

63. Does the Gram/Nagar Panchayat work effectively for the development of the people in general Dalits in particular in your village/town? Yes /No? Please explain---------------------

64. Are Dalits of your village/town allowed to cast their vote freely in elections for the Gram/ Nagar Panchayat? Yes/No

    If yes, describe----------------

65. Are the elected Dalit Panchayat members discriminated and humiliated by other caste members in the meetings of the Gram Panchayat/Nagar Panchayat? Yes/No

    If yes, please give reasons-------------------------

66. Do the Dalit women elected in the Gram/ Nagar Panchayat participate equally and effective in the meetings as men do? Yes/No

    If no, please give reasons------------

67. (a) If no, whether they are discouraged/ harassed / humiliated by the male elected members of the other castes in the members of the Gram /Nagar Panchayat? Yes/No

    Please give reason(s)----------------

68. Has reservation in the village/Nagar Panchayat enhanced the power and authority of the Dalits in village/town? Yes/No please explain-----------------

69. Do the other members elected to Gram/Nagar Panchayat exclude the elected Dalit members from the decision making process pertaining to your village/town? Yes/No

69(a). If no, do they invite elected Dalit member(s) in the meeting(s) of the Gram/Nagar Panchayat and discuss the issue seriously? Yes/No Please explain---------

69(b). If yes, do they give the due respect or prestige to the Dalit members in the meeting(s) of the Gram/Nagar Panchayat? Yes/No please explain-----------

70. Do the people of upper and middle level castes take from and give suggestions to from the Dalit members about any matter related to village/town? Yes/No

71. Do the Dalits of your village/town approach the Thana/ C.O /B.D.O /S.D.M easily without any fear or trouble? Yes/No

    If yes, whether their grievances are listen to properly and sorted out immediately? Yes/No

    Please explain----------------------

Index

D

E

F

G

H

I